Praise for Deborah Lee Luskin's
Reviving Artemis

"This engaging memoir follows the trail of how hunting deer grounded a woman more strongly in her community, the forest, and herself—truly a joy to read."

—Tom Wessels, author of *Reading the Forested Landscape*

* * *

"*Reviving Artemis* is so much more than a story about a woman learning to hunt; it's a story about following your heart, finding your passion, challenging your fears, and building confidence. It's a story about growth and believing and trusting in yourself."

—Judy Camuso, Commissioner of the Maine Department of Inland Fisheries and Wildlife

* * *

"On its surface, *Reviving Artemis* is about becoming a deer hunter, but in its heart it is so much more: an honest, tender and engaging story about building relationship with land and community, about conservation, about reciprocity and responsibility, about death and change, about choosing to step bravely and humbly into the unknown."

—Ethan Tapper, forester, digital creator and the bestselling author of *How to Love a Forest: The Bittersweet Work of Tending a Changing World*

* * *

"Luskin's writing tracks like a hunt: moments of exhilarating poignancy interspersed with quietly sublime reflection. Her ability to relate the feeling and experience of the woods—especially from the perspective of a new hunter—is remarkable."

—Lou Tamposi, *Cow We Doin'* (Substack)

* * *

"Hunting stories are as old as recorded time. Mostly told by men. *Reviving Artemis* is a woman's story through and through with a lot to say to all of us. Deborah Luskin is an honest and self-aware writer with a keen sense of language."

—Tom Bodett, author, storyteller, voice actor, woodworker

* * *

"Deborah Lee Luskin is an important voice for women who take up hunting as adults. As she spins her story, she comes face to face with mortality, past pain, gender, and the conundrums that come any time we begin to truly engage with the sources of our own lives."

—Erika Hawsare, author of *The Age of Deer*

* * *

"I found the book to be a delight to read and the title is perfect! It's the story of a woman's evolution into the world of not only sustenance hunting but the culture of hunting."

—Kelly Price, Vermont State Game Warden, retired

* * *

"In *Reviving Artemis*, Deborah Lee Luskin answers the call to enter the woods with courage and perseverance, starting a new chapter in her life. Like Artemis, Luskin becomes a protector of wild nature, and she understands the deep interconnectivity between her personal life, the forest, and her community."

— Jesse C. McEntee, *Next Adventure* (Substack)

* * *

"Luskin's insights are not just limited to the woods. With a sharp intellect, she opens new doors of awareness about community and connectedness."

—Kate Troll is an Alaskan adventurer, columnist and author of *All in Due Time, A Memoir of Siblings, Genealogy, Secrets and Love.*

REVIVING ARTEMIS

THE MAKING OF A HUNTRESS

A MEMOIR

Deborah Lee Luskin

Sibylline Press

Sibylline Press

Copyright © 2025 by Deborah Lee Luskin

All Rights Reserved. Published in the United States by Sibylline Press, an imprint of All Things Book LLC, California. Sibylline Press is dedicated to publishing the brilliant work of women authors ages 50 and older.

www.sibyllinepress.com
Distributed to the trade by Publishers Group West

ISBN Trade: 9781960573759
eBook ISBN: 9781960573766
Library of Congress Control Number: 2025933376

Cover Design: Alicia Feltman
Book Production: Aaron Laughlin

HUMAN AUTHORED: Any use of this publication to train artificial intelligence (AI) technologies to generate text is expressly prohibited.

In Memory of Jan Rutherdale

Fragments of previous published essays and broadcasts appear in this text as follows: essays in *Vermont Magazine* in the 1990s; feature stories in the online magazine *EasternSlopes.com* in 2015; *The Commons,* Windham County's Independent Weekly, published "He Was My Grandfather" in 2018, sections of which appear in Chapter Eight; bits and pieces of some of the more than 200 commentaries broadcast on Vermont Public Radio between 2006 and 2018.

This is a work of nonfiction; however, some of the first names have been changed, and some last names omitted to preserve friendships and protect privacy.

Permission to use the Posewitz quotation:
Published by Falcon Guides an imprint of
Globe Pequot Publishing Group (2002)
Chapter, "The Place of the Hunter"
Authored by Jim Posewitz

REVIVING ARTEMIS

THE MAKING *of* *a* HUNTRESS

DEBORAH LEE LUSKIN

"For more than a million years our ancestors were socially organized, using tools and hunting. In North America 10,000 years ago, they hunted beaver as large as bear, ground sloths as tall as giraffes, long-horned bison, caribou, horses, musk ox, and mammoths. As recently as 300 years ago, hunting and gathering societies were common throughout the world. We are the children of these generations of hunters."

—Jim Posewitz, *Beyond Fair Chase: The Ethic and Tradition of Hunting*

Men have had every advantage of us in telling their own story.

—Jane Austen, *Persuasion*

ONE

CALLED TO HUNT

This is the unlikely story of a woman born in mid-twentieth-century postwar America, into a suburban tribe that hunts for bargains and houses, a people who navigate highways around large urban centers; a clan who think "game" means tennis, baseball, and Parcheesi. Even though all three of my brothers earned merit badges for marksmanship as Boy Scouts, I'm the one in my family who owns a rifle, sits in the woods, and waits for game.

As a suburban kid and an urban young adult, I'd been a downhill skier. Early in my Vermont life, I switched to cross-country skis, walked on dirt roads, hiked on blazed paths, and grew peas, tomatoes, and squash. When I turned sixty, I hiked the length of Vermont on the Long Trail, the oldest recreational footpath in the United States. But I wanted to step off the groomed trails into backcountry wilderness. Without knowing where I was headed all this time, I felt a force pulling me beyond the tamed landscape of recreation and agriculture, into the untracked woods—but how would I navigate without written trail signs? I don't remember when or where I heard the answer, but it came through loud and clear: *Learn from the deer.*

Some of the most astute naturalists and conservationists I know are traditional Vermont deer hunters who not only know how to navigate through the forested landscape; they know how to be still and observe. But these men grew up in the woods, noticing the interconnections between the deer's habits and habitat since boyhood, while I'd been playing hopscotch on the sidewalk in front of my house or building cardboard homes for my Trolls indoors. In adolescence, I read nineteenth-century novels about lonely girls, pursued literature in college, and learned geographical navigation on Manhattan's signposted grid. From literature, I learned to read human behavior, but I didn't know how to read the land.

At sixty, I had nothing to lose; my three daughters were grown, my marriage intact, and my fertility complete. I was no longer tugged by the moon; I was now in tune with the sun. Being unmoored from the tides of fertility was profound. After years of cycles that buffeted my body with tears and desire, I was now above tree line, my mind clear. This annual rhythm is slower than the lunar tide that once ruled me. This solar rhythm allows me a deeper experience of the seasons and a longer view, both backwards into the lived past, and forward, toward death. It's from this vantage point that I see how insignificant I am within the vastness of the natural world. Or maybe I'm just willing to take risks I wouldn't have taken before I became aware that my time's finite: it will run out. Either way, I feel liberated in the face of death, as if this is my season of autumn foliage, ablaze and gorgeous before I return to the earth.

For thirty years, I'd been fencing the wilderness out of the garden where I grew vegetables in rows straight as typed text, editing beets and beans the way I manipulate words. Then, one day I looked up from weeding the carrots and saw beyond the pastoral landscape and into forest that dominates Vermont. Now, instead of taking comfort in old foundations, stone walls, and logging roads that molder in the woods, I found myself looking beyond the evidence of human endeavor and was alert to live animal signs. It was as if the centrifugal force of the Earth's rotation was forcing me out of the garden, off the blazed trail, away from the civilized use of the outdoors. By learning to hunt, I was spinning into a new orbit.

* * *

Before I heard the call to hunt, I'd witnessed the spell that hunting can cast. I met ordinary, clean-cut fellows who stopped shaving in

September, grew silent in October, and went feral by Opening Day. There's something about tracking deer through the woods and pitting themselves against nature in nature that sets these hunters right, even if, at the end of two weeks, they haven't shot a deer.

Before I heard the call, I'd appreciated the value of hunting for good management of the herd. I'd seen deer starving in late March as the snow shrinks and they come down from their winter yards searching the valleys for browse. I've seen mangled deer too weak to outrun neighborhood dogs, and deer too famished to successfully cross a road before an oncoming car.

Thanks to Vermont's robust hunting tradition, I heard hunting stories long before I shot a deer. A neighbor who doesn't usually say much waxes eloquent in season.

"How'd it go this morning?" I once asked when I saw him in his red-checked shirt.

His eyes lit up. "I saw a six-pointer, but I couldn't get a good bead on him."

He continued with details of landscape and wind and sight lines as I nodded, recognizing his passion for something I didn't yet understand. I marveled at this whole field of knowledge of deer behavior and the way of the woods, not because I'm especially interested in how deer think, but because I'm fascinated by humans, and hunting is deeply human.

I was twenty-eight when I moved to Vermont for the summer—and never left. I've now lived more than half my life in this rural state where hunting is ubiquitous. According to the *Big Game Management Plan for 2020-2030*, published by the Vermont Fish & Wildlife Department shortly after I started hunting, Vermont has a hunting participation rate of about fourteen percent—way above the four percent national average. Living among hunters made me curious about hunting, so curious that I once accompanied a hunting friend into the woods with a camera. But this was back when I was still learning to farm, when I was doing my best to tame the landscape rather than read its wildness. It was before I knew how to sit still.

For the first thirty years that I lived in Vermont, I stayed out of the woods during hunting season. I was never worried a hunter would mistake me for a deer, but I recognized that for the sixteen days of rifle season, something primal overtakes these hunters; they need the woods to themselves. Then, as I approached sixty, this primal urge overtook me—an urge strong enough to overcome a lifelong fear of getting lost in the woods, an urge so insistent I would learn to shoot a rifle despite an enduring fear of firearms. When I heard the call to hunt, a voice from the universe vibrated inside me. It was a sensation I couldn't ignore.

It would be more than a year between the time I was called to hunt and my first morning in the field. It would be a year of alternating fear, effort, new knowledge, and preparation. Regardless, I knew almost as soon as I was summoned by this force I can hardly describe that I would write about it, because writing is how I make sense of the world. Somehow—perhaps in the same way that I knew I needed to hunt—I knew I would narrate this story of walking into the woods alone, with a rifle, in the dark.

* * *

I seem to have been working my way backwards through human history: leaving the city, raising domestic livestock, keeping bees, nurturing an orchard, and cultivating a vegetable garden before making tentative forays into foraging fiddleheads, ramps, and black trumpets. Simultaneously, I had been facilitating book discussions in libraries, giving lectures around the state, and telling stories on the radio, in print, and in cyberspace. Ironically, it's only now that I see how these two activities—hunting and storytelling—are so intimately related. We tell stories to educate, persuade, and entertain, and we now do so over many platforms, from the campfire to the internet. Storytelling is central to human experience. So, too, is hunting.

The fairy tales and TV shows of my childhood were variations on the theme of princes rescuing princesses from captivity and *Father Knows Best*, narratives mirrored in my suburban neighborhood, where men hunted achievement and women gathered groceries; where men earned money, and women cooked dinner; a world order as bruising as it is untrue.

While we don't know the content of the oldest stories from the oral tradition, I can guess that many of them had to do with the hunt, given the number of deities who presided over hunters and hunting, a pantheon that included many goddesses. Artemis is the Greek goddess of wild animals, the wilderness, and the hunt, childbirth, child welfare, and chastity; Diana is her Roman counterpart. Both are familiar figures in Eurocentric storytelling, but there are many other ancient goddesses from other traditions. A short list includes goddesses from ancient Egypt, Finland, the Caucasus; Norse goddesses, Hindu goddesses, Slavic and Thracian goddesses; and Inuit goddesses; all with names that are now largely unfamiliar: Neith, Pakhet, Mielikki, Dali; Skathi, Devana, Bendis; Arnkuasgsak, Nujalik, and Pinga. These deities held sway over the hunt; they also held powers as healers and protectors, not just of humans, but also of animals and the Earth. These goddesses were believed to protect the health of the forest and clan, promote fertility, make medicine, and reign over winter, mountains, and moons. Of all these goddesses, I only knew a little about Artemis, mostly from art, where she's routinely depicted as tall, slim, small-breasted, and fleet—none of which describes me. But as the mother of daughters, I knew how to nurture girls and women; as a gardener, I knew how to care for soil. In becoming a hunter, I would learn about stewardship of the wild.

* * *

Before Artemis became known in Greek mythology as the virgin goddess of the hunt, she was worshipped at a temple dedicated to her as a goddess who protected women, children, and wildlife. The Temple of Artemis at Ephesus dates back to the Bronze Age. Whether the temple was first built by Amazon warriors or other worshippers is uncertain.

What is known is that the Temple of Artemis served as a place of pilgrimage and worship for both women and men. It was important enough to be rebuilt three times, each time more grandly than before. The first temple was destroyed by a flood in the seventh century BCE. A second iteration was destroyed by fire, possibly arson, in 356 BCE. The third Temple of Artemis at Ephesus was the largest, deemed one of the Seven Wonders of the Ancient World, of which only the Great Pyramid still stands. This third temple, which was larger than the Parthenon, survived into the Common Era and is mentioned in the New Testament. The spread of Christianity and the persecution of pagan worship led to the temple's gradual neglect, aided by Goths, who raided Ephesus in 268 CE.

The Temple of Artemis housed the earliest known sculptural representation of the goddess, a bronze and alabaster figure from the second century BCE. While the original statue is lost, copies of it have been found throughout the ancient world, where Artemis was first worshipped not as the daughter of Zeus, nor as the twin sister of Apollo, nor as a virgin, but as the "great mother goddess." Across her chest hang spheres, as if she has many breasts, though some scholars insist the spheres represent the testicles of sacrificial bulls. Breasts or balls, the statue is a depiction of female sexuality, fertility, and power.

I grew up in a world ruled by a male god in a time when archeologists had long been operating under the assumption that all prehistoric hunters were male, despite the long lineage of female hunting deities. Recently, when archeologists in Peru dug up a 9,000-year-old skeleton buried with a hunting toolkit of stone projectile points and animal-processing tools, they assumed they'd found the remains of a male hunting chief. But the bones and tooth enamel indicate that the skeleton found at the Wilamaya Patjxa site was a female between seventeen and nineteen years old. Archeologists are now asking how common it was for women to hunt in pre-Columbian times by reviewing previous assumptions and data.

I didn't know many women hunters when I heard the call, nor did I know that women currently make up the fastest growing cohort of hunters in the United States. In fact, I didn't know much. Five years later, I still have a lot to learn. But when I felt that overwhelming physical sensation, as if gravity were pulling me sideways into the forest, when I heard that unbidden and unmistakable call to hunt, I answered it.

This is my story.

TWO

GETTING STARTED

Call it kismet or coincidence, but shortly after the imperative to hunt entered my bloodstream, I had a call from Tim Jones, my editor at *Eastern Slopes*, an online magazine for outdoor enthusiasts in the Northeast. The magazine had previously sent me to review an alpine ski resort, to learn whitewater kayaking, and to cover a community service project in the Umbagog National Wildlife Refuge. Now Jones asked, "Do you want to go to Doe Camp?"

"What's that?"

"School for adventurous women," he said. "I can get you a spot for the winter retreat."

While we were talking, I checked out their website. "Can I take any classes I want?" I asked.

"What do you have in mind?"

"Hunting, rifle skills, and game calling."

I could have capitulated and signed up for advanced snowshoeing, Nordic skating, and winter camping, but I already had those skills. Here was a chance to learn hunting skills—from and with women. I wanted to go. I remained silent.

"Our audience isn't the hook-and-bullet crowd."

I let his words hang in the air.

Maybe he heard me think, *I don't need this job.* Or maybe he sensed I shrugged. I waited a moment more.

Just as I was on the verge of saying, "The people who run Doe Camp certainly think women are interested in hunting," Tim Jones said, "Okay."

I drove to the Hulbert Outdoor Center in Fairlee, Vermont, on a Friday in early March, when fierce sunshine bouncing off the snowpack was the only sign of spring. Under a bluebird sky in brittle cold, participants ranging in age from teenagers to elders gathered to learn outdoor skills among other like-minded women. Some of the participants were repeat attendees; others, like me, were newbies.

Friday afternoon I made my way to the Center's library for Becoming a Deer Hunter, which gave me my first exposure to the nuts and bolts of hunting, taught by Murphy Robinson, tall, slim, and androgynous. Murphy was born in Iowa, raised in Maine, and now lives in mid-state Vermont.

One of the things Murphy likes about Vermont is how hunting is a right, protected in the state's constitution ratified in 1793. This right to hunt counters English game laws, where the landed aristocracy own game and access to it, and the laws against poaching are harsh. Murphy views Vermont's constitutional guarantee as consonant with the state's long tradition of sustainable rural lifeways. When Murphy founded Mountainsong Expeditions in 2012, it was to teach women the skills to hunt deer as part of living lightly on the land.

Raised a vegetarian, Murphy is now an omnivore who promotes ethical deer-hunting practices that go far beyond game laws and touch on the history, myths, and spirituality of hunting as a way of deepening our human connection to and honoring the forest that sustains us. Murphy appreciates the strong Vermont traditions of a sustainable food chain and local economy, and especially values Vermonters' willingness to live and let live. Murphy was socialized female, became a woman hunter at age twenty-eight, and now identifies as transmasculine and nonbinary. They understand the extra hurdles that female hunters face, and they have dedicated many years to helping aspiring hunters of marginalized gender identities learn hunting skills and ethics.

Eight other women gathered around the library table, all of them younger than me, most by a couple of decades. I wasn't just the oldest in the room; I was also the least experienced. Most of my classmates had at least fired rifles, and several had already been out in the field with their male partners. I was glad to be in a room with women, free of the male bravado that often infects hunting culture. Among these women, I felt safe, unembarrassed to ask the most basic of questions, and honored to learn from their collective experience.

In three brief hours, Murphy talked us through the essential legal requirements for becoming a hunter in Vermont, including taking a hunter safety class to earn a hunting license. Murphy showed us a hunting rifle and a compound bow, the two most common weapons for deer hunting, and explained the pros and cons of each.

The rifle looked more straightforward than the compound bow, which bore no resemblance to the simple long bow Artemis carries. This modern bow is a complicated-looking metal contraption with pulleys and a crisscrossed bowstring. Murphy told us it takes years to acquire the strength and skill to use a compound bow effectively, dispelling my fantasy of hunting with a classic long bow, which is even more challenging to draw, aim, and shoot. As a rank beginner who'd never shot a rifle, who didn't know her way around the woods, and who didn't yet know she needed skills to track a wounded deer, I was starting to understand what an enormous challenge I'd set for myself. I was already making a late start, trying to acquire skills most hunters learn over a lifetime, and I had only a fraction of a lifetime left.

Next, Murphy told us how deer communicate with vocalizations, rubs, and scent-laced scrapes that signal a deer's interest and availability to mate. This was the first time I'd ever heard these words. I didn't yet know the difference between a *grunt* and a *bleat* or a *scrape* and a *rub*, but I knew that learning the deer's language would help me find them and my way through the woods.

Throughout this presentation, Murphy repeatedly touched on the ethical issues of hunting, including a hunter's responsibility to the animal she's shot. Finally, Murphy strongly encouraged us both to practice shooting and to find a mentor. They said, "There's so much to learn, especially if you didn't grow up with hunting."

* * *

I needed a mentor, and I knew just whom I wanted to ask: Roger Brown, the first hunter I ever met.

Roger and I first laid eyes on one another in June of 1984. I'd barely settled into a Vermont cabin smaller than my New York apartment and was already at my desk by the window when I saw a branch fall on the power line and catch fire. With some trepidation at waking the world at five o'clock on a Saturday morning, I called the volunteer fire department. A half dozen unshaven men showed up and stood in the dirt lane a safe distance from the disturbance, arms folded across their chests, heads tilted up, watching the branch smolder.

Uncertain how to host a volunteer fire brigade, I asked if I could get anyone coffee.

"No thanks," they muttered, looking everywhere but at me, a female flatlander living alone.

Good thing; I only had two mugs.

Awkwardness persisted until, finally, the branch fell to the ground, and the men stamped the fire out.

"I'm sorry to get you up so early," I said as they prepared to leave.

"No, you did the right thing," the one in the white T-shirt said.

That was Roger, the fire chief, though it would be another year before I knew his name, or that he was a hunter, or how much he would eventually influence me.

Thirty-five years later, Roger confessed, "You were gutsy, Deb, living up there by yourself."

I was lonely.

That was the summer I decided that lonely was better than any of the duds I'd dated in New York, and the one date I'd had in Vermont with a guy who didn't use words of more than one syllable. After lunch with him, I foreswore dating and mating; I was better off on my own. A few weeks later I met Tim, the new doctor in town.

We met on the first Saturday in August, at Hospital Fair Day, an annual fundraiser for Grace Cottage Hospital, a nineteen-bed rural outpost that was providing the kind of primary care now called "patient-centered" long before that term came into use. I took one look at Tim and thought, *This man looks tired*. A few weeks later we ran into each other at a gas station. This time he wasn't haggard but smiling and curious. We talked. He asked if I had a phone in my cabin.

I did.

He asked for my number, and if I had something to write with.

"I'm a writer. Of course I do."

Some weeks later, the phone rang.

It was Tim.

When I learned that he'd graduated from Oberlin College a year ahead of me and loved *Pride and Prejudice*, I broke my rule about conducting first dates in public and invited him to my cabin on his next day off. Two weeks later, he showed up for dinner.

We talked. We discovered about two hundred common acquaintances, and not just Obies. I was good friends with his high school girlfriend, someone I'd met in England. Since I'd already decided never to marry, I had nothing to lose by being my authentic, articulate, and intelligent self. I explained metonymy, and how letters embedded in Jane Austen's novels serve as instructions on how to read fiction.

"I could marry you," he blurted.

What chutzpah! We hadn't even kissed!

The following May, we bought a two-hundred-year-old, story-and-a-half Cape on the West River on the condition that I had a room of my own. I chose one of the two upstairs. The staircase was too narrow to bring up my desk, and the room had only one electrical outlet, which was insufficient to run a computer, printer, and desk lamp. The room faced the river, but had knee-wall windows at floor level, under the slanted ceiling, and no view.

"We'll renovate," Tim said. "I've got the name of the guy who worked for the previous owners."

That would be Roger, who met with us to discuss what we could do in the two months before we moved in. The two men talked R-values, low-e glass, and circuit breakers. I wanted to discuss budget and time.

In 1985, I was supposed to be writing my dissertation, *Jane Austen and the Limits of Epistolary Fiction*. I had sublet my New York City apartment, moved out of my rustic cabin, and was living at Tim's apartment until his lease ran out. I had no place to write, so I was anxious for the renovations to be finished. These included installing a window big enough to hoist my desk through and give me a river view. Until that happened, I did what I could to accelerate making the place habitable. I worked with Roger, doing demolition in advance of his Skilsaw, then sanding and priming in the wake of his taping knife. He hired the floor sanders; I applied the polyurethane after they left.

I knew he wasn't too keen about working with me. After that first conference about the remodel and in the way of small towns, word got back to me that Roger called the new doctor "pussy-whipped." I was shocked into silence, but continued to prime, paint, and sweep up.

After a few weeks, Roger and I began to talk over lunch. I'd slurp a cup of yogurt; he'd pull out a cooler packed with blue-shelled boiled eggs from his laying flock and a pile of wild-game-on-white sandwiches.

We'd mostly talk cooking. It seemed the one really safe subject between us. He'd tell me about his three freezers filled with bear, caribou, and venison, and how, after work, he'd throw a slab of wild meat on the gas grill.

I showed him the piglet we were raising in the backyard and said, "Look, two hundred pounds of meat growing right here. I don't even have to hunt for it."

"Yeah," Roger replied, "and for all that work you just end up with a lot of pork."

One day I complained to Roger about the groundhog that was raiding the garden, an agricultural pursuit Roger approved of, although he couldn't fathom why I wasn't growing potatoes. "What the hell is *arugula*?" he wanted to know.

The next day, he showed up for work with a rifle, which he propped alongside the new window he was framing. Halfway through the swing of his hammer, he picked up the gun and nailed the groundhog to the back lawn. "I guess that one won't bother you no more."

I was impressed, and Roger could tell. The next day, he brought photographs of a recent trip to Canada, where he'd hunted the caribou that was now in his sandwich.

Tim and I moved into the house at the end of June, before the renovations were finished. I painted my study in August, and in September I resumed commuting weekly to New York to teach freshman composition, leaving the finish work to Roger.

Roger returned from the Labor Day weekend unshaven and started to talk about what jobs we'd finish next year. Gradually, he stopped talking. I was perplexed, still imagining an end to Sheetrock before winter. Had I somehow offended him?

By the end of October, just after we slaughtered our pig, Roger—now bearlike behind his full beard—packed up his tools. "Goin' huntin'" was all he said.

I stared alternately at the receding tailgate of his pickup and the uneven gaps between the wall and ceiling where trim board was to go. That's when I realized just how long winter would be. To console myself, I phoned for a haircut, but my hairdresser's answering machine said to call back in January. *Gone hunting.*

By November, with the foliage fallen, the tourists departed, and the woods feeling unsafe, I took to wearing bright colors and walked on paved roads instead of dirt lanes. The chill air popped with gunfire. If Roger shot his deer, would he come back to work?

"No," said my friend Helen, whose family has lived in Vermont as long as stone walls snaked through the woods. It was she who told me the truth: "He'll be back in the spring."

"*What?*"

She patiently explained: hunters like Roger and her husband, Dennis, follow the herd across New England, hunting deer in different states during different seasons with bows, then modern rifles, and then old-fashioned black-powder guns.

"You mean your husband will be hunting for months?"

"Well, he'll come home, and he'll go to work, but he won't really be back—I mean, he won't really be there for us—not until the season is over."

"And you just accept it?" I've known wives who've filed for less.

"It's seasonal behavior," Helen said matter-of-factly, "as unavoidable as shortened daylight in November. I mean, one of the reasons Dennis married me," she continued in a perfect non sequitur, "is because I like to hunt, too."

"Okay," I said. "Take me with you."

So, long before I heard the call to hunt, she did.

I loaded film into my camera and found warm, red clothes that didn't make noise—which meant my high-tech ski parka hung in the closet while Tim's oversized woolen jacket hung on me—as Helen led me into the woods before dawn on Opening Day.

Helen had already scouted where we'd sit. As the gloom faded into a gunmetal day, she pointed out a series of depressions in the ground. "This looks like a place where deer have been sleeping," she told me.

I took her word for it.

Helen was hoping the deer would come home with daylight.

We hunkered down in silence to wait.

No buck came into view.

From time to time Helen silently shifted her rifle, scoping the thicket some fifty yards away, behind which, she assured me, an eight-pointer could be lurking. I sighted my camera in the direction she pointed her gun. Even if such a mythical beast were to emerge from behind the wall of hemlock, I was shaking with cold, unable to steady the camera in the dim light.

Hours into our vigil, the red squirrel who'd been chattering all morning began to shower us with the detritus of the pine cone it was shelling. It was at that moment, stone cold and bored beyond measure, that I suddenly understood the red squirrel's language.

Go home, it scolded. You don't belong in the woods. You're not a hunter. The deer aren't going to come.

I attempted to rise, but unused to the discipline of keeping a woodland vigil, I was too stiff to budge.

Go back to your garden, the squirrel said.

I envisioned sitting on the warm earth between rows of beans and tomatoes, deep in the meditative act of weeding.

"Helen," I willed my frozen lips to utter, "I'm a farmer."

With aching limbs, we stumbled out of the woods.

For the next three decades, Tim and I grew fruits and vegetables, kept a laying flock and beehives, and switched from raising pigs to raising chickens for meat.

* * *

Roger had been a big part of our lives during the ten years we lived in the old Cape. During that decade, Roger plowed our driveway, delivered firewood, added an upstairs bathroom as our family grew. We had three children in less than four years. I managed Tim's medical practice; he saw patients, covered the emergency department every third night, rounded on his hospital patients every weekend, and delivered babies, who inevitably arrived on his night off. As the practice grew, we needed more space, purchased a restaurant, and hired Roger to convert it into Tim's medical office.

By the time the kids were three, six, and seven, we'd outgrown the antique Cape and moved ten miles away, into a five-year-old post-and-beam house three times the size of the old one, and four times less effort to heat. Roger installed bookcases when we first moved in, but there was nothing else for him to do after that. Nevertheless, we kept tabs on one another, as one does in a small community like ours. For a while, Roger was an in-patient at Grace Cottage, for rehab after a double knee-replacement; Helen was his nurse. Roger's son is the longtime CFO at the hospital where Tim works.

Roger and his wife, Janis, are also among my longtime and loyal readers, from my early days as an editorial columnist in the local paper to *Living in Place*, my current blog, where I write about rural life, politics, and aging. When I phoned to ask if he'd mentor me, I confessed I didn't just want to learn to hunt, I wanted to write about it.

"If anyone can explain hunting to folks who don't know anything about it, Deb, it's you," he said.

"Yeah, Roger. That's nice of you to say. But what are the chances I can learn to hunt?"

"You can. I know you can. I've seen you set your mind to do something and do it." Before we hung up, Roger agreed to an interview.

He was outside when I drove into his yard. Roger folded his arms across his chest. Before I was out of the car he was saying, "The first thing you need to know about hunting is tree huggers badmouth hunters." He shook his head at the ground. I leaned against the car door. "Teachers badmouth hunting. A lot of people frown on it." He dropped his arms and sighed. "But a hunter does more for animals than anyone else." He looked me in the eye. "The twenty-nine words," he said, as if I knew what he was talking about.

I raised an eyebrow and tilted my head.

"The twenty-nine words of the Pittman-Robertson Act." Roger was referring to the 1937 law ensuring that hunting fees and taxes support conservation, and recited the twenty-nine words by heart. "'And which shall include a prohibition against the diversion of license fees paid by hunters for any other purpose than the administration of said State fish and game department.' It's hunters that pay for conservation, not tree huggers. Hunters protect wildlife habitat with an 11 percent tax on guns and ammunition. And that money can't be spent on nothing else. That's what those twenty-nine words mean." He was frowning. "And everybody benefits. People don't pay no special tax on their cameras to shoot pictures of animals. It's hunters who pay." He shook his head at the ground again, then looked me in the face. "That's what you're up against, Deb, if you want to hunt."

If I'd never left the city, if I'd never met Roger, I'd probably be one of those people who disparage hunters.

"My grandfather hunted," Roger said. "Everyone around here hunted." Roger grew up a few miles from where he lives now. "I was ten or eleven when I got a job so I could buy a gun. It's a .22 JC Higgins from Sears, Roebuck. I bought it myself, with money from my paper route, and I still use it to shoot squirrels." He gave me a sly look. "They make a holy mess in my trailers." He's referring to the truck trailers tucked into the woods on his property and filled with lumber, equipment, and supplies.

"I'm surprised you've never built a barn," I said. Roger's a skilled craftsman who's built houses from the ground up and renovated buildings from the inside out.

"Trailers are on wheels." He smirked. "They're not taxable."

I steered the conversation back to hunting. He named two boyhood friends with whom he had ongoing, year-round competitions for how many squirrels and partridges they could shoot. "That was our recreation," he said. "You didn't have nothing else to do. It wasn't until I was fifteen or sixteen that my parents got a black-and-white TV with one channel." He made a frame in the air with his fingers to show how small his parents' first television set was. "Nowadays," he sighed, "kids have so many other things to do."

Roger was unsupervised when he was hunting and fishing. There was a local man who kept wine in the brook. "We got into that. And I didn't go to school much. Janis mastered my mom's signature, so I could work." Roger and Janis have been married almost sixty years. "I skipped classes to milk cows, cut hay, and do whatever needed doing that would earn me gas money. To keep your car running, you had to work. Gas was eighteen cents a gallon at the farm pump." In the 1950s, there were three operational dairy farms in town, now long gone. "I worked twelve hours a day, from daybreak to after dark."

"But you graduated?"

Roger smiled. "Janis wrote my papers." Roger can't remember if he was last or second to last in his graduating class of sixty-three. Janis was class valedictorian. She was on track to attend the University of Vermont, but she and Roger married instead. Four months later, their son was born, and three years after that, their daughter.

Roger supported his family by working, mostly outdoors, for a local excavating enterprise driving heavy equipment six days a week and picking up spare jobs on the local farms haying, milking, and clearing fields. By the time Roger came to renovate our old house, he was forty. He was still working hard, but in business for himself, which is why he could walk off the job to go hunting.

Roger looked me in the eye and said, "Hunting is total freedom."

"So how do I learn?"

"Let see how you shoot. Do you have a rifle?"

I told him I had a .22. What I didn't say is I'd never fired it.

* * *

The first time I fired any rifle was at Doe Camp. The range was no more than a lean-to on one side of a modest clearing in the woods, facing targets nailed to trees in front of a steep hill to stop stray bullets. The hill also blocked the feeble sun. Thankfully, my anxiety about handling firearms generated enough heat to mitigate the cold air snaking under my layers of fleece.

Of the four of us who reported for Rifle Skills and Marksmanship class, two were experienced hunters, one of whom brought her own deer rifle to test and to adjust her scope for accuracy, called "sighting in"—still a mystery to me. Another woman was as clueless as I was, and we couldn't have asked for better instructors.

Larry Hamel and Dick Bayer are complete opposites in appearance: Larry is tall and wiry, with long gray hair and an Old Testament beard. Dick, on the other hand, is short, clean-shaven, and solid. Neither man said much, nor did I learn how they were qualified to teach rifle skills; they simply demonstrated deep knowledge.

We started with gun safety, then mechanics. From an arsenal of weapons heaped on a picnic table, Larry chose what he thought was the best fit for each of us. I fired a succession of .22-caliber rifles, from antique to modern, single-shot, with magazines and with clips. I didn't appreciate these mechanical differences until the following year when I went into the woods with a rifle for the first time. On this cold morning, it took all my concentration to handle the weapons safely while Dick kept me supplied with ammo and quiet encouragement. Using my yoga training in mindfulness and breath work, I discovered that I'm a pretty good shot, hitting the bull's-eye time and again.

I quickly learned that a .22 is not a deer rifle, nor are all guns the same. Larry handed me an M-4, a military rifle that kicked hard against my shoulder. Next, I fired an AK-47, which didn't even look like my idea of a gun. It's all sinewy metal and angles, lightweight and lethal. It's made for killing people—many and quickly—not for deer hunting.

At the end of the session, I retrieved my targets. Across the array of rifles I fired that morning, I hit my mark every time, but I was ambivalent about my success: proud to discover that I'm such a good shot and uneasy that I didn't have poor aim as an excuse to give up hunting right then. My life would be so much easier if I could just stick to the comfort of homegrown food and hiking trails, but at some inarticulate level, I knew that learning to hunt was my path to finding my place in the natural world. I also knew that trying to ignore this call to hunt would be as bad as ignoring the words that rise inside me, words it's my job to commit to the page. Somewhere between resignation and curiosity, I accepted that I would have to learn more about firearms and buy a deer rifle of my own.

* * *

Despite my inexperience handling firearms, and without ever intending to own any, we had three in the house: two rifles and a handgun. Tim learned firearm safety as a boy but had no interest in handling guns. I didn't even know what distinguished one from the other, except that the handgun looked especially lethal.

"That's because it's designed to kill people," my husband explained.

The pistol had belonged to Tim's father, who moved in with us at the end of his life. We found the gun after he died. It was in the bottom drawer of a steel toolbox that my father-in-law kept on his dresser. The box wasn't locked, and the gun wasn't loaded.

But still.

We had no idea the gun was in the house, or for what purpose.

Pops had been ill; had he considered taking his own life? He'd been a prisoner of war in Germany after the B-26 he co-piloted was shot down in 1944. He acquired the pistol between being set free and returning Stateside, a time he described as chaotic and perhaps the most dangerous of his service. Did he hold on to the handgun to feel safe? Or was it a souvenir of survival? Pops was a private man and a gentle soul. In the ten years I knew him, I'd seen him angry just once, and even then he didn't raise his voice, but reverted to the flat Midwestern drawl of his youth to indicate his ire. I had a hard time imagining him pulling a trigger. Finding the pistol after his death cast a wrinkled shadow on this man whom Tim so closely resembles and still deeply loves.

Pops taught organic chemistry at Dartmouth and lived in the house he shared with his youngest son, Andrew. It's a Federal-style antique that Pops and Andy were always planning to renovate, even as they trudged through the snow to the outhouse while forever discussing just how. The house fronts a dirt road, with acres of wilderness beyond the gardens in back. After he retired, Pops purchased a deer rifle "to keep the damn squirrels out of the orchard." But Pops had end-stage kidney failure, and his retirement days were mostly occupied by self-administering peritoneal dialysis, brewing tea, and reading. I don't know whether he ever fired the Remington before he came to live with us. In addition to indoor plumbing, we also had heat. After he died, we inherited both the rifle and the handgun.

The third gun in our arsenal was a single-shot, bolt action .22 that had belonged to my Aunt Joan's brother Larry, who'd been on the marksmanship team at Midwood High School in Brooklyn. While it now seems unthinkable that a public high school in New York City would host an after-school activity involving guns, such programs were common immediately following World War II. Larry graduated in 1948.

When Aunt Joan and Uncle Dave bought their summer place in Vermont, Larry gave the rifle to them. Uncle Dave stowed it in a closet, where it sat unused for twenty-five years. When Tim and I moved into our first house, Uncle Dave gave the rifle to us.

Following tradition, we also kept the rifle in a closet and forgot about it—until varmints raided the henhouse. Vowing revenge, Tim dusted it off and bought ammunition. This was back when Tim was on call every third night, and my parents would frequently visit, providing much-appreciated help with our three young daughters. One evening when Tim was on call, Dad carried the rifle out to the chicken coop at dusk. I accompanied him for the stakeout.

I'd never seen my father hold a firearm. I knew he'd been an infantryman during World War II, but Dad spoke about his army experience so rarely that I remember the first time he ever mentioned it to me. I was thirteen and still clueless that I occupied a special place in his heart as his only daughter, or that my older brothers, then aged fifteen and seventeen, were causing him the grief that sons cause their fathers. Dad and I were cleaning the kitchen after dinner when he told me,

"When you're seventeen, you think you know everything. Being shot at in combat changes that. If I still had the skill, I'd shoot past your brothers' ears so they'd learn what it's like." As far as I know, my father never owned a gun after leaving the service; he did, however, possess a mordant sense of humor slanted toward hyperbole.

That night, Dad and I sat out by the coop, feeding the mosquitoes while waiting for the culprits killing the chickens to show up. We were about to give up when two baby raccoons appeared. I exploded with invective, giving those two such a tongue-lashing they fled. No shots were fired.

The firearms we did have when I was growing up were water pistols, a cap gun, and an air rifle, and my brothers never let me shoot the air rifle. As Boy Scouts, they wore uniforms, went camping, and learned field craft, including firearm safety. Dad served as an assistant Scoutmaster in my older brothers' troop and as chairman of the troop that he helped establish for Jonathan, the youngest. My mother briefly wore a yellow kerchief around her neck as den mother to a basement of Cub Scouts. But my Brooklyn-born mom wasn't interested in Scouting when I raised the issue of Girl Scouts, and I didn't press her. As the only girl among boys, I'd already figured out that becoming a Girl Scout would have opened up yet another avenue of ridicule from my brothers, who, typical for boys of that era, acted as if being a boy was better than being a girl. I grew up believing this to be true.

* * *

I had briefly considered hunting deer with a camera instead of a rifle. I knew naturalists who have a deep knowledge of wildlife and don't kill it, so at Doe Camp, I attended a workshop on Critter Calling for Hunters and Photographers. The workshop was taught by Bradley Carleton, a professional guide, avid bird hunter, and four-time state champion in duck calling. In his earlier life, he sang opera. The class, as they say, was a hoot.

Bradley taught us a few of the 105 different known geese vocalizations: the basic honk, the moan, the rasp, the murmur, the whack, the chuckle, the laugh. Next, we learned turkey calls: the cluck, the purr, the gobble, and the putt. We also inspected different mechanisms hunters use to reproduce these calls in order to lure birds within shooting range. In the process of learning what birds have to say to one another, I realized how deaf I've been in the woods. No longer. Now that I knew what to listen for, I could imagine eavesdropping on woodland conversation instead of just passing through the woods on my way to a summit.

What the animals say is closely related to what they do, so listening to their talk is a way of learning what's happening in the forest. Crows are the town criers, alerting those in the understory of approaching predators, often starting a chain reaction of avian chatter. Deer are herd animals with their own language for alerting one another to perceived danger: sniffing to indicate suspicion; stomping to specify certain but undetermined menace; and snorting to signal a real and imminent threat. Fawns whine when they're nursing—or when they want to; they bleat when they're content; and they cry when they're in distress. Bucks speak a language of dominance with grunts, snorts, and wheezes. A doe will grunt to let others in the herd know she wants to socialize; she lets out a high-pitched bleat when content; and she will sound a kazoo-like bleat to let a buck know she's ready to mate. Hunters who learn how to imitate these sounds can call game to them, and humans who understand animal language can hear the complex drama of forest life. But I don't want to talk to the animals, nor trick them into coming toward me just to take their photograph.

I have a love-hate relationship with photography dating back to the days of black-and-white film, which I used to develop and print myself, a process I loved. But I never knew what to do with the piles of snapshots I felt obligated to take of my family. Five years into motherhood I stopped snapping photos entirely. I didn't like holding the camera between me and my children. I wanted to be present for their birthdays, sporting events, and performances, not document them. When the iPhone came out in 2007, I thought that having a telephone that was also a camera was one of the stupidest ideas of all time. Now it's the only camera I use, and I'm always snapping photos, but I still have never spent the time developing a system to index them. At least digital photos don't collect dust.

My friend Kathy, from Maine, takes fantastic wildlife photos, and she's developed a workable digital filing system so she can find them again. With her camera and enormous lenses, she's captured stunning images of wildlife in Alaska, Florida, the Galapagos, Iceland, and Zambia. These photos have helped me acknowledge certain truths about myself, namely: I'm more interested in becoming intimate with the landscape of home than sightseeing in faraway places, and photographing wild game isn't high-stakes enough to motivate me to learn how the flora, fauna, weather, time of day, time of year, and animal behavior are all interrelated, because I don't just want to read the landscape.

I want to eat it.

* * *

Shortly after returning from Doe Camp, I met Aunt Joan and Uncle Dave for lunch. Joan and Dave were New York City schoolteachers who spent their summers in Vermont. In the mid-sixties, I started visiting them for weeks at a time. It's mostly due to those visits that I came to Vermont for the summer in 1984.

As soon as the server handed us our menus, I started telling Joan and Dave about the critter-calling class at Doe Camp. "I learned that deer burp, grunt, and bleat," I said, enthusiastic about my new knowledge.

Aunt Joan peered over her menu and snapped, "Did you learn what sound they make when they're shot?"

"I bet it's a better death than the pig whose bacon you just ordered."
And just like that, we were taking sides.

To my dismay, Joan changed her order from a BLT to a salad with shrimp.

I didn't mean to shame her, but I also didn't like being scolded for learning more about the natural world from which we humans are becoming increasingly alienated, even as we're degrading it by what we eat.

I said nothing about Aunt Joan's choice of farmed shrimp raised in place of factory-farmed bacon. I'm sure the chickpeas and lettuce in my hummus salad also exploited laborers and burned fossil fuel on the journey from faraway fields to my restaurant plate. The ethics of food in our industrial age are complex, leaving each of us to make food choices based on an alphabet of attributes, from Affordability, Beliefs, and Culture to Yeast and Zest, for the profound connection to Earth and clan that comes from preparing and sharing food. It's this complexity that informs our personal choices, and, as with so many other hot-button issues, none of us is consistent or rational, so it pays to be tolerant.

I never would have snapped at Aunt Joan for ordering a bacon, lettuce, and tomato sandwich if I hadn't felt attacked for learning about the language of deer, or for wanting to harvest local, wild, organic meat.

* * *

Before I ever set foot in Vermont, I learned it was possible to harvest wild food from the sea. During my childhood in the early 1960s, my family vacationed in a rented cottage on eastern Long Island. Most mornings, we four kids donned "life preservers," as PFDs were called then, joined Mom and Dad aboard a wooden rowboat with a *putt-putt* engine, and motored out to a drawbridge, where we'd anchor. After the excitement of threading the hook into the mouth of our live bait, we dropped the line into the drink and baked in the sun. Occasionally, the wake of a passing boat would interrupt our deep boredom. Mom would slather us with Coppertone. Greasy and fragrant, we'd sink back into the hot wait, hoping that somehow, in all the vast water around us, a fish would find our baited hook toothsome enough to swallow.

Occasionally one did.

Then one of the poles would bend.

"I've got something!"

"A bite!"

"The net!"

Pandemonium in the small craft.

"Slow and steady," Dad would say as he reached out to help. We'd all lean over for the first glimpse of the catch, but Dad would order us back. "Steady the boat!"

It was flounder we were after, and sometimes that's what we caught: a fish that swims horizontal to the sea bottom, white on one side and dark green-brown on the side with both eyes, like a cartoon. Having a fish flopping on the bottom of the boat woke us to hope that maybe we'd catch another. The captive fish would be placed in a bucket of seawater. When I found staring at the sea unbearable, I stared at the helpless fish. Against improbable odds and vast boredom, we'd caught a fish! But I also recognized in the flounder's confinement to a bucket my own predicament of being held captive in the boat with mounting pressure on my bladder, leaving me no option but to hold still and endure.

Back at the cottage, Dad showed me how to sharpen the knife, open the fish, identify the guts, and examine the contents of its stomach, so I could see what the fish had eaten for its last meal. After Dad scraped off the scales, he fileted the fish, peeling off the backbone and ribs, which looked like a fragile, two-sided comb. The head, tail, fins, bones, and guts all went into the canal beside the cottage; the fillets went into the fridge.

At low tide, we motored out to the mudflats for clams. I was too little to rake, so I carried the bucket and watched the mud flow clear from the rake's metal basket every time it was drawn to the surface. Sometimes the basket held only rocks or seaweed, but any clams too big to fall through the wires were ours to keep. I guarded the bucket with care. Cherrystone clams were even more delicious than fish.

We ate whatever we harvested for dinner at the patio table. Tight-lipped clams opened like the mouths of baby birds. Mom dished a few onto each of our paper plates. As soon as they cooled enough, I'd pluck the soft muscle, dip it in melted butter laced with lemon juice, and plop it into my mouth. It was as succulent as the yolk of an egg. If we'd caught a flounder, Mom breaded and baked it so that the outside was crisp and the inside soft. The grownups squeezed lemon on theirs; we kids passed the ketchup. On days when we didn't fetch food from the sea, we ate hotdogs or hamburgers and fresh corn.

I also had my first experience harvesting cultivated food during one of those summers. Mom plunked Jonathan, a baby, down between the strawberry rows and handed him berries while the rest of us picked our own. Across the row, Michael, my oldest brother, filled three baskets before I filled one. He kept shouting, "I found a jackpot!"

Whatever a jackpot was, it had to be more interesting than the sun beating down on my head or the straw scratching my legs. It was in that strawberry patch that I learned how language can provide respite from boredom, and how the accumulation of berries in a basket is a prize.

* * *

Most of the food I ate growing up came from the A&P, a grocery store that would fit inside the grab-and-go section of ready-to-eat offerings at one of today's giant supermarkets. The A&P sold what I call "whole foods": foods that were presented as harvested and sold with limited packaging. Mom placed apples and oranges in brown paper bags and handed them along with a clutch of bananas to the Vegetable Man in charge of the produce section. He weighed and priced the fruit with a wax crayon on the bags and directly onto the peel of one of the bananas. Only some produce was prepackaged, like cellophane-wrapped iceberg lettuce; shriveled heads of garlic, two to a box with a see-through window; and unripe tomatoes cradled in a faux-basket of white plastic. The butcher behind the glass case offered whole chicken and ground beef, which he wrapped to order in brown paper and tied with string. Cottage cheese came in a waxed cardboard container from a dairy case stacked with golden boxes of oleo and yellow cartons of Velveeta, which I grew up thinking was cheese. Mom used these ingredients to prepare the dinners we ate with gusto: spaghetti and scrambled eggs, hot dogs and baked beans, ground beef in meatloaf, meat sauce, chili, and burgers. On special occasions, she braised a brisket or made a lasagna.

It wasn't what we ate that mattered as much as the rituals of dinnertime, when the six of us took our places around the yellow Formica table that filled the nook just off the kitchen. Dinner started with salad into which Mom always added a dollop of cottage cheese and tossed with a sweet and sour bottled dressing that made it all palatable. We waited while Dad doled it out, youngest to oldest. This salad ritual was our grace that ended when Mom picked up her fork. We ate "good bread" with the salad, meaning delicatessen pumpernickel or rye, served without butter. Dinner followed.

Some Friday nights and when we had company, we ate in the dining room with linen and silver. On Fridays, we blessed the Sabbath candles. As the daughter, I lit them. Dad said Hebrew words over the braided bread, which we tore with our hands. We all raised a glass for a taste of blessed wine. Invariably, we ate roast chicken, which Dad carved at the table. If we had company, there might be a bakery dessert. The food of my childhood was ordinary American fare, but the ritual of eating it made a lasting impression about the holiness of food.

* * *

To hunt, I needed a hunting license. To get a license, I had to pass an online self-study course and then sit for the state's in-person hunter safety exam. I planned to knock off the online course while staying in my brother Jonathan's San Francisco apartment for a DIY writing retreat while he was at an artist's residency. I spent a week at his place, brainstorming how to include ideas about food, civil discourse, human impact on the environment, and gender into my imagined narrative about learning to hunt, while also working through the hunter's education course. But the main reason I was in California was to visit my eldest daughter in her new West Coast life.

When Mim traveled in Rwanda, Kenya, Tanzania, and India, I knew she'd come home to pick up her mail. But when she moved to California earlier that year, she informed the post office of her new address. As delighted as I was that Mim had become the competent, creative, independent, and self-supporting adult we'd nurtured, I never imagined the poignancy I'd feel when she left to make a home of her own.

Mim was teaching at a school within walking distance of Jonathan's apartment. My plan was to study all morning and meet up with her when school let out. I logged in to *Today's Hunter* and began studying. The course, reading materials, and exams are written at a sixth-grade reading level. I have a PhD in English Literature and expected this to be easy, but I soon found that answers to simple-sounding questions like "What is a firearm?" were utterly opaque to me. What, exactly, *is* a firearm?

During the week I was in California, I studied the different kinds of rifle actions: bolt-, underlever-, pump-, semiautomatic, break, and revolving. I paid closer attention to the different kinds of safeties, the mechanisms that block the action and prevent a gun from firing. Safeties also come in a variety of styles, but none is fail-safe. When I read this, I wanted to give up.

Instead, I walked through the Mission District to the school where Mim was teaching life skills to parenting teens. She introduced me to her co-workers, who told me how much they loved working with her. I so admired Mim's courage and determination to move across the continent, find meaningful work, and thrive.

Back in Vermont, I continued studying what I needed to know to pass the test, much of which I no longer remember, like how to pattern a shotgun, hunt from a boat, or install a tree stand. I was operating on a need-to-know basis, adhering to Albert Einstein's advice: "The only thing that you absolutely have to know is the location of the library." Einstein lived before the World Wide Web. These days, if you can find your smartphone, you can ask Lady Google; she knows everything.

I did my best to commit information about rifles and hunting safety to long-term memory. Much of it is both obvious and sobering, like muzzle control, identifying your target before shooting, muzzle control, carrying a rifle safely in the field and across obstacles, muzzle control, maintaining a safe zone-of-fire, muzzle control, hunting sober, and muzzle control. But as one of my graduate school professors was fond of saying, "Reading ain't thinking. Writing is." Something similar is true about firearms: I could only learn so much by reading about guns; what I really needed to do was practice.

* * *

After we discovered Pop's guns, we'd consulted our friend Gunther Derby about how to get rid of them. Gunther collects firearms of historical interest. He did some research on the handgun and reported back that the pistol is a Walther P38, probably manufactured late in 1942 at the factory in Zella-Mehlis, Germany. He explained that there were still machine marks that would normally have been buffed out and that the individual parts weren't all stamped as was usual, leading him to believe the gun's manufacture was rushed and likely made by slave labor.

I had no idea a firearm could tell a story. Gunther's research taught me to think of guns as historical artifacts. I wish I knew the whole story behind Pops owning the Walther, though I'm not sure Pops would have ever told me. We gave Gunther the pistol on permanent loan; he bought Pop's rifle for his daughter. For sentimental reasons, we kept the .22 in the family.

Inspired by Gunther's research, I did some of my own. Our twenty-two caliber rifle is a Harrington & Richardson Model 365, manufactured in about 1946 in Worcester, Massachusetts. It's what's known as "a plinking rifle." In today's world of long-range, high-velocity automatic rifles, this one is decidedly low-octane. Only a few thousand of them were made; Larry's is number 1195. It's a beautiful artifact with a walnut stock and its original Lyman 55 rear peep sight. But owning a gun and learning its provenance is not the same as knowing how to use it.

Despite their early socialization, my brothers have grown into peaceable men with passions for sailing, skiing, surfing, sea kayaking, tennis, and squash. They're not gun owners, and they're scattered from coast to coast, so it's doubtful they could have helped me anyway. Tim had the knowledge, but no interest, so I emailed Gunther, who lives nearby. Would he help me learn to shoot?

"Absolutely," he fired back. Had I ever fired a rifle? When? What caliber? "If you are just starting out, it would be advisable to begin with a .22."

I was pleased to report that I'd fired a .22, a .30-06, an AK-27, and an M4.

"It sounds like you've seen enough action to qualify for the SEALS," he emailed.

"My understanding is that SEALS can hit their targets," I replied. I'm still not sure why I downplayed my skill at that moment. Did I think my sharpshooting was really a fluke? Or was this some misguided, hard-to-shake notion about femininity: that to be a good shot was unladylike? Since when did I ever profess to be a *lady*?

Gunther invited me over for a gallery tour of his collection, warning me that his guns are primarily historical in nature and not really designed for hunting. He assured me that they were all in working order, but some are hefty, dating back to the 1800s; his most modern rifles are from World War II. "Come over and decide which rifles you want to shoot by handling them first."

Instead of a man cave, Gunther retreats to a second-story aerie of several rooms. One room has a cathedral ceiling with windows at one end and a high wall hung with firearms on the other. Gunther is tall, but he still needed a ladder to reach the firearms. He gave me a history lesson with each rifle as he handed it down to me: underlever, as in the Westerns; bolt action; semiautomatic; carbine, a short-barreled rifle from cavalry days; and an M1.

"I think that's the rifle my father carried," I said.

Gunther handed it to me.

"Yikes, it's heavy!"

"Ten pounds," he said. "Do you know where your dad was?"

I told Gunther what I knew. My dad landed on Utah Beach on the ninety-third day after D-Day and, as he put it, "walked across Europe." He was wounded in Germany in February 1945, sent to a hospital in England, and was in London on V-E Day, when the lights went on for the first time in six years.

I knew this from the letters my dad wrote to my mom while he was overseas. She returned the originals to him on his seventy-fifth birthday. Dad typed and annotated them with memories of army life, complete with photographs and copies of military documents. He titled it *War Story* and sent bound photocopies to us kids.

Gunther explained what made the M1 such a warhorse: It uses the .30-06 Springfield cartridge, the United States Army's standard ammunition from 1906 until the 1970s. It's semiautomatic, meaning it fires and reloads every time the trigger is pulled. It has an eight-round clip, and when the last round is fired, the empty clip automatically ejects, locking the bolt open for swift reloading. As soon as a new clip is inserted, the bolt snaps forward, and the first cartridge slides into the chamber, so the rifle is ready to fire. It has fixed iron sights, and it's easy to clean in the field, making it an effective firearm for an infantry soldier in Europe during World War II.

Despite his many months in a foxhole, Dad's letters only mention guns once, and it isn't his own. He writes to "Blondie" (later my mom), shortly after landing in France:

Another man was killed by having a rifle aimed at him (by himself or by another of our soldiers) and the "unloaded rifle" went off. No one was ever shot by a loaded gun—they were always "unloaded." The basic rule with guns is: Never point them at anybody or anything unless you intend to shoot.

This is what I learned as "muzzle control."

In consultation with Gunther, I chose four rifles to try, including the M1. We reconvened the following week at the home of Lester Chaffee, a mutual friend who has a woodpile in his backyard to serve as a backstop to the assortment of rotten pumpkins, tin cans, and plastic bottles filled with water we set out as targets.

Lester is a little older than Gunther, a little shorter, and a lot less garrulous. I've known these two for over twenty years, but they've known each other that much longer. They're also in the same line of work, pushing pencils at desk jobs past retirement age. *Decent* hardly does them justice, and I know I'm lucky to have them introduce me to firearms. But I was nervous.

For one thing, I'd already forgotten what made the rifles Gunther brought along different from each other. One was the M1 and another was an underlever, but was it also the carbine? I reminded myself that to learn, I have to accept ignorance. This is hard.

I was also unsettled that the guys were shooting pistols, which hardly jibed with my idea of these two mild-mannered men. Worse, they were shooting from a standing position: legs wide, arms outstretched with both hands gripping the gun, as if they had the bad guys in their sights and meant business.

And I was stymied: there was nothing for me to lean on or steady myself against, so I sat on the grass and braced my elbows against my bent knees. Meanwhile, Gunther's entertaining banter, filled with arcane information about each of the rifles, distracted me. I shot high. I didn't just miss the targets; I missed the woodpile. I tried lying on my belly. I was fighting humiliation when at last I made a pumpkin explode, but I was still flustered. Nevertheless, I kept at it. With their encouragement—or was it insistence? —I fired a handgun, which was easier than firing the historical rifles that recoiled. My right shoulder would be sore the rest of the week.

Both Gunther and Lester seemed to be enjoying themselves; it's possible they were just amused at what seemed like the impossible task I'd set for myself. Unless a large buck stands broadside in an open field at thirty feet and doesn't move, there's no way I'll ever get off a clean killing shot. And deer simply don't hang out in conditions like that in Vermont.

Clearly, what I needed was a lot more practice. The .22 I owned was a perfect gun for that, but it hadn't been fired in who knows how long. Gunther suggested that I take it to a gunsmith.

"Is there one you recommend?"

"Mike Theodorou, doing business as The Windham Armorer," Gunther said. "He's skilled, local, and affordable—and also a tad eccentric," adding, "He's a double amputee, just so you're prepared."

* * *

Mike worked out of his modest two-story home located in the section of town where Brattleboro's factory workers once lived, back when Brattleboro had factories. The entrance to Mike's house had been retrofitted for a wheelchair. I followed the instructions he gave me over the phone: ring the bell, identify myself through the speaker, let myself in, and descend wooden stairs to the cellar. The stone foundation walls and low ceiling came into view as I descended. When I turned, I saw Mike, a man with no legs, few fingers, and an aura of kindness. He was sitting in a wheelchair tucked into a space crammed with tools and appliances, all within arms' reach. I handed him the rifle.

"Nice," he said, opening the bolt and looking down the barrel. "You've been storing it with the muzzle up," he said, shaking his head. "No good."

I couldn't place his accent.

He raised his large brown eyes. "You have to keep dirt and moisture out of the barrel." He swiveled so that when he lifted the gun to his shoulder it was facing a far corner of the room, away from me. "Where did you get it?"

I told him the story of the gun's migration from Midwood High School in Brooklyn to rural Vermont.

"It's in good shape."

"Can you check it out, make sure it's safe?"

"Sure. I clean it, make sure it works. It cost maybe fifty bucks." He pulled one of those old-fashioned claim tags with a string threaded through a reinforced hole and wrote my name and number on it. "You have a hunting rifle?"

"Not yet."

He pulled out a catalog thicker than the New York City phone book of my childhood and started paging through it. "I have lots of good deer rifles." He flipped the tissue-thin pages, pointing out rifles and telling me the pros and cons of each. I looked over his shoulder, but I couldn't read the fine print. All I saw were the prices in boldface. Four digits. Yikes.

As if Mike was privy to my thoughts, he settled his index finger on a rifle he recommended and said, "This is retail. I give you a better price."

While we were talking, the phone rang. The answering machine was on speaker, so I heard the caller's arrogance as he told Mike how to fix his firearm and how much the repair should cost. Mike scowled but didn't pick up. The next time the phone rang, a different customer described what was wrong with his rifle and asked if this was something Mike could fix.

Mike took the call. "No problem," he said. He gave the caller his federal firearms license number so the guy could send the gun through the mail.

We resumed talking.

Mike told me about his boyhood in Greece, working in a foundry long before anyone thought about workplace safety, so I assumed he lost his legs in an industrial accident as a teen, before arriving in the United States.

I liked this man, and if there had been another chair and I didn't have other errands, I would have stayed longer, but I had to get on with the day.

"I'll call you when it's ready. Next week. Do you have ammunition?" Before I could answer, he said, "I can sell you a brick at a good price."

"What's a 'brick'?"

"Ten boxes of fifty rounds."

Five hundred rounds ought to help me learn to shoot. "Sounds good."

A week later, I returned to retrieve my rifle and ammo. I wrote Mike a check.

"It's a nice gun," he said, handing it over.

"Thank you. I'll be back."

But it was almost a year before I was ready to buy a rifle, and when I called Mike, his answering machine said, "Thanks for calling. I'll be out for a while." There was no invitation to leave a message.

I called Gunther to find out if he knew what was the matter.

"Cancer's back."

* * *

I'd only fired the .22 once in the months since picking it up from the gunsmith, so I was nervous when I returned to Roger's to "sight it in"—gun-speak for adjusting the metal loop I look through so the bullet hits what I'm aiming at.

Roger has a range behind his house and had set up a shooting bench of molded plastic and bent chrome that reminded me of the white desks attached to red, yellow, and blue seats from my high school days. We clamped my rifle into a vise and used sandbags to support the barrel.

Roger nodded at the target set into a pit dug into the hillside. "That's about thirty-five yards. Let's see what you can do."

I sat at the desk, took aim, and fired.

We sauntered from the bench to the target. Roger plucked a twig from the leaf litter, broke off an inch, and stuck the stub into the hole where the bullet entered the target just above and to the right of center. "High and outside," he said, like he was calling pitches.

We strolled back.

I watched Roger adjust the sight with the turn of a screw. "Try that."

I sat down, put on my hearing protection, took aim, and squeezed.

We journeyed back to the target. Roger stuck a piece of twig in the second hole, in the strike zone.

He made another adjustment.

I fired again.

We walked back to the target.

Home run.

"Well," he said. "You can shoot, that's for sure."

"But I can't hunt deer with this," I said, taking the .22 out of the vise. I knew I needed a more powerful firearm to hunt deer. "Where does a person buy a deer rifle?

Roger told me about the different gun shops in the area. There's the one he won't go to. "They treat me like I don't know nothing about firearms." There's another he won't recommend. "They're kind of a rough crowd, and maybe not such a nice place for a woman." He mentioned Cabela's, a big box store, the kind of chain I try to avoid.

"What about Sam's?" Sam's is the local outdoor outfitters where I buy hiking gear, snowshoes, sleeping bags, tents, backpacks, yoga clothes, winter jackets, jeans, socks, wool shirts, and even the occasional dress. I've walked past the hunting department where they sell licenses, fishing tackle, bows, and rifles, but I've never bought anything there.

"You can go there, if you want."

"What other choice do I have?"

"I've got some rifles you could try."

"One you'd sell me?"

"I might," he said. "Follow me."

We walked the long hallway into the house. The hallway bisects what used to be two garage bays that have been closed in. Antlers of all sizes stick out from both walls like a forest of bare branches.

"Sally, Dennis's girlfriend, she calls this 'Antler Alley'" Roger said. Since Helen died, I'd stayed in touch with Dennis through Roger; the two men are longtime friends.

"I can see why."

Roger lifted a six-point rack from the wall and turned it over. "Nineteen ninety-two," he said, reading off the back of the skull, where he'd written the date.

"Do you remember where you shot that one?"

He lifted his eyes from the antlers in his hands and gave me a look that said, *You've got to be kidding*. "I remember every deer I ever shot." He told me how much this deer weighed. I'm now pretty sure that if I'd asked him what the weather was like and what time of day it was when he took the shot, he could tell me, no problem. His memory for every hunt remains vivid, including where he was, what rifle he used, where the shot landed, and how he managed to drag the animal out of the woods. It wasn't till a few years later that I learned he kept a written list. In his lifetime, he's taken over seventy deer—so far.

We entered the house and descended to the basement, past a parade of boots waiting on the steps: steel-toed logging boots, rubber mud boots, lace-up hunting boots, felt-lined snow boots, and a pair of hip-high waders. Roger showed me some of his hunting gear stored in giant plastic bins, all neatly labeled: Spring Bear Hunting (filled with insulated rain gear); Canadian Cold (with boots Neil Armstrong might have worn on the moon, only black). Woolen overalls and jackets hung from the rafters along with the giant chain saws for his winter work in the woods. Roger had me feel the fabric of the hunting clothing he thinks is the best.

"Does Sam's carry this?" I asked, suspecting they didn't.

"You have to buy it direct from the manufacturer," he said of his top-of-the-line woolens.

"But how do you try it on?" My heart sank.

"They come to the hunting show at the Big E. End of February."

Drive to a hunting show in Massachusetts? I didn't think so. It's not that I wouldn't learn a lot about hunting and hunting culture; it's just that I don't care for highways or crowds. Besides, February was on the other side of this year's hunting season. I was working to be licensed and armed by November, so the Big E event wouldn't do me any good.

I didn't say any of this out loud as I followed Roger to the corner of the basement, where I expected to see one of those steel gun safes that look like a super-sturdy filing cabinet. Instead, we came to a cement-walled room built into the corner of the foundation. The fireproof door was as thick as a bank vault's, with a combination lock built in. The room was about the size of a full bath—only this room was crammed with firearms. One wall had rifles roosting in long, narrow pigeonholes; another wall had shorter compartments for pistols. A third had shelves sagging under boxes of ammo.

"Wow. That's a lot of guns." An understatement.

"I hunt with some. Some are collectors' items."

I knew better than to question what people collect. Without ever setting out to start a collection, I own a drawer full of classic Pyrex bowls. Designed in the 1940s, a set includes four different-size bowls that nest: yellow, green, red, and blue. My friend Kelly gave me my first set over thirty years ago, and I started picking up more at flea markets and yard sales. I use mine daily, have given a set to each of my kids, and keep extras in reserve, just because.

Roger told me about the Remington Model 700 Classics, a set of collectors' rifles. He bought one every year for over twenty years and then sold them to buy the winch, fork, bucket, and York rake to go with the shiny orange Kubota tractor parked outside. Even so, there's only room enough inside the gun safe for Roger, so I stood outside as he pulled out one rifle after another.

"This is Ma Bell."

"Ma Bell?"

"Yeah, because you can reach out and touch someone with it."

"I remember that ad." He handed me the rifle.

"This one's Old Thumper."

I remember guns' names better than their specs. I think Ma Bell's a bolt-action 7mm STW, but I don't remember what that means. Old Thumper's a 300 Weatherby Magnum, whatever that is.

Ma Bell has a dark, green stock made from some kind of composite material. "I want a gun with a wooden stock," I said.

"Why do you say that? Wood's heavy." He nodded at the rifle I was holding. "That's six and a quarter pounds."

I frowned. I didn't know what a rifle was supposed to weigh, or even why weight mattered.

Roger told me about hunting in Nova Scotia, where it's wet all the time. "The wooden stock delaminated. I won't never buy a hunting rifle with a wood stock again."

Hmm. I'd just learned two things: Roger doesn't like a rifle with a wooden stock, and I'll be hunting in the rain.

"So I can't hunt with a wooden rifle in the rain?"

"Vermont's different. It's not an island in the North Atlantic."

Fair enough. By now, my brain was saturated, and I was done for the day.

Roger told me he'd choose some rifles for me to try.

Before I left, I told Roger about my plan to hike the Long Trail.

"Tim going with you?"

"No. I'm going with a friend from college."

"Another woman?"

"Yeah."

"You best be carrying bear spray."

"I wasn't planning on it."

"You better," he said. "It doesn't just work on bears."

"We'll be fine." I wasn't worried about bears on the trail; black bears are shy. But humans? I hadn't even thought about them.

THREE

HIKING

Jan and I met in college. We became friends our senior year, when we were among seven women known collectively as The Red House, an off-campus dump with seven bedrooms, two bathrooms, and mice. Jan and I were the only ones willing to set and empty the traps, but we really bonded over cross-country skiing at night.

After we graduated, Jan lived in Oakland and I lived in Manhattan. When I visited her in California, we did things: We skied in the Sierra Nevada by day and we slept in the back of her Pinto at night; we bathed in the Calistoga mud in the morning and tasted Napa Valley wine in the afternoon. When Jan visited me in New York, we talked. She'd tell me about her family, her friends, and her adventures, and I'd tell her about mine. Then she moved to Alaska and I moved to Vermont. For most of our long friendship, we lived parallel lives far apart. Even after the advent of email, we only corresponded by snail mail about once a year. Jan's Christmas letter would arrive about March. I'd reply with a Valentine in July.

It didn't matter. We'd pick up mid-sentence whenever we were together again. Because we knew each other's backstories, we could move immediately into the present. Jan was a splendid storyteller; I listened spellbound. And when it was my turn, Jan listened so intently, I knew I was heard.

Jan was an outdoorswoman whose motto was "Just say *Yes!*" and who welcomed adventure. At the sight of a grizzly, she reached for her camera; when a fellow hiker was stranded by an avalanche, she organized the rescue; when the sea plane failed to arrive at the end of a wilderness paddle, she hitched a ride on a passing yacht. But the previous year, Jan had travelled from Alaska to tell me in person that her marriage to the man she'd known since she was fourteen and had been married to since she was twenty-two was ending. It was the first time in our forty-year friendship I'd ever seen her distraught. As she was getting ready to return home, I blurted, "Do you want to hike the Long Trail with me?"

"Yes!" She flashed her luminous smile. "What's that?"

We scheduled the almost 300-mile hike from Massachusetts to Canada for the following summer. It's the trail that Tim and I had been section-hiking for the past thirty years and still hadn't finished. What I was proposing to Jan was a through-hike, where we'd hike the entire distance in one go. I was surprised how relieved I was at the prospect of hiking with Jan rather than Tim.

* * *

Tim grew up in New Hampshire and had been climbing in the White Mountains since he was a boy. He's summited all but one of the forty-eight peaks over four thousand feet, some more times than he can count. We started climbing these mountains together during our courtship, continued through each of my pregnancies, and talked about climbing the last one together, back when it seemed likely I'd catch up. But it took my knees a week to recover after a four-day weekend when we left the kids with my folks and hiked thirty-eight miles over six summits for a total elevation gain of fifteen thousand feet. Instead of feeling chuffed at my accomplishment, I thought it was another instance of not being good enough. That's when we switched from peak bagging in the White Mountains to section-hiking the Long Trail along the spine of the Greens.

After a few years of weekend overnights near home, we'd reached mid-state and set out on a forty-one mile hike over eleven peaks in five days and called it "vacation." I'm trained as a literary critic and see metaphor and allusion everywhere. I wasn't just at the midway point of the Long Trail, but also midway through my life's journey, and like the narrator in Dante's *Inferno*, I found myself in a dark wood. One day, we walked from eight in the morning until seven at night, covering fourteen grueling miles. The next day, we climbed the Great Cliff of Mount Horrid. (I'm not making these names up.) Even weighting Tim's backpack with forty pounds to my thirty didn't slow him down. Nevertheless, I expected to keep up, driven by that childhood belief that to be *good enough* I had to be just like the boys. Despite birthing babies, I still mistook equality for sameness and thought I was supposed to be able to match Tim step for step, even though he's over six feet tall, nimble as a goat, and indefatigable.

He waited for me every hour or so. When I caught up with him in Romance Gap, his nose was in a tattered paperback. He looked up. "I want to read you a poem."

I dropped my pack. "All I want is water."

He looked wounded.

After slaking my thirst, I tried to sound reasonable. "You know, I'd like a chance to sit and read poetry, too."

"But we've only gone four miles!"

This was supposed to be another fourteen-mile day. I hoisted my pack and toiled on. A mile later, we crossed Sucker Brook. That did it—I was a sucker for leaving the planning of this trip to Tim. His idea of a vacation was feeling like a forced march. By the time we entered the Breadloaf Wilderness, we still had four miles to make the night's shelter, including almost nine hundred feet of elevation to the crest of Burnt Hill.

I was burnt, all right, so Tim shifted into hyperdrive, doubling back to carry my pack. He loves playing the knight in shining armor; I hate being a damsel in distress.

When we made camp, I finally spoke up. "I like hiking," I said. "In moderation."

"You mean you'd like to have fun that's enjoyable?"

This is an old joke between us.

"Yeah. A vacation that's not just work."

* * *

After Jan's visit, I spent the summer revising a novel, blogging, recording radio commentaries, and writing bread-and-butter copy for a major medical center. But that was just work. Summer in Vermont includes tending the vegetable patch, picking berries, and raising chickens for the freezer—tasks whose doing is determined by weeds, ripeness, water, and feeding, all of which can be complicated by insect infestation, predator activity, and dramatic weather events.

Interspersed with these imperatives are others unique to summer, like cooling off in the river and planning a week off the farm—also known as vacation. Tim and I planned to bike the C&O Canal towpath from Cumberland, Maryland, to Washington, DC, until I broke my ankle on a routine hike to the summit of Stratton Mountain, the closest peak to where I live. We went on vacation anyway, but instead of biking point to point, we hopscotched with the car so I never pedaled more than fifteen miles while wearing my Aircast. My ankle healed, but my confidence took a hit: how would I be able to hike the Long Trail?

A broken ankle should have been no impediment to target practice. I'd planned to spend part of the summer learning to handle the .22, finishing the hunter safety course, and navigating through untracked woods—skills I needed to develop in order to be ready to hunt when Jan and I returned from our adventure. But I didn't.

Any number of afternoons that summer I thought, *Today's a good day for target practice.* But I never locked the dog in the house or set up a target, Instead, I took Leo for a walk, or I picked up a book and read. Deep down, though, I knew procrastination was a manifestation of ambivalence. What I didn't know was what aspect of learning to hunt I was most ambivalent about: being off-trail in the woods by myself, carrying a rifle, or shooting a deer.

I was also ambivalent about my status as an empty-nester. Not only had Mim moved to California, but Naomi, my middle, moved to Brooklyn; and Ruth, my youngest and her partner, flew off to teach English in the former Soviet republic of Georgia. But I wasn't left alone. My ninety-year-old father moved to a senior residence in nearby Brattleboro. He'd been married to my mother for sixty-six years and endured widowhood for two. It was the first time in his long life he'd ever lived alone. I visited him several times a week and helped him with tech support and hearing for his worn-out ears. I also drove him to the indoor pool where he became popular with a group of middle-aged ladies.

Despite my full and satisfying life, I still felt the desire to hunt thrumming like the *basso continuo* in baroque music, repeating harmonic variations of the question, How am I going to learn?

* * *

It turned out that one of the hardest things about going for a 272-mile hike was carving out the time to do it. My freelance life was busier than ever. Editors I'd worked for were calling me with new assignments; editors I didn't know were pitching stories to me; the Vermont Humanities Council had me driving around Vermont for their Speakers Bureau; the Brattleboro Area Hospice asked me to develop a literature-based reading program about end-of-life issues; the local Osher Lifelong Learning Institute invited me to give a series of lectures on Virginia Woolf; and I received grant funding to teach memoir writing at the local library. This was in addition to writing a biweekly post for Live to Write—Write to Live, the blog of the New Hampshire Writers Network about the business and craft of writing; bimonthly commentaries for Vermont Public Radio; weekly posts to Living in Place, my own blog; and teaching both for the Vermont Humanities public programs and running a weekly writing circle out of my home.

It's true that I like pumping out so much work. It's also true that hunting in November seemed a long way off. I hadn't even planted the vegetable patch yet, and hunting comes after the harvest. But truest of all, I was focused on hiking the Long Trail with Jan.

I had initially proposed the hike in a flash of intuition that it would do Jan a great deal of good. But as our departure date approached, I started to list the ways I could benefit, too.

1. I saw the hike as a chance to press my reset switch. For some time, I'd been publishing exclusively short-form pieces. Meanwhile, two long-form projects had been languishing: one in rough draft and the other in my head. I wanted to return to these projects, and I knew that a long walk would help me regain the capacity for long thoughts.

2. My idea of a good day is one spent at my desk and not in the car; I don't like to leave home if I don't have to, and I try to limit my driving to what's necessary. For most of my teaching and speaking gigs, driving is necessary. If this hike went well, I'd travel only by foot.

3. In my regular life, I eat dirt-to-dinner a lot of the time, which is delicious, environmentally sound, and labor intensive. I was looking forward to a month of food-as-fuel: Jan and I were packing instant meals of fast-cooking grains and freeze-dried beans and greens. We'd have no extensive prep on the trail; all we'd have to do is boil water.

4. Since transplanting myself to Vermont, I'd put down roots so deep that I often found it hard to leave. But I know the world's bigger than my seventeen acres, and I wanted to remember to stay grounded without being stuck. As we walked the length of the state, we'd be on the move all day and would take shelter in a different place each night.

5. Despite efforts against entropy, I live a cluttered life, with piles of books and magazines on every surface, closets full of shoes for every season, a wide variety of outdoor wear, drawers full

of headlamps and compasses, cross-country skis going back to the wooden-ski days, and enough snowshoes, ice skates, boats, paddles, and personal floatation devices to outfit a small camp. I hoped that carrying my food, clothing, and shelter on my back would help me learn how little I actually need.

6. As a self-employed writer, I'm always setting goals and assigning myself tasks and organizing my time. I was looking forward to life on the trail, where day after day all I'd have to do is hoist my pack and hike.

7. While I'd love to make it to Canada, I knew there were a lot of reasons I might not. My goals were to walk as far as I could and to have fun. When a former colleague learned about my adventure, she said, "I'm envious that you can go on such a journey while the rest of us slog away at our computers." I was hoping that after slogging through the woods for a month, I'd return to my computer with renewed enthusiasm, concentration, and joy.

8. This would be the longest spell away from home since the summer I lived in Paris when I was twenty-three, and longer than I'd ever been away from Tim in over thirty years. He would be both keeping the woodchucks out of the garden at home and resupplying us along the trail in addition to doctoring. We'd come to depend on each other, he and I, to the point where I've become more competent in tasks where I already excel (time management, vegetable production, household finances) and more dependent on him for his strengths (firewood, snow removal, orienteering). Instead of following Tim into the woods, as I had for the last three decades, I'd be hiking with Jan.

9. I'd be unplugged and offline while hiking, eliminating the greatest distraction of my modern life.

10. My daily walks at home always loop back to where I start; on the Long Trail, I'd be hiking away from home, day after day, to an unknown destination that would reveal itself one step at a time.

Jan and I blocked out thirty days for the hike, starting in mid-August. We video chatted weekly, discussing what gear we already owned, how much it weighed, and what we needed to borrow or buy. Tim didn't think gear mattered as much as getting in shape.

"Don't you think you should practice hiking with your pack?" he asked—repeatedly.

"I just need to hike," I replied, not hiding my annoyance.

A dozen years earlier, when I'd signed up in December to run a half marathon in May he said, "Really? That's not enough time to train."

It was.

I knew he meant well, but I had enough self-doubt for us both. All I wanted from him was encouragement. It came as an invitation in early July with fine weather in the forecast.

"Let's go for a hike!" he said.

I accepted.

"How about Moosilauke?"

I've climbed this 4,802-footer in New Hampshire several times. Its name means "the bald place," and the top of the mountain is above tree line, with sweeping, 360-degree views.

Tim was already thumbing through the guidebook. "What about the Beaver Brook Trail for something new?"

"Read it to me."

He read in a soothing monotone, as if the trail description was a lullaby and the hike something I could do in my sleep.

"*It passes the beautiful Beaver Brook Cascades ... The section along the cascades is extremely steep and rough, making this trail the most arduous route to Moosilauke in spite of its relatively short distance ... with many rock steps, wooden steps, and hand rungs ..."*

"It sounds tough," I said.

"But beautiful. And just a two-hour drive."

I was thinking about it.

"We'll make an early start."

"You mean get to the trailhead before three?" I was smiling now. I'm the early riser, not him.

The next day, I wrote for a couple of hours before Tim woke up and said, "Let's hike!"

We enjoyed a robust and leisurely breakfast, made sandwiches, and arrived at the trailhead just before noon.

I climbed to the music of the falling water and stopped to enjoy the view of the cascade tumbling over a collage of gray granite slabs, green lichen, and white water. I was mesmerized by the falls until I imagined slipping into the torrent. I stepped back and continued upward. When the trail left the stream, I was overcome by a thirst I recognized as a symptom of anxiety. Happy to rest and drink some water, I relaxed. In hindsight, it was a great pitch. The rest of the hike was just ordinary-beautiful: a rocky trail through mostly eastern hemlock and balsam fir, with occasional views over the Jobildunk Ravine.

When we reached tree line, we leaned into the wind and soon joined other hikers perched on the rocky summit. Some of the hikers were closing in on the northern end of the Appalachian Trail at Mount Katahdin in Maine, just four hundred miles away. I was happy where I was, with clear views of the New Hampshire Whites, the Vermont Greens, and New York's Adirondacks off to the west.

I was tired on the way down and concentrated on my footing next to the waterfalls. We stepped out of the woods at a quarter to six. Six hours on the trail. I wondered if I'd be able to hike this much day after day on the Long Trail.

I had a hint two weeks later when Ruth and Ian, back from their year abroad, joined us backpacking in the White Mountains. They're long-legged hikers and have both through-hiked the Long Trail, Ian twice. I carried a thirty-pound pack over four 4,000-foot mountains. When we stepped out of the woods three days and twenty-three miles later, Ian said, "Deb, you can do the Long Trail, no problem. You'll crush it."

It was just the encouragement I needed.

* * *

It was mid-August when friends dropped us off at the trailhead in Western Massachusetts. Jan and I heaved our packs onto our backs and staggered under their weight. With poles to help us balance over the rocky terrain, we started hiking the three miles through the woods to the Vermont border, where a sign welcomed us to the Long Trail. We created our own fanfare by snapping a photo. While there was no registration to hike the trail, the Green Mountain Club required we document our hike in order to qualify for their official recognition when we finished—a certificate and a patch.

The day was hot and oppressively humid.

About twenty minutes in, I panicked. "We're never going to make it by September eighth"— so Jan could catch her flight back to Alaska.

"What do you mean?" Jan asked.

"We're going too slow," I said, trying to imagine reaching Journey's End at this pace.

"But we just started!"

"We slow down when we talk."

We decided the storyteller would walk behind the listener, who'd set the pace.

An hour later, we sat on a trailside log and ate lunch. By three in the afternoon, we reached the first shelter, where we rested and snacked. It was still hot and sticky, but the woods provided shade, so we pushed on.

By seven that evening, we were still walking. The light was fading from dim to dark. My fear rose like swamp gas. "What are we going to do if we don't find the next shelter?" I failed to keep the worry out of my voice.

"We'll get there," Jan said. "It can't be too far now."

I hoped so. I was glad one of us was calm.

A few minutes later, the shelter came into sight. Relief washed over me. We made it. Now we could make dinner, eat, go to sleep. But Jan said, "I'm going to wash up."

As if we were modern day followers of Artemis, we walked downstream for a sponge bath. It felt luxurious to remove the day's salt from my skin and pull on my camp shorts and shirt, slip my feet into my Crocs.

It was fully dark by the time dinner was ready. We cooked the meal that weighed the most and ate by the light of our headlamps; brushed our teeth by the light of the stars; slept the sleep of the footsore. When we broke camp after breakfast, my pack was two meals lighter, and so was my heart.

I asked Jan to fill me in on the divorce, now final.

"I'll start with the day of discovery." That's lawyer-speak for the day she found out that all the texting between her ex and his co-worker was the start of the emotional infidelity that developed into the real thing.

And so our long talk began.

For the first half of the hike, where the terrain is relatively easy, Jan looked backward, retelling the story of her marriage from beginning to end. As we made our way northward, the mountains became higher, the terrain harder, and the views above tree line more spectacular. Each time we reached a summit, we could see where we'd been and gain a glimpse of where we were going.

Then Jan walked ahead. For all her adventuring around the world, she'd never been in the northern forest before. She stopped to photograph the varieties of fungus, remarked on the thinness of soil covering the glacial till, and didn't understand how we could cross so many roads seemingly in the middle of nowhere. I gave her my Speaker's Bureau lectures about the history of settlement and transportation in Vermont, the history of Vermont politics, and the difficulty of bringing broadband to rural Vermonters, all based on my research for a trilogy of novels set in the fictional town of Orton. Usually, each lecture took about an hour, followed by Q&A. On the Long Trail, we measured conversations in miles—and kept all the wildlife away.

We talked and walked for eleven hours a day. Some days we covered seventeen miles; other days we ran out of steam and hiked just eight. But we never ran out of stories. After the halfway point, I confessed my plans to start hunting. Jan told me about her older daughter, who had just harvested her first deer. That small bit of information opened a sliver of possibility that I could actually do so, too.

* * *

Jan and I were born within five days of each other, and we'd just turned sixty. We'd both cared for our parents into old age; only my father was still alive. We were now more often in awe of our daughters than we were worried about them. We were on the threshold of new territory: Jan was as surprised to find herself single as I was to be married.

After the first humid, muggy week on the trail, we had remarkably good weather, and on the trail, we had remarkably good luck and no drama. When Tim met us with our last resupply, we knew we would finish. A few days later, we basked in the long view from the final summit, imagining ways to shape meaningful lives for what we thought would be the next thirty years. We reached the Canadian border elated, tired, and changed. Between Massachusetts and Canada, Jan stopped telling the story of blame and regret. She changed her story: She was now an independent woman who could accept every invitation to adventure that came her way. And she did. Since her separation and divorce, she'd traveled in Vietnam, biked in Croatia, rafted down the Colorado, and paddled through the Gates of the Arctic National Park. She fell in love and learned to value time by herself.

For me, hiking the Long Trail was good preparation for hunting.

I learned how much light there is between dusk and dawn. Put another way: I learned how little light I actually need to see in the dark. I learned how pleasant it is to be outdoors in the rain, how precious a resource water is. It had been a dry summer, and water was scarce during our last five days. On our last night, we stayed at a shelter whose water source was a shallow well, but the bucket for priming the hand pump was empty. We dropped our packs and carried the bucket a mile back to the last stream crossing, adding two more miles to what was already a hot, nine-mile day. And that was okay: without the pack, I floated through the forest, carrying only the water jug. The September afternoon light slanted through the tall fir, staining the bits of visible sky blue, peach, and pink. Back at the shelter, we primed the pump, filled all our water vessels, and left the priming bucket brimming. I learned that adversity is also opportunity.

Thanks to Jan's example, I also learned how to stay calm in the woods. Thanks to Tim's essential support—resupplying us weekly with clean clothes, chocolate, and bourbon—I was reminded that our marriage is one of mutual dependency, and that asking for help isn't the same as being helpless.

Most importantly, hiking the Long Trail reinforced the truth that the way to reach a long-term goal is to meet shorter, daily ones. Each day on the trail, we advanced a few more miles toward Canada. Each day at my desk, I add words to the page. When I started hunting, I learned that each day in the field brought me greater literacy of the woods, but overcoming my fear of getting lost was a heavy lift.

* * *

The first time I was lost in the woods was in the back seat of a '56 Chevy. We were on our way to visit family friends in New Jersey. Dad was driving, Mom navigating; Jonathan, my youngest brother, sat between them on the bench seat in front. I sat in back between my older brothers, Michael and David.

We turned off the main road and turned again onto a lane that narrowed and became grass. Dad hit the brakes and slammed his hands against the steering wheel.

"Hell's bells, Nisi! Can't you read the map? This is the goddamn dam!"

For a moment, the car was as quiet as the shade cool. Trees arched over the lane, submerging us in the dark, as if we were underwater and running out of air.

"Are we lost?" I asked.

"Don't cry!" Mom snapped.

I started to sob.

A brother kicked my shin. "Crybaby!"

The panic I felt on the dark lane, the tension in the car, and the memory of humiliation of that day rises like swamp gas when I find myself lost in the woods.

The geography of my childhood had little to do with untamed woods. Our house was in the middle of a suburban block a thirty-minute bus ride from The City, as we called Manhattan. We had a front yard for show and a backyard for play. It wasn't a big backyard, but we weren't very big, either. My three brothers and I were born between 1951 and 1959. We were among the pack of nearly two dozen kids who lived on our street. These were the kids we played with, kids whose parents we called Aunt Harriet and Uncle Arthur instead of Mr. or Mrs., and kids at whose tables we ate lunch or supper if that's where we were at noon or six. During the school year, we were outside from the moment the dismissal bell rang until Mom called us in for supper at six, unless it was raining and we remembered to watch TV.

Our first TV was a giant glass tube Dad built into the wall of the basement playroom. Right from the start, my parents restricted our viewing to the half hour between five-thirty to six on school nights. We watched either *Superman*, which I loved, thanks to Lois Lane, or *The Three Stooges*, which I thought was a documentary of my life with three brothers. As soon as the show ended, we ran upstairs to wash our hands and take our places at the table. While we were glued to the TV, Mom made dinner and Dad returned from The City. We were also allowed to watch Saturday-morning cartoons while Mom and Dad slept in. Sunday evenings, we all watched together. One Sunday, we watched the Beatles on *The Ed Sullivan Show*. Most Sundays, we watched *The Man from U.N.C.L.E.* until *Mission: Impossible* replaced it.

During the summer, we were outdoors as soon as we swallowed our Rice Krispies until it was too dark to see. After we discovered flashlight tag, we stayed out until the batteries ran down. We entertained ourselves. It helped that we could walk to our destinations: to school, to friends', the candy store, the public library, and the town parks. I always knew where I was and how to get home except for the time David, my middle brother, led a group of us into a swamp at the park. At least it seemed like a swamp, with the reeds towering over us and soggy grass beneath our feet. When we could go no further, David passed around his canteen shaped like a flying saucer encased in a green canvas jacket for a sip of warm water. He then cut us each a sliver of peach with his jackknife before leading us back onto the park's asphalt path. It was a mystery to me how he knew how to find the way out, but I was relieved that he did.

For the most part, we were outdoors and unsupervised. The neighborhood grown-ups gathered on our screened porch after dinner, the tips of their cigarettes glowing in the falling dark. I overheard recurrent words, like *Rusk*, *McNamara*, and *Kennedy*, but they didn't mean much until President Kennedy was assassinated and became JFK.

We were the baby boomers, born between 1946 and 1964, children of the generation that grew up during the Great Depression and came of age during the Second World War. Our newly middle-class parents provided us with opportunities they never had, like family vacations, music lessons, and orthodontia.

* * *

It was time to put my fear of getting lost in the woods to bed and learn to follow the deer. Tim was clear he had no interest in learning to hunt, but he was supportive of me doing so, and willing to help me gain confidence in the woods. So early on a Saturday in late October, we set out on a walk to scout for deer. Our upper field sparkled with frost, and the yellow beech leaves amplified the sunshine. The day was effervescent, and branches waved as if signaling farewell to the season of growth. Or maybe they were welcoming the season of rest, when trees stand bare and absolved from the imperative of photosynthesis and reproduction.

We entered the woods across the road from our house, where there are no blazes, so we can just wander. Well, Tim can; I follow. At least that's how it's been for the length of our marriage, when he's pointed out "rises" and "slopes" and "ridge lines" to me. I've stood beside him and nodded, as if I could make sense of the forest for the trees.

Sometimes, he has pulled out the geologic survey map and a compass to show me on paper how we had arrived on a ridgeline, or what our choices were to find our way home. I've had momentary flashes of insight, just as I did back in eighth-grade algebra, when the teacher wrote a theorem on the board. I could follow her chalk marks with excitement at their lucidity and precision, but when confronted by problems on a test, logic escaped me and anxiety robbed me even of arithmetic. My repeated failures at math bred in me a visceral sense of distress: I'd stop breathing, I'd hear my pulse in my ears, and my vision would blur as my eyes filled with tears—the same feelings that overwhelm me when I'm lost in the woods. But now that I was following the deer, I was learning a new way to make sense of the forested landscape.

On this golden morning, my curiosity gave me the courage to take the lead up a steep pitch, heading northwest, with the stream that would lead me home to my right. In the past, when I'd ventured here alone, I either stuck to the old logging road or left an easily legible snowshoe trail to follow back. But on this morning, I was keen to spy deer and orient myself to the landscape rather than to the signs of human usage. I noted the white pine giving way to hardwoods. I followed last season's faint deer trails instead of the antique walls built back when these were grazing pastures for sheep. Red and yellow leaves littered the forest floor, brightened by the sun filtering through the thinning canopy of birch and oak. I sought signs of browse, where the deer nibble the tender ends of young trees, and rubs, where males scratch saplings with their antlers to mark their territory and let the females know they're around.

I didn't see deer signs, and I was neither disappointed nor surprised; the deer don't usually come down to our side of the ridge until late winter, when we see them cross our field en route to the river. The doe often summer in our lower field with their fawn, returning to the woods before we cut hay.

We reached the top of the ridge, where the forest shifts from south-facing hardwood to north-facing hemlock, from openness and light to the cool dark of the evergreen forest. I recognized this place between light and dark from a snowshoe last winter. I wandered deeper into the woods. I lost sight of Tim and wondered if he would follow me for a change. I was surprised by what felt like audacity, and I was pleased when I heard Tim's whistle—a signal we use when we need to locate each other at opposite ends of the house, in crowded art galleries, and now, in the woods. I whistled back. We walked toward one another till we met.

* * *

I blame being geographically challenged on Manhattan, where I lived for six years as a young adult. A good deal of the island is a compass, with avenues pointing north and streets running east and west. I quickly learned the anomalies, like the alphabet avenues when I lived downtown, and Amsterdam and Columbus when I moved to the Upper West Side. Back then, I was a runner, so I also learned the island's topography, which is anything but flat. I always knew where I was in Manhattan; in the woods, I've famously become lost—and panicked. Until now.

Instead of relying on human signs, like a blazed trail, an old road, or a stone wall, I was motivated to see the landscape with the eyes of a deer, which note contrast of light and dark rather than color, and register movement above detail. Instead of reading the human landscape, I was starting to decode the wild one. I smelled the difference between the leaves decaying in sunlight and the cool balsam of the evergreen glade. I heard the crows, jays, and juncos arguing or alarming one another. I suspected that if I learned the language of the birds, I would learn about other animals in the forest from their point of view. For the first time in my life, I was so absorbed by the life in the forest that I forgot to worry about getting lost.

Excited by learning this new literacy of reading the forest, I arranged to go out with Holly Smith Domanski, who's been hunting since she was twelve. She was now thirty-six and headed to the woods whenever her busy life as a single mom and full-time nurse allowed. We met on a sunny Sunday just a couple of weeks before rifle season and entered the woods behind the housing development where she lives.

I often forget how wooded and wild Vermont is as I drive through the landscape. Roadside settlement gives the impression that the state is populated and tame. It's not. As soon as we stepped into the forest behind the village, we were in deep woods.

Holly explained that deer take the path of least resistance, pointing out a game trail along a fading woods road. She showed me an old rub on a skinny sapling and inspected bramble for signs of browse. We stopped at the edge of a ravine where the trails funnel down to a seep.

"Deer might come here to drink," she said. "This would be a good place to sit. There are good backstops for safe shots, either against the ground or over there." She nodded to the opposite cliff.

We climbed, circling north. Holly swept the leaf litter with her hand. "No acorns," she muttered.

"We have loads at my house." I live only a few miles away, but I was learning how woodland habitats are as specific and varied as an anthology of poems, which seems like a good argument for scouting a particular hunting ground.

Holly said she doesn't bother. "Knowing where the deer are now won't tell you where they'll be in season," she said. I reminded myself that Holly's been hunting on her family's land since forever, so she knows her terrain. I envy her confidence and wonder if I'll ever be able to read nature fluently enough to find my way into—and out of—the woods the way I can translate alphanumerical signage into an urban address.

We stepped out of the hemlocks' shade and into the hardwoods, where bare trees scraped against a brilliant sky, a sight so beautiful it hurt.

Holly pointed out a fresh rub. We followed a trail toward a towering oak rattling its leaves. At its base, the ground was thick with acorns. Holly pulled a thermos from her backpack. We sipped coffee in a patch of sunlight and talked deer.

Holly answered my questions and told me things I didn't even know to ask. She doesn't use a tree stand; she builds a simple blind when she finds a good spot, clearing dry leaves so they won't rustle once she's settled. Only then does she pull on her warm clothing, which she doesn't wear hiking in. "You'd get too sweaty," she explained. "The deer will smell you."

I asked about scent-cancelling soaps and shampoos.

"Just don't shower." Her shrug was a silent *Duh*!

We fell into silence. Blue jays argued with crows. Small birds fluttered. A red squirrel froze. The woods were more than a page to read or a place to pass through. They were a stage of high drama where we were all players, even me.

I looked around. I'd never been in these particular woods before, but I had a sense of where I was. I wasn't worried about getting lost.

We finished our coffee, and I asked how Holly hides the scent of her pee.

"I go when I move from one spot to another."

This was important information.

Holly hesitated.

I waited for what essential knowledge was going to come next.

The church bell tolled in the village below.

She nodded. "You lead us back."

Slightly astounded, I did.

FOUR

LEARNING TO HUNT

After these confidence-building walks, I was determined to be ready to hunt when the season opened in mid-November, so I returned to Roger's to try on rifles. He pulled out four for me to shoot, including Ma Bell. It fired like butter and I wanted it, but it's a rifle Roger still uses and wasn't for sale. I fired the other three rifles a couple of times and knew immediately what fit and felt right, the same way I know how it feels to try on a garment that looks good and feels right—and how uncomfortable I feel when it doesn't. As off as I feel in ill-fitting jeans or a dress, I knew in my bones it would be worse with a gun. Fit over fashion is something I learned from my mother.

Mom was a tall, slender, long-limbed beauty with a taste for good, classic clothes. I think she hoped that if I wore the right clothes, my body would be transformed into one like hers rather than the one I have, which is like my father's: short and powerful. I did my best to please her. All through high school I wore the woolen slacks and A-line skirts that made me look more like a teacher than a student. My mother, in fact, *was* a teacher, and she dressed well.

Mom came by her clothes sense from her own mother, a milliner in her working days who sewed my mother's school clothes for the first twenty years of Mom's life and most of mine for my first ten. Grandma's skill taught Mom to appreciate quality craftsmanship, which Mom sought when she started augmenting her homemade wardrobe with purchases from the original Loehmann's, a place Mom described to me so often that I feel like I'd been there.

The Brooklyn store was the 1921 brainchild of Frieda Loehmann, a savvy retailer who bought designer overstock and sold it below retail. But there was a catch: the clothes weren't returnable and there were no dressing rooms. This didn't stop women from trying dresses on in the aisles under Mrs. Loehmann's watchful eye. She lived in an apartment above the store and, according to Mom's firsthand experience, frequently appeared on a balcony overlooking the sales floor. If she saw a woman trying on a dress she didn't think was a good fit, she'd say, quite audibly, "No, dear, that isn't for you." Invariably shamed, the woman would meekly hang the dress back on the rack. It was a technique Mom used to discourage me from purchasing the youthful clothes I preferred to her "classics."

By the time Mom initiated me into shopping at Loehmann's in the 1970s, Mrs. Loehmann had died and her son had turned the brand into a chain. The no-return policy was still in force, but these stores each had a single communal dressing room where I witnessed women of varying sizes wearing a stunning variety of undergarments as they tried on one outfit after another. There were big gals trussed in armored support and skinny ladies in skimpy lace. But the most memorable were the women shrink-wrapped into pantyhose without panties underneath. I was suddenly grateful to Mom for all those Saturday afternoons at Loehmann's, where I learned that good fit was as much about comfort as looks. But I was disappointed not to find a rifle that fit me on that first try.

Listening to Roger's hunting stories blunted my disappointment. His stories were my education, and since I was trained in parsing narratives, this was an effective way for me to learn. He told me about his previous year's hunt, when he shot a four-pointer from a blind at the top of the hill behind his house. It's a blind he can reach on his ATV, an adaptation he's had to make on account of his bad knees.

"I didn't see anything Saturday, Sunday, Monday. By Tuesday, I figure I'm now part of the landscape, because this buck just wanders into my sights. He's only got four points, but I can see he's a big one, so I shoot it."

"How big?"

"A hundred and sixty-four pounds."

For southern Vermont, that's big.

"You sit in the same spot all day?"

"You can't shoot a deer if you're not in the woods."

I'd hear this so often that I'll start saying it myself: *You can't shoot a deer if you're not in the woods.*

"I can sit in the woods all day," he said. "I've got everything I need in my backpack: sandwiches, water, pee-bottle, my book. It's peaceful." He paused. "Nothing else to do, nowhere else to be, no telephones." He shook his head and repeated, "I can sit in the woods all day."

A few days later, Roger called. "Deb, I've got a gun for you. A Ruger M77 with a .257 Roberts cartridge. I think you'll like it."

"When can I come try it?"

"It's new-in-the-box. Never been fired."

I'd never heard the term before, and didn't understand what, exactly, Roger was telling me.

"I can't let you shoot it, or it won't be NIB. It's part of my collection."

I translated "NIB" to "new-in-the-box." "So I can't try it?"

"You can come see it. See how it feels."

This was an unexpected turn of events.

"I think this is a good gun for you. I wouldn't sell it to you if I didn't."

I was still trying to understand how I could buy a rifle without trying it out, like buying clothes from a catalog.

"I've seen you shoot, Deb. You're a good shot. And the .257 has all the power you need to shoot a deer in Vermont, and it won't kick or weigh you down or make you flinch."

"Okay. I guess."

"If you don't like it, I'll buy it back. I ain't going to sell you a gun you don't like. I think you're going to like this one."

We made a date.

In the meantime, I fell into the rabbit hole of online gun forums and read the chatter about crooked barrels on M77s manufactured in 1986–89. Really? I called Gunther, the voice of reason.

"Don't trust what guys with nothing better to do have to say online about guns."

"But here's the thing," I told him. "I can't fire it before I buy it, it being new-in-the-box and all that."

"Do you trust this guy?" He meant Roger.

"Implicitly."

"Then buy it."

"It's a .257 Roberts."

"Yeah, the .257 Bob is a good choice for you: light-caliber, high-power. It's all you'll need for hunting in Vermont."

As always, I was amazed at Gunther's deep—and seemingly off-hand—knowledge of firearms.

I drove back to Roger's to buy the rifle.

I was as nervous as a seventh grader at her first girl-boy dance. Roger took the rifle out of the box, which was coated with thirty years of dust. But the gun itself was beautiful: walnut stock with hatching on the grip and forestock, a safety I could slide forward with my thumb, a five-cartridge magazine, a twenty-two-inch barrel, and a red rubber butt. I snugged it to my shoulder and it fit, like we were made for each other. Unlike clothes shopping, where I'd been bombarded by marketing images of feminine beauty, I had no idea what a woman holding a rifle should look like. It didn't matter. I asked Roger how much he wanted, and I wrote him a check for $500.

He threw in two boxes of ammo and told me to come back with a scope and a strap. He'd install them, and we'd sight in the rifle, so the scope and barrel would be accurately aligned. Roger anticipated my next question about whether the local sporting goods store sold scopes. "Yes," he said, "Sam's will have them."

At Sam's, I explained that I was a new hunter with good accuracy to about sixty yards, but I was untested in the field. "Honestly, I don't think I'd shoot at a buck at more than fifty," I confessed.

The salesman was about my age. "Then you don't need a high-powered scope," he said. He handed me one from the case. "Try that."

I held the scope to my eye and everything in the store appeared at arms' length—and I have short arms. What I saw was a glimmer of possibility: If I see a buck, I'll be able to take aim. I bought the scope and scoped Sam's for women's hunting garb. They carried none. Resigned to shopping at a big-box store, I crossed the Connecticut River to Dick's, located in a huge parking lot that serves a Target, a Home Depot, a giant supermarket, and a New Hampshire Liquor Store. The liquor store was the only one in this shopping center I'd been to before.

I paused just inside the door of the sporting goods emporium. It was enormous and filled with an overwhelming array of merchandise for golfing, fishing, tennis, ice skating, ice hockey, archery, weightlifting, and the like, plus the appropriate attire for each activity. A rack of vibrantly colored, name-brand long underwear briefly distracted me until I remembered: I already had long underwear; I needed warm boots. The shoe department was straight ahead.

There, I found an entire section of women's hunting boots of roughly two kinds: rubber pull-ons and leather lace-ups. I picked out a pair of waterproof lace-ups with 800 grams of insulation in my size, but they were too tight, and they didn't have the next size up in the store.

A clerk checked the online inventory. "There's a pair in the warehouse," he said. He looked up from the screen and smiled. "Shipping's free, and I can take ten dollars off."

I took the deal. A bit dazed, I bushwhacked my way around stacks of pre-fab hunting blinds and tree stands into an aisle filled with insulated blaze-orange camo that made my eyes ache. When I turned the corner, I came face-to-face with the same insulated suits in shocking pink.

Women are the one demographic of hunters whose numbers are rising. According to the U.S. Fish & Wildlife Service's *National Survey of Fishing, Hunting and Wildlife-Associated Recreation*, published approximately every five years, the number of registered female hunters in the United States has grown from 1.8 million in 2001 to 3.1 million in 2022, making up about 22 percent of all hunters. Manufacturers of hunting clothing and equipment are attempting to cash in on this growing demographic with a marketing strategy of "shrink it and pink it." The pink camo is right in line with the pink rifles I've seen online, including pink assault rifles available at a website devoted to "feminine & functional shooting gear & gifts." But I wasn't looking for pink. I wanted functional that fit.

There was no wool anywhere, so I shifted my sights to synthetic gear in muted green and brown. After several tries in a private dressing room, I settled on a pair of pants with six pockets and a jacket with three, both pieces claiming to be water-resistant and odor-canceling so deer wouldn't smell me. A pair of insulated glittens—fingerless gloves with a mitten flap attached—set me back almost as much as the pants, but if my hands get too cold to function, the whole gambit is off. I bought them. Then I checked to see if they had my ammo to augment the forty rounds Roger gave me. I had no idea how much I'd need to sight in my rifle, practice firing it, or shoot a deer, and thought it would be good to have more.

"Two fifty-seven Roberts?" the clerk asked. He shook his head.

Hmm. Had I bought an esoteric gun?

On my way out the door I ran into Kimona, a passionate hunter, on the way in.

"Will you go hunting with me?" I asked.

"Sure! That will be fun!"

But as I drove home, I knew I still wasn't ready to hunt. I needed something more, though I wasn't able to articulate exactly what.

* * *

At Doe Camp, I'd been impressed by Murphy Robinson's ability to articulate not just the mechanics of hunting but also the ethical complexities of taking a deer's life, and the spiritual connections between the hunter, the quarry, and their shared, natural world. Murphy is versed in myths and magic of ancient cultures from around the world, which made me aware of how my own world view was more utilitarian than spiritual. Deep down, though, I knew the call to hunt was about more than putting meat on the table, that learning to hunt threatened the agnostic shield that protected me from organized religion. Maybe learning to hunt was opening a door for my dormant spirituality as well.

I was raised Jewish. This led to confusion in first grade, where after we stood for the Pledge of Allegiance, we sat and mumbled Psalm 23 into our folded hands. No one taught me the words. I learned them through repetition, but I wasn't sure if I should be saying them. At age six, almost all I knew about being Jewish was that it made me different from people who went to church. I assumed the prayer we recited in school belonged to churchgoers. By the time I reached second grade, the Supreme Court had decided that school-sponsored prayer in public schools was unconstitutional. I was relieved.

But synagogue services were equally baffling. I could read the transliteration of Hebrew prayers, but I had no idea what the words meant. I had almost no formal religious training. We were possibly the only Jewish family in Weston, Connecticut, when we moved there in 1966. The temple was in neighboring Westport. I would have liked to learn about Judaism at Sunday School, but the teacher had no control over the class and the other students were friends from their junior high. They spent Sunday mornings flirting in class or disrupting it. I was the outlier.

I dropped out for a while, but returned in high school to study with the rabbi.

"Weren't the dietary laws developed for health reasons," I asked, pleased to apply logic to religion. "You can get trichinosis from pork, and seafood would spoil without refrigeration in the desert."

"No," the rabbi said. "We follow the Kashrut Laws because God says to."

End of discussion—and my interest in religion—until I had a pregnancy scare in high school. I was so relieved when the scare ended that I borrowed Dad's car and drove myself to Friday night services in a fit of thanks. I arrived early and sat in the sanctuary, transported with gratitude to an all-powerful God who'd had the goodness to look out for me. Just as the service was about to begin, a woman sitting nearby tapped my shoulder. She looked familiar, but I was beyond the mundane reality of names; I was floating in the rarefied netherworld of rapture.

"Psst, Debbie," she said in a penetrating whisper. "You look so religious!"

My trance broke and sight blurred. I could barely focus on the well-heeled congregation, and when they rose for the opening prayer, I slid out and drove home. I lost my faith in organized religion and placed it in proven methods of contraception instead.

My three planned children tested my lost faith. They asked me questions like, Where does god live? Why don't we go to church? And how come we don't have TV?

I was more comfortable telling them where babies came from.

I did occasionally take them to church when Tim was on call and I needed a Sunday morning breather. They had supervised crafts in the basement; I had an hour of sitting on a wooden pew where the community had been worshipping for almost two centuries. I liked how the sun streamed into that lofty room through tall mullioned windows. I liked singing the hymns and hearing the biblical passages. I liked the hour of peace.

On the Sunday the congregation celebrated holy communion, however, I was tested. Rather than having celebrants come up to the altar, as I'd witnessed in the Catholic Church, the blood and the body of Christ appeared on a tray as cubes of white bread and thimble-sized glasses of grape juice passed from person to person, pew to pew. I didn't know what I should do and wondered if I'd be struck down if I partook.

That day, I was sitting beside Carlos Otis, the founder of the hospital where Tim worked. Dr. Otis was revered, feared, and obeyed. So as the tray with the host approached, he held it for me. "Take one," he said.

I did.

No thunderbolts. Just Wonder Bread.

Having children forced me to have faith. The summer the kids were nine months, three years, and four, we rode the tramway to the top of Cannon Mountain in New Hampshire. The four-year-old lost grasp of a stone she'd been clutching and watched it roll downhill.

"Why did it do that?" she asked.

"That's gravity," I said.

"Where does she live?"

"In the earth," I replied.

I looked across the horizon, inspired by the view and the sudden certainty that gravity is a female force at the center of the world.

Sometime in my fifties, I started practicing yoga. I loved both the physical exercise and the metaphors of finding and improving flexibility, strength, and balance. I found breathing meditation a helpful method of calming my body and focusing my mind. After a day alone at my desk, practicing in a room with others was both restful and social. It was a break from being my own boss and relaxing to have someone else telling me what to do for a change. And even though I was confined to the island of my own mat, I moved in unison with others. Yoga had become an important part of my life, and I was training to become a certified yoga teacher at the same time I was learning to hunt. But the training started with instruction in Buddhism with the expectation that we would practice mantra in Sanskrit. I completed the training, but I was clear that I had no interest in another religion in a language

I didn't know—except reading Vermont's landscape. *I will lift up mine eyes to the hills* ... Was Vermont my religion?

* * *

I remembered how Murphy Robinson taught hunting and asked Tim Jones if he would send me to Murphy's school to write a story about the Huntress Intensive Workshop.

He did.

At Mountainsong Expeditions, workshops "emphasize connection to nature, competence & skill building, and empowerment through learning and adventures." About half the programs are open to people of all genders; others are open only to marginalized genders: those who identify as women, nonbinary people, trans folks, queer people, and people who aren't yet sure. For the record: I'm a cisgender, heterosexual, white woman. I grew up with three brothers and have been married to the same man for more than half my life. Nevertheless, at the time of this workshop, a candidate embodying toxic masculinity was running for president of the United States. Being female—which poses inherent risks to personal safety even for a married, middle-aged female like me—felt especially risky in the woods.

To be clear, all the men who helped me learn to hunt were kind, patient, and respectful as well as knowledgeable and encouraging. But there are stories dating back to antiquity where women have not been welcomed as hunters, as in the story of Atalanta and the boar.

Artemis sends a wild boar to ravage Calydon after King Oeneus fails to honor the goddess of nature for a good harvest. Hunters from all over Greece come to help Oeneus's son, Meleager, hunt the terrorizing beast. Atalanta, a woman, joins the hunt. She's modestly dressed, wears her hair in a single knot, carries a quiver slung over her shoulder, and grasps her bow in her left hand. Meleager, Calydon's great warrior-prince, sees Atalanta's androgynous face and falls in love. But he's modest and focused on destroying the monstrous boar that threatens his father's kingdom.

The hunt takes place in an ancient forest, where the boar tramples the hunters' nets and gores their dogs. The hunters are too eager to take careful aim, but when Atalanta sees her chance, she shoots. Her arrow grazes the beast along its back and sticks behind its ear, wounding the boar.

Meleager is thrilled, but the male hunters are ashamed that a woman has succeeded where they haven't. They throw their shafts wildly. Disgusted, Ancaeus, an older hunter, shouts the hunters aside, claiming it's time for young men to learn women can't match a weapon wielded by a man. He raises his double-headed ax with both hands, and while he is poised to strike, the boar gores him in the groin. Unmanned, he dies.

At last, Meleager kills the boar. The men surround him, touch him, touch the boar, dip their lances in its blood. But when Meleager honors Atalanta for drawing first blood by giving her the boar's hide, snout, and tusks, the men grumble. Meleager's uncles tell Atalanta she's beautiful, but lovesick Meleager can't help her, and they snatch her trophies. Meleager slays his uncles, and Meleager's mother avenges her brothers' deaths by killing her son.

Among the women at the Huntress Intensive, I felt welcomed and safe.

The weekend workshop promised to touch all the reasons I was being called to hunt: harvesting healthy, wild food; understanding the woodland landscape at a new level; and connecting with something primitive pulling at my core, what Murphy calls "the power of the ancient Huntress archetype." Despite my tendency toward metaphoric thinking, I didn't yet see any connection between myself and Artemis, the young, virgin goddess of the hunt. I was no longer young nor virginal; I never considered myself anything but a fallible human.

* * *

Mountainsong's classroom was a circle of logs with a breathtaking view of the Worcester Range and, to the south, the distinctive silhouette of Camel's Hump, Vermont's most iconic peak. We were blessed with two warm, dry days and a cold, clear night illuminated by the full Blood Moon.

Of the five women enrolled in the course, only Tara, a sullen sixteen-year-old from Montana, was an experienced hunter. Tara's Aunt Karen, a well-meaning middle-aged woman who lived in Vermont, accompanied her niece. From Tara's resentfulness, I suspected spending a weekend camping with a bunch of old ladies learning to hunt in Vermont's cramped forest wasn't really her idea of fun. And Karen's deference toward, defensiveness around, and protection of Tara bespoke a troubled relationship that became increasingly evident as the weekend progressed.

Meghan, a thirty-something mother of two young children, had just moved from California. She was attending the workshop to connect to her new landscape and to learn new skills. She'd never hunted, but she'd collected road-killed animals for their pelts and was curious about when and how one could safely and legally claim a road-killed deer to eat. Meghan had a kind of curiosity and confidence liberated from conventional thinking I admired.

Lisa, closest to me in age, was a former Outward Bound instructor who now taught at a wilderness school in western Massachusetts. She wanted to revive the hunting skills of her ancestors, who were among the European settlers in Colonial New England.

Of all the people at the workshop—including the instructors, Murphy and Eric Garza—I was both the oldest and the one who'd lived in Vermont longest. Like Murphy, Eric shared his field-craft expertise with generosity and kindness. Originally from the Midwest, he'd been hunting for nine years, mostly with a bow. Eric's a self-described "scholarly entrepreneur," with specialized knowledge in the ecology of food systems, from foraged plants to Energy Use in Food Systems, a course he teaches at the Rubenstein School for Environment and Natural Resources at the University of Vermont.

Each experiential learning episode began and ended at the fire circle. In this circle, Murphy explained what to expect. After completing the activity, we returned to the circle to process what we'd just experienced, locking what we'd learned into our hearts and minds, and integrating these lessons into our whole selves. The two sessions I liked best were the ones that taught me new ways to interpret the landscape: scouting for deer sign and the mock hunt at daybreak.

We scouted for deer in a forest a few miles from base camp. Before entering the woods, we imaginatively transformed ourselves into deer and spent a few minutes inhabiting the forest verge as if we were *O. virginianus borealis*—members of the family Cervidae best known as white-tailed deer.

We turned ourselves into whitetails by circling clockwise to the beat of Murphy's drum as Murphy called instructions: We cupped our ears, because deer have keen hearing. We lowered our eyes, because deer see movement better than images. We inhaled deeply, because keenest of all is the deer's sense of smell. When Murphy stopped drumming, we entered the forest to sense it as deer do.

I know adults who would roll their eyes at such play, but I was alert in the forest as never before. I noticed the movement of a garter snake; I heard my cohort's footsteps; felt the air brushing my face; inhaled the pungency of autumnal decay. Using more of my senses allowed me to recalibrate my mind to see the woods from a deer's point of view.

We reported on our experience as deer before circling counterclockwise to unwind back into our human form.

Next, Eric led us along a trail into the woods, over a rise, and through a bog. We arrived at what he called "a kitchen"—where deer go to browse. What looked to me like low-lying scrub is really a well-stocked pantry filled with the tasty brambles on which deer feast.

We followed a narrow path—a "hallway"—leading from the kitchen to the "bedroom," located on a rise darkened by hemlock. Circular depressions in the fallen leaves revealed where deer made their beds. Anthropomorphizing how the deer use the forest helped me make sense of what had previously appeared as inchoate wilderness.

Surrounding the hemlock grove, we found where a buck had rubbed his antlers against a sapling, scraping off the outer bark so scent from glands on his forehead would be absorbed into the softer phloem, thus marking his territory. These rubs were in the margin where hardwoods met hemlock, as if we were standing at the threshold between the bedroom and hall.

We also searched for scrapes—places where a buck paws a bare a patch of ground and pees into it. His scent announces his availability to breed to interested females—and to warn other males off his turf. A scrape is the buck's equivalent of a profile on a dating app. By the time I walked out of the woods, I saw organization and meaning where previously I'd seen only the illegible tangle of underbrush. I'd had my first lesson in decoding the forest. But reading the woods is more than looking for signs, as I learned early the next morning.

We headed out for the mock hunt in the near dark of the setting moon. Murphy led us single file along a path through thick woods that ended at a stone wall. The open land on the other side of the wall was only marginally visible in the predawn twilight. We split up as instructed, each of us finding a seat along the wall, each out of sight of the others.

With the moon down and the sun not yet up, there was little to see and lots to hear: a rooster announcing dawn; increasing traffic on the state highway; an owl hooting goodnight and geese honking good day. With my ears open to the moment, I heard coyotes, turkeys, crows, a red squirrel, and blue jays. I also heard Murphy yell, "Bang!"—the signal that Eric, playing the mock deer, had been shot. I looked at my watch and waited thirty minutes before following the fake blood trail

Eric left for us to follow. This pause allows the deer to die without the additional stress of being chased.

I expected tracking to be harder, but I easily spotted the fake blood. I was keen to follow the deer's trail rather than a blazed path, and surprised that when I thought I'd lost the trail, it was because the deer was well camouflaged in front of me. Lisa pointed out the lump of Eric covered by a gray blanket beneath the low branches of a hemlock.

This tracking exercise allowed us to put into practice some of the theory we'd been learning, and gave us a chance to experience daybreak in the woods—to witness the line where light meets night slide across the land. At the end of the exercise, I vowed to make being outside both in the dawn and the dark a priority for how it sharpens my senses. But I still didn't know if I could ever shoot a deer. At rifle practice this time, I was way off my mark.

Target practice was more challenging than at Doe Camp. There, I hit a cluster of bull's-eyes in clear view at twenty-five yards. At Roger's, with my .22, I'd hit bull's eyes at thirty-five yards. But I still hadn't been back to Roger's to install the scope and sight in my gun. I tried not to think about how much I still had to do in the little time before Opening Day, like sight in my rifle and take the Hunter Safety Exam for my license. I forced myself to breathe and be present.

This time, target practice was in the woods, and the target was down a narrow shooting lane through the trees, whose fluttering leaves turned sunlight to dancing shadows. I couldn't find a stable shooting position crouched and braced against a fallen tree. We all took turns shooting Murphy's .30-06, pronounced "thirty-aught-six." It's an iconic deer rifle, but it felt like a cannon. And unlike the highly visible fluorescent targets we used at Doe Camp, the target here was drawn with marker on corrugated cardboard; I could hardly see it through the leaves, and each time I squeezed the trigger, the gun kicked. Of my three shots, two hit the target well outside the strike zone, and one missed the target entirely. I defaulted to ingrained self-doubt, assuming all the earlier shots I'd made on-target were flukes, and these missed shots were more accurate of my likely incompetence. My only hope was that my rifle would be a better fit. Sigh.

A well-advertised part of the intensive was the Sacred Goat Slaughter, for which Tara and her aunt didn't stay. After they left, Murphy told us that Tara—the experienced teenage hunter from out West—found the premeditated slaughter of domestic animals immoral, which was a new twist to the complexity of food ethics for me. It was the first time that I wondered whether it's better to raise an animal for slaughter or to take a wild animal from the woods. I still don't have a clear answer. For all her teenage discontent, I have to credit Tara for helping me see how hunting wild game is a form of animal welfare when compared to the treatment of factory farmed animals raised in concentrated feeding operations for mass-market consumption.

I felt as if we'd already put in a full day by the time we'd finished breakfast, but it was still early when a nearby farmer drove up with a young goat in the back of her truck. A male kid is expendable in a goat dairy; the farmer was glad to find a customer for this sweet boy. Murphy gathered us around the trusting animal. We laid hands on him and began to chant, "The earth, the water, the fire, the air, return, return, return, return," over and over to calm both the animal and ourselves.

* * *

There's no way around it: killing an animal is a Big Deal. Even under the most ethical standards, it's a violent act. According to Murphy, it's emotionally easier to shoot a deer at eighty yards than to slaughter a goat up close and personal. I already knew that taking the life of an animal I eat is a sacred act. In 1985, I learned the hard way that raising a pig was one thing, and slaughtering him, quite another.

We raised the pig in the first place, because, Tim assured me, "it's so convenient." The pig lived in the old cellar hole at the edge of our property, and we fed him the spoiled produce from the farmstand next door. Every evening I walked across a field to collect the leftover produce, and returned with a cart laden with spoiled peaches and old corn. I fantasized a freezer so full that I wouldn't have to buy groceries all winter.

My city friends thought it was disgusting. "You're going to eat it?" they asked.

"He's not a pet," I replied. No matter how much affection I felt for this pig, there was no question that he was destined for the table, not a spot on the couch.

"But how can you do that?" they asked.

Odd how people competent at riding New York subways during rush hour turn squeamish at the ritual of raising a pig. But in urban life, I remembered, animals meant cockroaches, pigeons, and rats. In just a year of country living, I'd already learned that the proportions of life change when measured in acres instead of square feet.

The pig grew from a thirty-five-pound piglet to a 250-pound porker: pink, happy, and oblivious to his fate. And that's what I'd tell my urban friends. "Look," I'd say, as I dumped a load of spoiled lettuce, melons and squash into the sty. "He loves to eat. What better destiny than to be eaten?"

The farmstand was planning on closing come fall, so I made a date with a slaughterhouse. On the appointed day, we woke early and lured the pig into a crate we'd built. It was heavy work, tricking him with a scoopful of grain. For the first time, I felt like a traitor, using the pig's gluttony to lead him toward death.

The morning sparkled as I drove across a valley shining with farms. The agrarian landscape reassured me that this journey was part of the season, the harvest, the cycle of nature. The feeling ended, however, when I parked in the slaughterhouse yard and a pig-faced man came out, pulled my pig by the ear, and kicked him into a pen. I'd imagined only a swift slaughter, not the indignity of my pig being treated like meat. I was relieved, a few minutes later, when I heard the pistol. On the drive home, with the empty crate rattling in the back of the truck, I decided I could no more sanction anonymous killing than I could eat anonymous meat.

We ate pork chops all winter, and come springtime, we bought two adorable piglets. We'd also made a deal with some neighbors experienced in pig slaughter. We'd raise the animals; they'd perform the slaughter. We'd divvy the pork.

The day appointed for killing the pigs arrived as naturally as the tourists in that season of cold nights and bright foliage. At seven in the morning, men from the village—men I knew by sight but not yet by name—were already splitting wood and filling a pig-sized, galvanized tub with water. I greeted them with coffee and doughnuts. They mumbled, "Good morning," accepted my offering, and continued building a fire under the tub in which we would later scald the dead pigs. Once the fire blazed, there were knives to sharpen, rope and tackle to hang. Meanwhile, the pigs grazed nonchalantly as nearly a dozen of us waited for the water to boil. We took turns feeding the fire and shooting the breeze. The atmosphere was cordial. Clearly, some of the men enjoyed showing Tim, their family doctor, something he didn't know how to do, and they all liked explaining country ways to me, a hick from the Big Apple.

When I tried to express my thanks for everyone's generous help, the most talkative fellow cut me short. "Just helping Doc put meat on the table." Back in the city, people often helped me carry my groceries home—the urban equivalent of helping me put food on the table—for a price: a fee for each bag and a tip for the enterprising youth. Here, no money changed hands.

At last, we were ready. Bob loaded his pistol and entered the old cellar. One of the pigs looked up. Bob shot him between the eyes. For a moment, everyone was still. And then our labor began. We bled the pig, hauled it to the tub, and dunked it. Four or five men rubbed the pig down with tools called candlesticks—shaped very like what they're named after. I watched as the men's rough hands rubbed away the wiry bristles, transforming the red-haired pig into what began to resemble an enormous, pink-skinned baby.

The men worked swiftly. Soon, the carcass swung by its hind legs on a rope hung in the backyard maple. Bob slit open the belly, and the guts tumbled out. In short order, the pig became two sides of pork. With hardly a pause, we moved on to the next. This time, Bob handed the knife to Tim, who obliged with a biology lesson, identifying various organs as they slithered out. I took photos for the family album. The serious mood of the morning turned festive as blood-spattered buckets filled up with offal.

We made neither headcheese, blood pudding, nor pickled pigs' feet, as no doubt we would have had this enterprise been one of survival rather than a rewarding agricultural pursuit. By two in the afternoon, we hung four sides of pork in the barn to cool overnight.

At the end of the day, we had blood on our hands, new friends in the village—and pork from pigs who died with dignity, without being kicked.

* * *

"The earth, the water, the fire, the air, return, return, return, return." Still chanting, a woman straddled the goat with the rest of us circling her. Those of us in the circle placed one hand on the goat, the other on the woman wielding the knife, so we were all connected.

One swift draw of the knife. We all held on, our chant softer and softer as the animal stilled. We stood, silenced by death.

We carried the goat to the shade, hung it from a tree, and began breaking it apart bit by bit, saving every usable scrap. Eric skinned the carcass; Murphy would use the pelt at the following weekend's hide tanning workshop. Eric then harvested the organs, including the guts for sausage casings. Murphy talked us through breaking down the animal into recognizable joints of meat. In a matter of hours, the goat was compost and food.

When we finished the butchering, Murphy guided us with drum and spoken prompts into the spirit world, where we were to check on the goat's spirit as a way of processing our part in its sacrifice. I didn't meet our goat in the spirit world. Maybe I was too tired to travel deep enough into that world to find him. I'd been outdoors for more than thirty hours by then, soaking up knowledge the way the earth absorbs rain until it's saturated. I couldn't take in any more.

Mountainsong Expeditions promises "journeys for your wild soul." Even though I didn't connect with the slaughtered goat's spirit, I did connect with my wild soul. I always thought my wild soul would roar and growl, be fierce, like a lioness. Over the weekend, I discovered that my wildness comes not from ferocity or bloodlust, but from a deep understanding that life takes place on a thin edge, surrounded on all sides by death. It was starting to make sense that Artemis was the goddess of wild animals and the hunt, of chastity and childbirth; after all, I was past childbearing, yet fertile with curiosity and ideas, telling stories to create change.

* * *

Just two weeks before Opening Day, I drove two-plus hours to Linwood Smith's Archery & Pro Shop in northern Vermont, arriving in time for the eight o'clock start of the all-day hunter's ed review that would end with the licensing exam. I brought the certificate showing I'd passed the online course and checked in, stunned to see seats for a hundred.

The room wasn't just crammed with chairs. Stuffed mounts of small mammals stood frozen in place on shelves that lined three walls. There was a fawn so young, I wondered if it had been "ripped untimely from his mother's womb" like Macduff in the Scottish Play. Skunks, weasels, ermine, and fishers, each with glass eyes and pert noses, posed on logs or other bits of habitat. Their eyes shone like jewels in the otherwise dingy room that soon filled mostly with kids come to test for their first-ever license, chaperoned by parents. There were just a few adult test-takers, including one man who appeared close to my age. Men and boys significantly outnumbered the women and girls, and most of the women looked to be the mothers of test takers. Maybe they already had licenses; I didn't ask. Once everyone was seated, a man in front announced, "If you are packing, please leave it in the car today."

Generally, hunters are strong on their right to bear arms. According to news reports, hunters showed up at the public hearings in 2018 to speak against the Vermont Legislature's proposed restrictions on high-capacity magazines following a thwarted mass shooting at a public high school near Burlington. The legislation passed and Vermont's Republican governor signed the law expanding background checks in private sales, raising the purchase age to twenty-one, limiting magazine sales, and banning bump stocks, devices that can drastically increase a firearm's speed of fire. Legislation allowing law enforcement officers to disarm and confiscate guns from people cited for domestic violence also passed. Despite the new legislation, Vermont's gun laws are still relatively liberal: there's no waiting period to buy a firearm, no permit required to carry a concealed weapon, no licensing of gun dealers, and no restrictions on buying firearms in bulk.

I don't grasp why hunters object to restrictions on automatic weapons and bump stocks, which are not firearms for hunting wild game in Vermont—or anywhere else, as far as I understand. I often wonder how unusual I am as a gun owner in America who supports gun safety laws, like requiring gun owners to be licensed and guns to be registered and insured, similar to the requirements for owning and operating a motor vehicle. Thinking like this leaves me in an uncomfortable nowhere land between those who believe the Second Amendment is as sacred as a biblical commandment, and those who believe no civilians should own any firearms of any kind. When I told a New Jersey cousin that I owned a rifle, she shouted, "I hate guns! I hate guns! Don't talk to me about guns! I hate guns," effectively prohibiting conversation.

I don't tell most of my friends that I own a rifle or that I'm a good shot. Most of them have never handled a firearm. Only my truly liberal friends ask, "Why hunting?" and then listen as I answer. But many friends and relatives who call themselves liberals don't want to know what's calling me to hunt; they think I've become a redneck because, as they see it, only rednecks, criminals, and cops own guns; reasonable people outside of law enforcement just don't.

When a cousin I hardly know visited from California, I expected him to be horrified when I told him I'd just bought a rifle.

"What kind of rifle?" he asked. "If I'd known, I would have brought some guns to shoot."

"*Guns*? Plural? You shoot?"

He laughed, then counted on his fingers, naming manufacturers and calibers in a language of numbers I recognized without real comprehension. "I think I have fourteen guns."

I must have looked incredulous, because he laughed again. "It's one of the world's great secrets: even Liberals own guns!"

When the test takers returned from stowing their firearms, Ken introduced our instructors, who were all trained volunteers. Ken was a veteran instructor; Joe was teaching for the first time, and junior instructors Hannah and Destiny were assisting. Their presence was consonant with the increase in girls and women learning to hunt.

In his next breath, Ken voiced an expectation of pushback. In an aggrieved tone he said, "Please show respect to our junior instructors. The idea that girls shouldn't be teaching the boys just pisses us off." Ken leveled his gaze at the boys in the room. "And just so you know," he stared everyone down, "Joe's their dad."

Nervous laughter.

Ken continued. "Let the instructors instruct. Don't undermine us while you're here." This time Ken glared at the dads. "We're teaching to the IHEA standards used in all fifty states, nine of Canada's ten provinces, as well as other countries around the world." That's the International Hunter Education Association. Ken sounded beleaguered. Do parents who hunt pass down outdated traditions? Or do some hunters find the entire licensing procedure an infringement on their freedom? I didn't know and couldn't ask; I had to pay attention so I could pass the multiple-choice test at the end of the day.

I was nervous. Given a choice, I'd always rather take an essay exam over a multiple-choice test. I'm good at writing exam essays; I've had a lot of practice. As an English major, I wrote many exam essays, including, once, a crackerjack essay on a novel I hadn't actually read. But there would be no essay on the hunting exam; answers would either be right or wrong, so I paid attention.

Joe told us we'd spend the morning reviewing firearm safety and the afternoon outside, shooting. The test would come at the end of the day. "If you need the test read, you need the test read," he said. This was to accommodate those with reading challenges. Joe finished his introductory remarks by asking that we please separate our recyclables from our trash. "Leave the place better than the way we found it. It doesn't just go for the wilderness."

The instructional videos included information that hunters formerly learned from their elders, when America was rural and hunting was a way of life. While generational knowledge continues in some families, that thread of knowledge broke as Americans migrated toward suburbs and cities. In 1949, New York mandated the first hunter education in program in the U.S. Now, it's required in all fifty states, using the IHEA curriculum designed to instill responsibility, improve skills and knowledge, and encourage ethical hunting practices.

This first video was about firearm safety, and included all the safety measures Roger employs every time he's handed me a rifle: opening and checking that the chamber's empty and the safety's on. Every time I've handed it back to him, he's peered down the barrel again. It's automatic with him, from years of practice. I vowed to make it automatic for me, too.

The next video, *Shoot, Don't Shoot*, dramatized hunting scenarios that freeze just before a hunter pulls the trigger. The words *Shoot? Or*

Don't Shoot! appear on screen, inviting viewers to decide whether the conditions are safe. The kids in the room shouted the answers with gusto.

While the main focus of the class was on deer hunting, the test covered the basics of bird hunting, too. When my neighbor Dean heard I was learning to hunt, he invited me turkey hunting. "It's loads of fun," he assured me. I gave him all sorts of reasons why turkey hunting wasn't for me: I can't devote any more time to hunting; I don't own a shotgun; I can't justify more gear for another kind of game, and turkey hunting requires significant camouflage to elude turkeys' keen eyesight, considered about three times better than humans'. I told Dean everything but the truth: I don't want to make a fatal mistake, either shooting another hunter or being shot by one. Besides, this was the year we were raising turkeys—heritage breeds—that are supposed to taste closer to wild birds than the hybrids found in the grocery store.

The last video of the morning was *The Last Shot*, based on a true story of two teenage boys who go hunting without their parents' permission, knowledge, or supervision. The boys get reckless, and one shoots the other, killing him. After viewing it, Joe asked, "What did they do that was wrong?"

Kids called out their answers.

"No safety!"

"The safety wasn't on!"

"No muzzle control!"

Joe interjected, "The boys had no muzzle control all day long."

"Wrong hold when they were walking through the woods!"

"The gun was loaded all the time!"

"They ignored the private property signs!"

"They were shooting into water!"

"They shot the signs!"

"There were no grown-ups with them!"

"They didn't have permission to use the gun!"

Joe used the movie to reinforce the cardinal rules of firearm safety. "Treat every gun as if it's loaded and keep it pointed in a safe direction. Once you pull the trigger, you can never take that shot back."

The kids fell silent and still.

The morning ended with visits from Jeff Hood, the chief hunter safety instructor for the county, and Lieutenant Dennis Amsden, the local game warden. Jeff had a special message for parents: "Stay ethical. Give positive reinforcement for a child's safe choices." Dennis said the same thing in more detail: "Since the mid-twentieth century, when hunter education became required, there's been a decline in hunter-related incidents."

We heard the word *incident* all morning, but rarely the word *accident*. *Incident* describes preventable events; *accident* is saved for events beyond human control. Both the online, self-study course and the morning's videos have drilled us in firearm safety: maintaining muzzle control, unloading rifles for safe transport, and storing them unloaded and locked, separate from ammunition. At home, I keep my ammunition separate from my two rifles and use trigger locks, which are inexpensive and effective.

Next, under the watchful glass eyes of the stuffed wildlife in that packed room, we discussed ethics. "Ethical behavior," as defined by the famed conservationist Aldo Leopold, "is doing the right thing when no one else is watching." In the field, hunters have to make ethical decisions.

Lieutenant Amsden described how the law and ethical behavior don't always align. "Game wardens," he explained, "investigate hunting-related shootings according to the legal standard, which is black and white. Ethical standards are high, but not always as clear. Just because something's legal doesn't mean it's ethical. Laws pertain to the community. Ethics are individual and personal." He gave an example. "Vermont doesn't have a wanton waste law, but that doesn't mean you shouldn't try to recover any animal you wound, or that you should kill a game animal you don't intend to use for meat or fur." States that do have wanton waste laws make it a crime to waste any part of a protected species.

"You have a constitutional right to hunt in Vermont," Amsden said, "but you have to have written permission to hunt on posted property. And to post land legally, a landowner has to go through some rigorous hoops." He regarded his mostly youthful audience. "During youth hunting weekend, all hunters must have landowners' permission, whether the land is posted or not. And you can't take a shot within twenty-five feet of the road."

The warden briefly described how state wildlife biologists work to determine deer density in different parts of the state, which in turn determines what constitutes a legal deer during rifle season. "So what do you do if you shoot a sublegal deer?"

He paused, then answered his own question. "If you shoot a doe or a spike horn by mistake, your best option is through field-side clemency."

Do the kids know what this means?

"First, self-report, but this only works for first-time offenders. Take the plea deal. Instead of a criminal violation, you will be offered a civil ticket; you'll surrender your tag, pay the state monetary restitution, and carry five points on your license for five years." He's referring to the "uniform point system" for hunting licenses, similar to that used for driver's licenses. Accumulate enough points, and a hunting license can be suspended.

The lieutenant concluded with reminders that feeding or baiting deer is illegal in Vermont. This is to prevent the spread of chronic wasting disease (CWD), a fatal neurological condition spread by deer, elk, caribou, and moose eating from common sources, such as a salt lick or a pile of apples. The part of this law I don't understand is that planting a food plot is allowed. I have a neighbor who has planted apple trees in the woods near his tree stand. Legal? Yes. Ethical? Hmm.

Despite the misting weather, it felt good to be outside after lunch. Several more men of various ages were now on hand to help out with this part of the day. One of them distributed compasses to everyone in the group. All we were told was, "Put red in the shed," meaning line up the red side of the compass needle with the arrow inscribed on the plate beneath it. When aligned, the arrow points north. Without waiting for questions, we were also told, "Always carry a compass! Don't rely on GPS! A compass doesn't rely on batteries!" I was glad I already knew how to use a compass and didn't have to depend on this thin bit of instruction.

Next, we entered the woods to watch a demonstration of installing a tree stand, which gives a hunter a perch above the forest floor from which to shoot. There's no question, a tree stand gives the hunter an advantage—literally—over the deer, but it comes at a cost, and not just for the equipment. First, it has to be carried in and set up. Once installed, the hunter has to haul her gear up with a line, and then clip into a harness to prevent falling out. As with the compass, we were given just cursory instruction about tree stand safety. I didn't care, because I wasn't interested. I'm determined to avoid gearing up beyond warm and waterproof clothing, a rifle, and a knife. Besides, a hunter needs landowner permission to install a tree stand, and I still didn't know where I was going to hunt.

I spent the rest of our time outdoors standing in line for a chance to shoot a variety of firearms. After a long wait, a man handed me a shotgun, another volunteer released a clay disk from a kind of pitching machine. I shot and missed. I stood on another long line to fire a .22. The line for firing a handgun was so long, I didn't bother. Yet again, I wondered what handguns had to do with hunting, or why people have them at all. I have good reason to dislike handguns. I have two friends who used them to kill themselves.

*   *   *

One evening in the late eighties, my friend Kelly and her husband were over for dinner. Kelly was suffering from one of the migraines that could lay her low, so she stretched out on the sofa in the darkened parlor while Tim and Clem finished prepping the meal. I brought Kelly a pillow, a blanket, and a glass of water. She thanked me and said, "Sometimes, I think it would be best if I just put a gun in my mouth and fired."

I thought this was hyperbole, until I came to understand the terrible pain that wracked Kelly's body as she fought to suppress searing childhood memories. She was the child of polio survivors, people who could barely care for themselves, let alone the child they'd never expected. Sometime in her childhood, Kelly's parents sent her to an orphanage. There, Kelly was brutalized by the nuns and humiliated by the other children when they discovered she had living parents, reinforcing Kelly's sense of being both unwanted and unloved.

Kelly had no children and delighted in mine, outfitting them with fantastic dress-up from her side business collecting and reselling vintage clothing: hats with net veils, silk slips, lace shawls, country frocks, and snap purses—dress-up the older two used in imaginative play that Kelly joined.

Kelly also bought them Barbie dolls. I wasn't a fan of such sexualized idols, but two things changed my mind. First, the two- and three-year-olds played with their dolls in ways I'm sure Mattel never imagined: they undressed one Barbie so the other could nurse, demonstrating that they understood one of the functions of breasts. And second, Kelly had a Barbie collection of her own. She played with her dolls all the time, and it gave her great pleasure to play Barbie with my daughters. As long as I wasn't required to swallow my feminist pride and play with these particular dolls myself, I let it slide.

In late November 1991, a ferocious migraine sent Kelly to Grace Cottage Hospital a few days before I was admitted in labor with my third child. Ruth was just a few hours old when I introduced her to Kelly in the hospital. Ruth and I went home the next day; Kelly stayed till after Thanksgiving. The weekend after the holiday I roasted a turkey, Tim mashed potatoes, my brother-in-law Andrew baked a pie. Kelly and Clem joined us.

The following month, Kelly visited frequently while I was anchored to the couch with a new baby latched to my chest. Kelly was healthier and happier than I'd ever seen her, even as she told me about the dark memories of childhood trauma that were surfacing in therapy. Her good mood continued through New Year's Day, when our family spent the afternoon at Kelly and Clem's. The two older girls played with Kelly's Barbies; Tim and Clem held the baby and watched football; Kelly had me try on vintage clothing she'd just bought at auction, giving me first pick before she consigned it.

On her way to work the following week, she bought a handgun on Main Street, and during her mid-morning break she walked into the woods and pulled the trigger with the gun in her mouth.

* * *

I thought of Kelly as I stood in the chill mist observing the scene of mostly children lining up to fire rifles, shotguns, and handguns. I'd never heard this much gunfire in my life, and I wondered what I was doing here when we were corralled back indoors.

Finally, and with much fanfare, we were given the written test.

It was easy.

I missed the name of a particular way to carry a rifle and passed with ninety-eight percent correct. My card proving that I'd passed this final hunter safety exam was already printed and laminated. I was now entitled to apply for a hunting license in all fifty states. It was just after three o'clock.

I returned to my seat to wait.

At three-thirty, Joe said, "The IHEA says this course is eight hours long, but we'll let you out early."

What message does that send about ethics, I wondered, as I started my long drive home.

FIVE

MY FIRST SEASON

Rifle season was just twelve days away when I finally brought my rifle over to Roger's to sight in. After he mounted the scope and attached the shoulder strap, we walked up to his range, where he'd set out the bench, gun vise, and sandbags we'd used to sight in my .22, only this time we were a hundred yards from the target—more than twice as far than before. Once Roger secured the rifle into the vise, I slid into the seat, peered through the scope, and focused on the target, which seemed impossibly far away. Both of us put on ear protection. I adjusted my body to the stationary rifle. It was awkward. Uncomfortable. I fired.

We walked to the target. High and outside. Ball one. Back at the bench, Roger adjusted a knob at the side of the scope to move it into alignment with the barrel. I took another shot. We walked to the target. Lower, but inside. Back to the bench. Another adjustment. Another shot. If this had been a ball game, I would have loaded the bases on walks. My confidence was tanking, but Roger remained calm despite his obvious discomfort walking the two-hundred yard round trip on his bum knees after each shot. He persisted, and so did I.

In time, we brought the scope and the barrel into alignment. I took the rifle out of the vise. "I'd like to take a shot as if I were in the field."

"Go ahead."

I halved the distance, knelt, and brought the gun to my shoulder. Already, this felt better than firing from the bench. With the target in sight, I inhaled and squeezed the trigger on the exhale.

We strolled back to the target yet again. Roger put his finger on the bullet hole just above the bull's eye.

"Good enough?" I asked.

"Yeah. You just killed a deer."

My confidence soared for as long as it took to amble back to the bench. But as I helped Roger put the sandbags away, I felt my confidence leaking away. I still didn't know where I was going to hunt. I loved the idea of hunting with Kimona, the friend I ran into at Dick's, but I wondered if that was wise. Kimona and I don't see each other often, and when we do, we talk, talk, talk. But I didn't want to hunt alone. I assumed Roger would take me. I was counting on it, but I needed to ask him.

"I don't think so," he said, meaning, *No*. "Dennis's camp? There's no place for a woman."

The gender thing.

"It's just four bunks." Roger frowned. "I won't even stay there. The wood stove's between the bunks and the one door. There's no other way out. It ain't safe."

Roger had been the town's fire chief for twenty years.

"If you don't stay there, where do you go?"

"I drive up at three in the morning, so I'm in place a half hour before dawn."

I was momentarily seven years old again, in the family car and frightened by the dark woods and my father's anger.

"So where can I hunt?" I managed to control my voice, but my brain was on fire. How will I ever find my way in the woods? How will I find my way out? What if I shoot a deer? And why, oh why, have I chosen yet another solitary pursuit, as if writing weren't already lonely enough?

"Let me talk to Dennis," Roger said.

I changed the subject and told Roger that I looked at a knife with a short, fixed blade that the salesman at Sam's recommended.

Roger said, "I use a Wyoming blade." He started walking back to the house. "C'mon, I'll show you."

I followed him back to the basement, where he showed me a knife with a pointed blade for puncturing the skin; a safety blade, like a letter opener, to unzip the hide; and a hook to attach to a rope to drag or hang the animal.

"And in the unlikely event that I shoot a deer, how do I gut it?"

Roger mimed how he does it. I tried memorizing his moves. "But all hunters field dress their animals different," he said. "Especially the hunters who enter the pools for the biggest bucks." I vaguely remembered Helen telling me about this: hunters put money in a pot at the big-game reporting stations at the start of the season, and the hunter who reports the biggest buck at the end wins the money. "Those guys leave as much as they can in the body cavity to boost its weight."

I heard Roger's disapproval.

"You can win a thousand dollars at some of them," Roger said. "Especially if you get a buck at the beginning of the rut. By the end of the rut, a buck can lose thirty to fifty pounds, 'cause he don't eat while he's chasing the does."

When I left, I held on to two pieces of information: Field dressing an animal is an art, not a science—I'd slaughtered animals before, so I could figure it out—and best to get a buck at the beginning of the rut.

I also decided it was time to start making decisions on my own. The next time I was in Brattleboro, I went to Sam's and bought the knife with the short, fixed blade that fit my hand.

* * *

The weekend before rifle season started, Tim and I slaughtered three of the six turkeys we were raising instead of the twenty-five chickens we usually put in the freezer. The turkeys were a heritage breed and they grew slowly, which we weren't used to. Previously, we'd been raising hybrid chickens, bred for putting on weight quickly. It took only six weeks for those day-old chicks to reach a table-weight of four to five pounds. When we let them grow for eight weeks, we ended up with giant roasters, seven pounds and more.

We'd had killing frost, so the grass was dead, the insects gone, and we'd started feeding the turkeys commercial grain; if we kept them longer, we'd have to feed them a lot more. We'd also been hauling water from the house since pulling the hoses in for winter.

That sunny Saturday, we wrestled three birds to the chopping block. The turkeys were hard to contain and difficult to pluck. Once plucked, we discovered we'd been duped by their plumage. They were hardly bigger than last year's chickens, and not the eighteen- to twenty-pounders we'd hoped for. We fed the remaining three for a few more weeks.

I should have been out scouting on this last weekend before rifle season started, but it was also Youth Weekend, and I didn't particularly want to be in woods filled with eager young hunters. Besides, I still didn't know where I was going to hunt. I tracked Dennis down by phone. He told me there were lots of deer on the land he was logging. I could hunt there, just ten miles south of where I live. We made a date to meet Friday afternoon—the last possible daylight before Opening Day. I didn't like waiting till the last minute, so I did what I could on my own to prepare during the lead-up to rifle season.

On Monday, I drove ten miles north to Roger's for target practice with my new rifle.

Roger and I talked circumspectly about the upcoming election. He said he didn't like Trump, but he didn't trust Hillary. "She'll take away my guns."

"That's not how government works," I said. Despite disagreeing about politics, Roger and I still like each other. "In a democracy, no one ever gets everything they want. Everyone gives a little to meet in the middle. And no one's talking about taking away hunting rifles."

On Tuesday, I voted for five women at the top of my ballot: president of the United States, governor of Vermont, two state senators, and my state representative.

On Wednesday, the election of the three state legislators who represent me in Montpelier gave me some comfort that in Vermont, at least, there would be legislative compromises.

On Thursday, I drove to the Alstead Gun Shop in New Hampshire, where they had three boxes of cartridges for my rifle in stock. I bought them all.

On Friday, I met Dennis on the land he was logging: a forty-acre parcel on the east side of a ridge, owned by a fellow in Brattleboro who planned to sell after Dennis harvested the timber.

"Is it okay for me to hunt here?" I asked.

"He hasn't been here in years," Dennis said, motioning to a sad-looking deer camp sited in the scrub. "And it's not posted."

We were standing at the landing, where limbed, full-length logs were staged for transport to the sawmill. The skidder and forwarder were parked and silent, like sleeping mastodons. Their giant treads had flattened the immediate landscape and scarred the mud.

"C'mon," Dennis said, waving me to follow. "I'll show you some places to sit."

Dennis is compact and fast. I caught up when he slowed down to point out hoof prints in the churned earth. "The deer come up from the river right through here." Dennis swept his arm in the direction the deer traveled and kept moving until he saw a chewed raspberry cane. "See?" he held up the ragged twig. "They'll be here in the morning, eating browse." Dennis told me he and the boy he's taken under his wing saw deer here the other evening. "Derek shot his first deer, a six-pointer, last weekend." I was jealous, not that Derek is eligible for Youth Weekend or even that he shot his first deer. I was jealous that he had Dennis to take him, and that he'd be joining the others at Dennis's deer camp. I was ticked that neither Dennis nor Roger would do the same for me—not because I didn't have Derek's native enthusiasm, but because I'm not male.

Dennis pointed to the places where I'd likely see deer and have a clear shot. We worked our way to the top of the ridge, where he was currently logging. After Dennis left, I stayed to figure out the lay of the land, grateful for the logging road that led to the ridge where hemlock forest met the oak. I searched for good places to sit, following a trail marked with blue tape until I hit the property line flagged with orange. I followed the orange tape downhill, hunting for scrapes, rubs, game trails, and places to sit with a wide field of fire and clear shooting lanes overlooking the clearing where Dennis said the deer would feed.

I found a seat where I thought I'd see deer, grateful to Dennis for showing me around, and relieved to have a place to hunt. I was alone in the sunshine, surrounded by woods, trying to imagine returning before dawn by myself. Dennis made it sound easy, and I already had a good sense of this patch of land. Even so, I was having trouble believing that this was happening, that I was actually going to come back here alone, in the dark, with my rifle.

* * *

But I wasn't in the woods when legal hunting started at a half hour before sunrise on Opening Day. I was at Roger's for more target practice. I planned to head out before dawn on Monday, the third day of rifle season, when I knew that Dennis would be felling trees after eight. I'd need him to help me drag the deer I shot out of the woods. Despite my decision, I was feeling sorry for myself, lonely, and out of my depth, so I invited Kimona to scout the land with me late Sunday afternoon.

Kimona Alin trained as an orthopedic surgeon, practiced family medicine, and was briefly my primary care physician before she had children. As much as I understand how full-time clinical practice is incompatible with having babies and raising kids, I was disappointed when she switched to emergency medicine. She was knowledgeable and funny and easy to talk to about my innards. She now worked the night shift in the emergency department at the hospital where Tim works. I didn't know when she slept.

Like many women who hunt, Kimona learned from her partner, the passionate hunter she married. Jim outfits her with top-of-the-line equipment and takes her on big-game adventures out West and in Canada. "It's how we spend time together," she told me. In fact, Kimona had already been out that morning, well concealed from wildlife in a blind that Jim set up for her along a game trail. "A fox passed within feet of me, then a coyote, but no deer," she said. I sensed she had deer fever, and she's a famously good shot.

When we arrived at the landing, two pickups and a car were parked there, all with out-of-state plates. "Other hunters," I said, already spinning deadly fantasies. In the first, one of us is shot by a man who hasn't seen a deer all weekend and doesn't want to drive back to suburbia before shooting *something*, and a woman crashing through his hunting grounds is fair game. In another, one of us shoots a hunter camouflaged in a deer costume, with antlers. I'm pretty sure that if I were a male hunter, a jury would acquit me. But I'm a female hunter, well aware that I'm trespassing on male territory, despite a long tradition of hunting goddesses.

Kimona nodded at the parked vehicles. "Etiquette says we can't park here. Let's park further up."

I followed instructions.

It was already late in the day. We had just over an hour before sunset, an hour and a half until legal hunting ended. Kimona left her insulated seat cushion in the truck. I wondered if I should carry my daypack, carefully outfitted with buck knife, rope, and rags—the equipment I'd need for gutting a deer.

"Leave it," Kimona said.

"But what if we get a buck?"

"I'll call Jim. He'll be here in an instant. I never have to do that."

I was still chasing the fantasy of self-reliance, determined to field dress any buck I shot. The night before, I'd watched four videos demonstrating how to gut a deer in the field. Each hunter did it slightly differently, emphasizing what I already knew from slaughtering chickens, turkeys, and pigs: It's not rocket science; it's food prep. The principles of evisceration are all the same and all geared to preserving the meat by working quickly to cool the carcass and taking care not to nick the intestines, gall bladder or spleen. As I'd just learned from recently slaughtering turkeys, the larger the animal, the easier it is to eviscerate once it's dead. The challenge is to shoot a deer so that it dies quickly, without puncturing its gut, then gut it. I'm not just willing to do this; I feel obligated to care for any animal I harvest to eat.

I was a bit amazed to be leading Kimona, an experienced hunter, into the woods, and I was pleased that by dead reckoning I brought us onto the logging road that ran to the top of the ridge. My goal was to scout a spot I could reach in the dark that would afford me a good view of deer returning to bed down as the sun rose.

We were trudging uphill when Kimona stopped. "What's jingling?" she whispered.

I stood still. "I don't hear anything," I whispered back.

We resumed climbing.

She stopped again. "Walk," she commanded.

I stepped forward.

"It's you. What's in your pockets?"

"My cartridges."

"How are you going to shoot a deer if they're not in your gun?"

"I've never hiked with a loaded rifle."

"You have to load the gun."

"I will. When we're in place."

"Then you have to put your cartridges in different pockets so they don't make any noise."

I did, and we carried on. I'd come out to scout the land; I still wasn't ready to hunt.

The logging road was steep and the machines had churned the earth, so hiking up was slow and hard and our breath came ragged. Kimona was ahead and flapped her hand low, indicating, *quiet.* "Hear that?" she whispered. She was peering into the woods filled with burnished beech leaves.

Crunch. Crunch. Crunch.

I heard it.

Kimona lifted her rifle.

I squinted in the direction of her muzzle. Like Kimona, I was sure it was a buck, and my gun wasn't loaded. I must have jumbled what I'd learned in hunter ed, thinking I wasn't supposed to walk with a loaded weapon. But if that's the case, why did we learn all those different ways to carry a loaded rifle?

Now I remembered Kimona slipping a clip into her rifle when we left the truck. Belatedly, I understood the difference between a clip and a magazine and wished I'd bought a different rifle. If I had a clip, I could have just slid it in when we parked and been ready to shoot my first deer. But I pushed buyer's remorse aside when I remembered how finicky the clips were on some of the rifles I tried at Doe Camp.

"I thought we were just going to scout the land," I said.

"I never have to scout." Kimona said. "Jim does that." He sets her up; she shoots.

We left the logging road and entered the woods. I steadied myself against trees as I climbed over blowdowns.

Kimona followed. "Try not to touch the trees," she said. "It leaves your scent. The deer will smell you."

Something else I never thought of.

We walked through dark hemlock and came into a stand of oak at the top of the hill. The super moon rose like a headlight, huge and white. We circled back to the logging road and followed it out.

I dropped Kimona off and headed home, thinking about how I'd assumed she'd know how to scout and field dress a deer. I did learn a couple of important lessons from her: Load my rifle. Don't touch trees. I also learned that I already had basic hunting knowledge. As much as I wanted a mentor to take me out, I knew the best way for me to find my way in the woods was to hunt on my own.

It was full dark as I turned the car into the driveway.

Tim was pulling out in the truck.

We both stopped and rolled down our windows.

"Where are you going?" I hoped he hadn't been called back to the hospital.

"Looking for you."

"I'm here."

"I'm glad."

I wasn't the only one who was nervous.

* * *

The night before my first hunt, not even Tim's soft snoring lulled me to sleep, so I stopped trying. At four a.m., I brewed coffee to drink then and filled my thermos for a second cup later. I tried to be both quiet and methodical. I carried the coffee down the hall to the office, where the dog sleeps and where I'd set out my hunting clothes the previous night. Leo opened one eye and shut it. I started pulling on layers. It was dark but not cold: mid-forties and windless. I packed extra clothes in my daypack: dry socks, glove liners, neck gaiter, hat liner, and chemical hand and foot warmers. I was too nervous to eat, so I packed a calorie-dense sandwich. The plan was to meet Dennis at the landing before dawn, but he texted at four-thirty, saying he was running late, I should go without him, and good luck. I drove off alone in the dark. As the truck shuddered along the washer board dirt road, I remembered how, against all assurances that Tim would be by my side during childbirth, I ended up in labor alone.

This was back in 1988, when Tim and his two colleagues still delivered babies at Grace Cottage. Inevitably, Tim had a patient due the same week as me. His colleague Ed would deliver her if we went into labor at the same time. Tim said this was unlikely, but I knew better. Two years earlier, Tim had to pass a pregnant patient on to Bob, the third member of the medical staff, in order to attend our wedding.

Tim's patient was in the birthing room under Ed's care when we arrived at the hospital. They tucked me into a little-used room with two hospital beds and a jumble of unused furniture. Bob doctored and Tim coached as I labored. After a while, a nurse came for Bob, saying Ed needed some help.

Time passed with Tim by my side.

The nurse returned. "Doctor? They need you."

Tim went, and there I was, in what felt like a storeroom, in labor, alone. If only I'd known about Artemis back then, I'd have invoked the goddess of childbirth to aid me.

* * *

There were no cars parked along the road near the log landing that morning, meaning no other hunters—at least for now. I loaded my rifle by the light of the cab, shouldered my pack, and headed up the logging road. It was still night, but not dark. I couldn't see the moon, just its light reflected off thinning clouds. I climbed the rutted road to where the hemlock and hardwood met in an area logged the previous year. Raspberry was already colonizing this patch, where I'd seen hoof prints and Dennis had pointed out a scrape.

The night was fading into day as I made myself cozy between a tree and some slash. Thanks to the walk behind the village with Holly, I remembered to clear the brittle, dry leaves out of the way, so I could shift in my seat without making noise. I pulled on extra layers and sat with the wind in my face, braced my elbows against my knees and peered in the direction I expected the deer to arrive. I was uphill and downwind, all good.

I saw or heard the wildlife around me: red squirrel, gray squirrel, chickadee, Golden-crowned Kinglet, blue jays, and oak leaves like bronze birds floating in for a landing. I noticed a white moth with gray markings, hardly distinguishable from a bleached log a hand's breadth from my face. As far as I could tell, I was the only human in this part of the forest. A tree fell and I heard it.

The sun was up and the day warming when I started to lose focus. I observed the orange tape marking the property line flapping like an anemometer at a distance. I took aim through my scope just to check the view, only to discover the dense scrub wouldn't allow a clean shot. I ate my sandwich, happy to be outdoors as the world woke. I was practicing a breathing meditation when I heard a truck door slam, then the engine of the monster machine roar to life.

I was too sun-doped to leave my seat and greet Dennis, so I listened to the music of the chainsaw and trees cracking before I traversed the hillside away from their noise. I found a rock outcrop in more-open woods. This perch was better, but I was restless and hot. When I heard the machine hauling a load of logs out of the woods, I walked out.

"We're cutting the hemlock now," Dennis said after he shut down the engine. The silence ached. "Just beyond that, it meets some oak. That would be a good place to wait. I may even join you tomorrow morning."

"See you tomorrow, then." I headed home.

The next day, I'd already been sitting for a couple of hours when Dennis and Dale, a sawyer, arrived. I followed Dennis across the ravine into the woods. He gestured toward groves of hardwood and evergreen facing off like pieces on a chessboard. "That's what they like," Dennis said. "The safety of the hemlock and the food from the oak."

We stepped into a silent cathedral of conifer, where needles muffled our footsteps and the treetops filtered the sunlight. Dennis scanned the immediate landscape and pointed to the base of a hemlock. "Sit here. A buck will be by within the hour."

I believed him.

He returned to work.

I sat for an hour. Then two.

I moved into the oak, faced the hemlock, and waited for another hour before heading back to my world to work on my lectures about Virginia Woolf, then visit Dad.

On the third day, I headed out even earlier. I climbed the hill by moonlight. I found a spot where I could sit with my back to fallen trees that gave me good cover. This was where Dale said he'd seen a buck. The landscape came into focus with dawn. I was intent on what was in front of me when I heard crunching from behind. It's the same sound I heard with Kimona. My buck?

My brain narrated instructions: Turn slowly. Make no noise. You'll have to shoot from kneeling. You might be able to rest the barrel against the tree that was your backrest.

I peered through the tangle of beech and hemlock slash from the logging operation. The deer was right there! I had a perfect view of its tail as it bolted.

Did it know I was there? Did it smell my excitement despite my scent-blocking clothes? Or did something in the forest alarm it, something that has nothing to do with me?

It didn't matter: I saw it. I thought my way through the challenges of shooting a deer as if I were planning the logistics of cooking and serving a complicated meal to a crowd, replaying the whole episode and creating a new curriculum for myself:

1. Learn how to shoot from different positions, not just sitting.

2. Find a seat above the ravine rather than embedded in it for better sight lines, and so the smell of me floats above the deer's nose.

3. Be in place before sunrise so the woodland can swallow the noise of my intrusion.

Creating this list made me feel like I was starting to think like a hunter.

The next day, I went out tired. It was raining—hard—and the landing was all puddles and slick mud. The truck slid. I shifted into four-wheel drive and escaped to the road without getting stuck. Mud sucked at my boots on the logging road as I worked my way uphill. I slipped to my knees a couple of times, breaking my fall with one hand while holding my rifle above the muck with the other. My effort was rewarded when I reached the carpet of hemlock needles, where the walking was easy, quiet, and nearly dry. Sitting on a rock at the base of a tree above the ravine, I enjoyed a comfortable view of the scrubby glade below. The ravine walls narrowed, forming a natural funnel that would force any deer to pass well within my range.

If I weren't hunting, I wouldn't have been in the woods on a misty, rainy day, and it was lovely. It reminded me of hiking the Long Trail with Jan, of being outside in sun and rain, both day and night. I wondered how I could spend more time out of doors in all weather until I realized: I'm already doing it.

By the end of the first week I was feeling confident about staying oriented within these forty acres. On Friday, I hunted in the morning and was back at my desk after lunch, when the phone rang. It was Dale, the sawyer. He'd just seen the buck.

"It's an eight-pointer. You should come over."

I went.

I was nervous about hunting in the afternoon. Tracking, gutting, and dragging a deer out by dark seemed beyond my abilities. But it didn't matter: When I returned to where Dennis and Dale had been logging and I'd been hunting all week, the men had already left, and so, it seemed, had the deer.

* * *

I didn't hunt on the weekend. We slaughtered the last three turkeys, harvested the Brussels sprouts, and prepared for the usual multi-day Thanksgiving lalapalooza, when our nearest and dearest and their friends and relations arrive by train, plane, and automobile while I strategized sleeping arrangements and menus. Easier years we were just ten; Herculean years we were twenty-eight. Of course, everyone helps with the cooking, eating, and cleaning, and mostly it's fun. But I was grateful that hunting offered me an excuse to get out of the house and take a break from being in charge.

Hunting on Tuesday and Wednesday mornings was unremarkable, except that I felt both distracted to be missing the ongoing house party and relieved to be out of the crowded house. I'd like to believe that if there were deer about, I would have noticed, but I was oblivious. I was thinking about how I was taught about the Pilgrims in 1963, when I was in second grade and Columbus's discovery of America was presented as an unqualified success that logically led to eating turkey on the fourth Thursday in November. It was years before I realized that my grandparents hadn't been there. They'd arrived from Eastern Europe centuries after the *Mayflower*, aboard the *Aquitania*, the *Czar*, and the *Kaiserin Auguste Victoria*. They disembarked at Ellis Island, not Plymouth Rock.

I was also learning how hunting involves a great deal of sitting with my back against a tree, allowing my mind to wander. I wondered about the Abenaki who once hunted these woods, and how quietly they moved through it, how very lightly they lived on this land, and how simply being outside and observant leads to knowledge about the forest's flora and fauna.

My mind wandered through the woods to memories of Helen, the extraordinary friend who long ago had taken me into the woods to hunt with my camera, washed my kitchen floor when I was ordered to bed in a failed attempt to avoid a miscarriage, invited me to go with her to check out Savannah, the mare she brought home, and Hurricane, the colt she raised into a stallion for stud. Helen even coaxed me into the woods on horseback, where the mare's ears swiveled like radar, scanning for danger. More often, we hiked through the woods. Helen led me to a den of porcupettes, showed me owl pellets, deer sign, claw marks where a bear scratched a tree for bugs, and other talismans of wildlife to which I was blind on my own.

Helen had curiosity and compassion for all living creatures. She observed their behavior and gave them extraordinary care, once rescuing an infant mouse that she fed with a doll's bottle and then tucked into her bra to keep warm between feedings. In addition to her dogs and a cat, she had an ever-changing menagerie of mice, rats, ferrets, and doves in her house, not always in their cages. I'm not fond of wildlife indoors, and I was unsettled when the dove flew at my head.

Different as we were, Helen and I met at the intersection of experience and language. Helen was a fine writer and a good friend. One snow-covered Saturday toward the end of the century, she phoned, sounding low. In addition to a family history of depression, Helen had suffered some childhood trauma and a sexual assault as an adult.

"Do you want me to come over?" I asked.

"Yes."

"Stay safe until I get there. Promise me."

"Okay."

"I'm on my way."

Ordinarily, I'd be preoccupied with chores and my three young children on a Saturday when Tim was on call, but for the life of me I can't remember where my kids were or how I was able to leave home. I drove up the valley and then up the mountain to the log home where Helen lived. Neither Dennis nor their daughters were there. Upstairs, I found Helen and her dogs in bed.

Her despair was beyond my ken, so I called the hospital and explained the situation to Tim, who was both Helen's friend and her physician. He arrived and sat on the side of the bed, still wearing his woolen jacket as he held Helen's hand. I heard only the susurration of their words, indistinct to my ears, until Tim turned to me and said, "Helen has agreed to sign a contract stating that she won't harm herself. She wants you to write it for her."

I sat on the same loveseat where six years earlier I'd written Kelly's eulogy while Helen took care of my kids. This time, I was writing a contract for living.

On this day in January, when the snow lays like lace on the leaf litter and pale light illuminates the woods; on this Saturday, in the home I built with Dennis, the home we made for our daughters, I make this promise to my husband and my children: that I will do my best to feed the horses every day, muck their stalls, give them grain and hay, fill their water, turn them out to pasture, and call them back to the barn. I will take the dogs with me, nipping at my heels, and I will congratulate Hazel every time she slaughters the wild mice, but not, please God, the tame ones in the kitchen.

I will wake in the morning, see my daughters off to school, dress and go to my job. I will carry on even when the burden of living seems daunting. I will carry on. On this day, I make this oath to keep living. Amen.

Just then Dennis walked in, unaware of what was going on.

"Deb has written a contract for Helen to sign," Tim quietly explained. He asked me to read it aloud.

When I finished, Dennis said, "Well, hell, that was kind of poetic. If you'd asked me to write it, I would have just said, 'I promise not to kill myself,' and be done with it."

I handed the paper to Tim, who gave it to Helen to sign.

Then I drove home, proud of Tim for his kindness, and yet saddened by what I'd done. I already sensed that this rescue would cost me Helen's friendship, and it did. Did I pull away, or did she?

Helen was hospitalized sometime after she signed the contract. For the next fifteen years, we saw one another less and less. Despite her severe depression and several hospitalizations, Helen finished college, divorced Dennis, became a nurse, and remarried. Throughout her life, Helen found solace in the woods, where one fall day, she shot herself.

I think Helen would be proud of me for learning to hunt.

* * *

After the hoopla and feasting on Thanksgiving, I hunted again on Friday, which was magical. I was sitting in what had become my regular seat overlooking the ravine, the place where I'd actually seen one deer and hoped to see more. Late that morning, I did: a large doe sauntered into the newly cut slash. Another followed. And another. Five in all, each doe smaller than the one ahead, like a set of graduated matryoshka dolls. Rifle season is for bucks only.

My inner narrator started talking. Can you get a bead on them? Just to feel what it's like to take aim?

I lifted my rifle, but saw only black.

What's wrong with my rifle?

The lens cap was still on.

I exhaled, removed the cap, and brought the scope to my eye. I trained the muzzle on the kill zone of the lead deer.

Yeah, if this were a buck, I could pull the trigger.

I lowered my gun and watched the parade vanish into the woods.

I sat a little longer, not really expecting it to get any better.

It got worse.

I heard shots just over the ridge. One—two—three—four—five. Then six—seven.

I lost count.

Has someone taken out the five does? It's illegal!

* * *

In the story of Artemis and Actaeon, Actaeon and his companions have spent a morning in wanton killing, slaying animals until the mountainsides are bloodstained and the hunters' weapons are caked with blood. Actaeon calls off the hunt, and the hunters disperse, but blood lust leaves Actaeon inattentive, reckless or predatory, depending on who's telling the story. He wanders through the forest and happens upon a secluded and sacred glade where Artemis and her nymphs are bathing. Not expecting to be interrupted, Artemis has set aside her lance and unstrung her bow. She is disarmed and naked—vulnerable.

Actaeon sees them. As soon as the nymphs detect him, they crowd around Artemis to shield her body from the mortal's sight. It's too late, and Artemis flushes with anger. Without arrows at hand, she splashes Actaeon and tells him to boast that he's seen her naked—if he can. But she's turned him into a stag. He can neither speak nor outrun his own hunting hounds, who pursue him to death.

* * *

I'm no Artemis. I didn't know for sure if what I heard was wanton killing, but I wasn't going to stick around to find out.

The shots still echoed in my head.

Wanton killing?

I hope not. They were so beautiful.

And yet if one had been a buck, I would have pulled the trigger. I had a good shot ... in range, with plenty of time to take aim.

It was the last day of the hunting season for me, and on my way out of the woods, I knew that if a buck ever came within range, I was capable of shooting it—and willing. This seemed like a good lesson for my first year.

SIX

WAITING TO HUNT

Once the sixteen-day rifle season ended, I had to wait three hundred and forty-nine days before I could try again.

Winter passed. I didn't think about hunting as much as I thought about writing about hunting, but my ignorance about deer and their habitat was so vast that I could barely put words on a page. I buried myself in other work, developing grant-funded courses to teach, chairing the Brattleboro Community Justice Center's Citizen's Advisory Board, and doing my best to help Dad, now ninety-one, negotiate the world as his balance wobbled, his eyesight dimmed, and his cognition dulled.

Bare ground was visible at the end of March, when I saw an announcement for a Vermont Fish and Wildlife meeting about the proposed changes to hunting regulations for the coming year. The idea of attending a lecture about hunting appealed to the academic I'd been trained as, and I'd always been a good student. Good, not brilliant, but diligent, earning my degrees—BA, MA, MPhil, PhD—by following the set path blazed as clearly as a well-marked trail: attend class, take notes, write papers.

* * *

I'd earned enough high school credits to skip my senior year, find a full-time job, and learn what working was all about. But this was before taking a gap year was commonplace, and my father squashed the proposal. "You'll have your whole life to work. Stay in school." I did as he said, attended my senior year of high school, and spent the summer after graduation blundering around Europe, looking at buildings and art, eating bread and chocolate, and sleeping on trains.

It was hardly The Grand Tour I'd anticipated from reading nineteenth-century British novels. It was the heroes of those novels who traveled freely. When heroines traveled, they were accompanied by chaperones whose very presence kept their charges safe from Italian train conductors' wandering hands, chaperones whose stern presence discouraged men from making rude gestures, chaperones whose withering looks stopped the breath of those who would whistle like wolves. I'd imagined traveling with the freedom of a hero, but I was a young female traveling with another girl who was frequently mistaken for my younger brother, and I attracted sexual attention I didn't want.

My goal in high school had been to attend college; my goal in college was to graduate. But it was at my commencement, my skin blistering in the Ohio sun while Marcus Raskin droned on about nuclear disarmament, that I realized I was supposed to have found a husband by now. I felt stupid for not having realized this sooner, and more than somewhat betrayed by my mother, who'd been such a force for "getting into a good college" during my high school years, but silent about what I might do afterward. Silence is hard to interpret, so I applied and was accepted into two English graduate school programs. My college advisor, Phyllis Jones, encouraged me to pursue an academic career. When I declined at the University of Chicago and deferred my acceptance at Columbia, Phyllis took me out to lunch and said, "It's hard to raise a family in a city."

Phyllis and I hadn't been close, and I found this frank declaration that she expected me to want a family and a career presumptive. Phyllis was tenured when I was a freshman, had her first baby when I was a sophomore, and arranged to job share with her tenured husband. At that lunch before graduation, Phyllis was heavily pregnant with her second child, and she complained that the college was getting more than two half-time faculty for the price of one, since both attended department and faculty meetings in addition to their half-time teaching loads. It was said as a warning, backed by Phyllis's confident assumption that I wanted what she had. My immediate plan, vague at best, was to move to New York, become self-supporting, and write.

I had neither role models for female bachelorhood nor money, so my first post-graduate gig was painting the interior of my parents' living room, dining room, and front hall. With the four-hundred dollars I earned, I moved into Aunt Joan and Uncle Dave's house in Brooklyn while they summered in Vermont, and I looked for a job.

I was prepared to wait tables, even though I hadn't been good at it during the two weeks I subbed for a friend in college. When I told Mom my plans, she said, "Don't you want to do something with your BA?" I wanted to support myself so I could write.

My former high school college counselor was now working in publishing, and she told me about an entry-level job at Octagon Books, an imprint that specialized in republishing scholarly works. It was a subsidiary of the trade publishers Farrar, Straus & Giroux. I took the job with the understanding that, in time, I could follow Lila, my predecessor, into a position in the trade division. Lila was my age and wanted to move out of her parents' uptown apartment where she had grown up. We found an apartment and became roommates and friends.

I started reporting to work at a battleship gray desk with a push-button phone and an IBM Selectric on which I typed letters that took one of two forms: The first was to the original publishers of out-of-print scholarly tomes, offering a pittance to republish them. The second letter was to the printer, giving instructions for the modest print run, including the color of the library binding: dark red, navy blue, or deep green. This left me little else to do but endure my boss's brute inquisitiveness into my sex life, listen to his off-color jokes, and watch the clock on the ConEd building on Fourteenth Street move ever-so-slowly toward five o'clock.

It was 1978, thirteen years before the Senate confirmation hearings where Anita Hill's testimony against Supreme Court Nominee Clarence Thomas introduced the term "sexual harassment" into the mainstream. In 1978, I had no language to describe my predicament at work, and no idea that I had any recourse. Even if I'd known Artemis's stories, I'm not sure I would have read them as I do know. Like almost every woman I know, Artemis suffered unwanted sexual harassment, assault, and—in some versions—even rape.

Alpheus, the river god with a history of sexual assault, suffered unrequited love for Artemis and planned to abduct her. Artemis learned of his plan and hid in plain sight by smearing herself with mud, becoming indistinguishable from the riverbank. In another story, Artemis rescues Arethusa from the predatory Alpheus by turning the nymph into a spring.

Stories of Artemis and the mortal Orion vary. In one version, Orion rapes Artemis. In another version, Artemis and Orion are playmates, soulmates, and then lovers. Apollo becomes so jealous of Orion's relationship with his sister, he tricks Artemis into killing Orion with an arrow. Bereft, she turns Orion into a constellation.

When Artemis discovers that Calisto is carrying Zeus's child, she's said to punish the nymph by turning her into a bear. But it was Artemis's father who raped Calisto, her good friend. Could it be that Artemis's anger is for Zeus, and that by transforming Calisto into a bear, Artemis is making her friend safe from further violation?

These stories about Artemis redefine female chastity from meaning abstinence to meaning self-determination. Instead of denying Artemis's sexuality, the stories tell of a female deity helping women maintain control of their bodies and exacting justice against those who attempt to force themselves on her or her nymphs.

* * *

I lasted nine months at Octagon Books before I revived my application to Columbia, figuring I'd rather read good literature in graduate school, which I believed would be a meritocracy free of sexual predation, maybe even of sexism. I'd been well-treated at Oberlin, where many of my professors were women. Only one male professor made a pass at me in college, a pass that was easy to deflect. I was his wife's student, not his, so there was no threat to my academic progress—no retaliation for ducking the embrace—just a rude awakening that marriage didn't necessarily insure fidelity. I was naïve enough to be shocked. But it was no better when another male professor singled me out on account of an essay I'd written about Jane Austen's *Emma*. He said, "It's the best student essay I've ever read," then offered me a job babysitting his five-year-old son.

Part of the allure of going to Columbia was the prospect of working with Carolyn Heilbrun. She wasn't only an academic who by then had authored *Toward a Recognition of Androgyny* and *Reinventing Womanhood;* she also wrote mysteries as Amanda Cross. I enrolled in Professor Heilbrun's seminar, British Fiction Between the Wars, which was terrific, except for one thing: Heilbrun was hostile toward me. It turns out I was not alone. Whispered stories of female students she undermined were rampant. In 2004, I met a man at a conference who'd been her student. He confirmed what I'd suspected. "No question," he said. "She was sexist. She favored men. She favored *me*."

Of course, Heilbrun was subject to intense sexism herself. She was the first female to receive tenure in Columbia's English Department, where she held an endowed chair. But when she retired after thirty-two years, she told a *New York Times* interviewer that her "name in the catalog gave Columbia a reputation for encouraging feminist studies in modernism. Nothing could be further from the truth." I know this to be true.

I did well at Columbia. After earning my master's degree, I was awarded two research assistantships to help pay my way. I no longer remember the work I did for a Shakespearean scholar, who was brusque—but brusque was better than abusive. Martin Meisel, by comparison, gave me clear instructions about what he wanted me to research, and he thanked me for it, both in person and in the acknowledgements to his prize-winning work, *Realizations: Narrative, Pictorial, and Theatrical Arts in Nineteenth-Century England*.

I started teaching Freshman Composition at Columbia College in 1982, the last year the school was all male. One of my students was a prince from the United Arab Emirates who came to my office to complain about his grade. He stood, tucked his tie into his jacket, and looked down at me. "Ms. Luskin," he said, his British accent squeezed between his teeth. "Haven't you heard of a gentleman's C?"

"Yes," I answered, "but you have to earn it."

He turned on his polished heel and walked out.

I'm telling these stories for two reasons. The first is that I believe the sexual abuse I experienced as a child and didn't remember until half a century later taught me to expect harassment and abuse—and endure it. The second reason is that in March, when my ignorance about how to learn to hunt overwhelmed me, I defaulted to my academic training, believing that attending meetings, classes, and lectures would be a good way to learn about hunting.

* * *

At the Vermont Fish and Wildlife meeting, about fifty white, mostly middle-aged men were in the audience. I was one of the four women in the room. Of these, two were presenters and decades younger than me.

Nick Fortin, a big-game biologist at Vermont's Fish and Wildlife Department (VFW), started with a grim data-driven report about the condition of Vermont's moose. Due to habitat loss and parasites, the moose population in Vermont was imperiled. In an effort to reestablish a herd of 3,000 of these giant but homely-looking animals, VFW was reducing the number of moose permits for the coming year.

Fortin's update on the deer herd was only slightly less dire, but for the opposite reason: overpopulation. Few hunters believe this, their general attitude being, if there are so many deer, why didn't I get one? But VFW scientists collect data the way baseball announcers collect stats, beginning with the winter severity index (WSI), calculated by assigning a numeric value to snowfall and temperature from the beginning of December through the end of April. This year's WSI was the lowest since 1970 and unlikely to change in the few weeks of data collection left in the season.

Mild winters mean more deer survive, especially more does and their fawns, so VFW was expecting an increase in the deer population statewide. In addition to mild winters, the loss of natural predators and a decline in hunting have allowed the deer population to swell. Even the estimated 3,600-5,500 deer fatalities due to motor vehicles on Vermont's roads are not enough to suppress the deer herd's growth.

But a larger herd is not necessarily a healthy one. Diminishing habitat combined with the deteriorating quality of food sources mean that the Vermont landscape can no longer support the increased number of deer. Invasive plants replacing native flora provide less nutrition, and habitat loss caused by development and forest fragmentation push deer into smaller areas. Even without knowing about WSI, I've seen the effects overpopulation and food scarcity each spring, when deer stagger across our fields, seeking early greens by the river. A herd of starving deer is not a pretty sight.

According to the state biologists, the deer herd was in poor condition back when the old-timers like Roger, my mentor, remember an abundance of deer. So why do the old-timers remember the size of the herd and not its condition? Because memory is selective, and because mid-twentieth-century winters were generally more severe than they are now. Back then, deer died of starvation months after hunting season ended, when hunters weren't necessarily paying attention to the size and condition of the herd, the same way I hadn't paid attention to what was going on in the woods since locking my rifle away.

The present century's decline in hunters has also enabled the herd to grow. In an effort to attract young hunters, Youth Weekend allows licensed kids under sixteen accompanied by an unarmed, licensed adult to shoot any deer, male or female, without restrictions. This is a boon for kids who have family members or older friends who can take these young hunters into the field and teach them where to go, what to look for, and to help them recover an animal, field dress it, and carry it out—the kind of help I'd wished for. When it came time for questions, I asked why there wasn't a weekend for new adult hunters the way there is for youth. Three years later, Vermont established a Novice Deer Hunting Weekend that allows a first-time hunter of any age to hunt with an unarmed mentor.

At the end of the meeting, I spoke with Theresa Elmer, a board member, who told me about the Women's Outdoor Program and encouraged me to check it out. Nicole Meier, the hunter education and outreach specialist at VFW, gave me her number, saying she could help me find a mentor. I didn't follow up with either of them; they're both from up north and I wanted to hunt near my home. But that might just have been a lame excuse, because the real truth was that it was the end of March, and hunting season seemed a long way off.

While I wasn't thinking about hunting that spring, I'd accepted invitations to give my popular Humanities Council talk about the history of transportation and settlement in Vermont come fall. As a result, instead of scouting for land in October and November, I found myself driving to all corners of the state, explaining how native footpaths were the foundation for all subsequent methods of transportation in Vermont, from the British military roads to the Interstate Highways. I was learning firsthand how work interferes with hunting and was starting to understand what Roger meant when he said, "Hunting is total freedom."

* * *

Fortunately, none of these speaking gigs fell on the evening in late October when the Conservation Commission in nearby Dummerston hosted a program called Deer in the Woods. I drove over the covered bridge to the former regional library, where I'd lectured about Jane Austen, Virginia Woolf, and the Long Trail. The room was packed with familiar faces. Nick Fortin, the state deer biologist, began the program with a brief history of deer in Vermont.

Deer and humans coexisted sustainably for the 9,000-12,000 years before Europeans arrived. French imperial activity began in 1540, and deer were still in "great store" in 1584, according to an early English account. Vermont became a state in 1791. By 1800, the population of non-native residents jumped from roughly 89,000 to over 154,000. For the next fifty years, settlers poured into Vermont, clearing land and hunting deer.

Vermont was about eighty-five percent forested when it became the fourteenth state. At the end of the Civil War seventy-five years later, only thirty-seven percent of the state was covered in trees, and the deer population was practically wiped out, along with wolves and mountain lions, deer's natural predators. Only a few deer survived in the Northeast Kingdom. In 1876, the state outlawed deer hunting, and stiff penalties were imposed: Anyone found in possession of "any wild deer or part thereof," was presumed guilty of poaching and fined fifty dollars. Additionally, the law allowed any dog found pursuing wild deer to be killed.

To remedy the lack of deer, a group of men from Rutland formed an association "for the purpose of restocking our mountains with this beautiful and valuable game animal." They purchased seventeen deer from New York State and turned them loose in Rutland County. To protect their investment, they offered fifty dollars to anyone furnishing evidence resulting in the conviction of anyone pursuing, taking, killing, or destroying the imported deer. The gambit worked, though slowly. It wasn't until the end of the century that the first regulated hunting season was held. In 1897, hunters reported taking 103 antlered deer.

Vermont's human population declined in the early twentieth century, and the deer herd increased. To counter deer damage to crops and orchards, the state permitted the harvest of antlerless deer—females and young males—during five seasons between 1909 and 1920. But the enduring cultural legacy of taking only bucks had already been established. Even though harvesting does is the most effective method of controlling the overall deer population, many traditional hunters, like Roger, dislike the practice.

"You shoot a doe," Roger told me, characteristically shaking his head. "Every time you shoot a doe," he frowned and rubbed his chin. "Every time you shoot a doe," he said again, looking me in the eye, "you're shooting her and all the fawns she'd have in her lifetime. Could be twelve or thirteen deer, because deer usually have twins, sometimes triplets." Roger was born in 1946. By the time he started hunting in his teens, the herd was booming.

By the middle of the twentieth century, with declining farmland for grazing, the deer started eating trees, damaging one of Vermont's most lucrative agricultural products: hardwood. Deer eat six to eight percent of their body weight daily. They prefer to graze on grass and greenery, but with less grazing available, deer will browse on woody vegetation. They're particularly fond of maple, oak, and ash saplings, which would grow into high-value timber if not nibbled to the ground. This is especially true in Windham County, where there is a great deal of privately owned forestland posted against hunting. These are beautiful, mature forests, but they can no longer sustain themselves or their timber value where deer have decimated replacement trees. Instead, faster-growing, lower-value trees are taking hold in the understory, including invasive species blowing in on the winds of climate change.

Following modern management practices, the Department of Fish and Wildlife has divided the state into over twenty Wildlife Management Units (WMUs) based on habitat and deer density. This allows VFW to apportion antlerless permits to areas where population control is needed most. To protect the forest and the health of the deer in the southeastern part of the state, VFW has initiated "a lower density objective" in two of Windham County's WMUs.

According to George Weir, a consulting forester, the deer have disrupted natural systems of forest regeneration that took thousands of years to establish. Oak has been browsed too many years in a row and won't recover, and the deer don't eat the black birch, beech, and buckthorn that has opportunistically moved in. "If we want to protect the high-value, browse-sensitive species of red oak, ash, and maple," Weir said, "twelve deer per square mile is too many. We must bring the deer density down to four or five deer per square mile."

Such a drastic reduction is sure to irritate deer hunters, especially those, like Roger, who remember seeing herds of fifty or more deer grazing on abandoned pasture at twilight when he started hunting in the 1950s. "Back then," he said, "everyone hunted. It was easy to get a deer."

Tim Morton, who has managed public land during a long career told us, "Deer are not distributed around the landscape equally, and heavy concentration is not good for the forest." Morton acknowledged the conflict between hunters, who want more deer than the forest can support, and landowners, who want high-value timber and the privacy of posted land. "It's a complex situation."

Morton said that in the southeastern part of the state the forests have never recovered from the deer overpopulation from the 1950s through the 1970s. "Forest management takes time, and mostly we've been concerned with overstory management, but it's the understory that's subject to browse." He acknowledged the reason why so many people came out for this event: Dummerston's forests are suffering. The deer have eaten all the high-value saplings; opportunistic invasive species are moving in; a recovery plan is needed for the understory, including regeneration of native plants, and more hunter access.

More hunter access was the reason I was there. Rifle season would open in just sixteen days. Dennis finished the job where I'd hunted the previous year. He was now logging up north. I didn't yet have anywhere to hunt. At the end of the Q&A that followed the presentations, I had a chance to announce that I was a new hunter looking for landowners willing to let me hunt on their land. I was hoping that the landowners who post their land "Hunting By Permission Only" would respond. They did: I collected several names right then, and more via email and phone in the following days.

* * *

I hadn't taken my rifle out of its case since the previous season. I'd often thought about shooting my .22 for practice over the summer, and I nearly did on an afternoon so clear and bright it made my heart both sing and ache to be alive. It was a perfect moment for target practice, but I couldn't bring myself to lock the dog in the house. I took Leo for a walk instead.

There's nothing like a walk to help me settle my mind and figure out what to do next. I'd run out of time to plink with my .22. I had to find a place to practice with my deer rifle, a place with a 100-yard range and no neighbors. I had an open invitation to shoot at Roger's, but I wanted to find out what a proper firing range was like. A Google search located four near where I live.

I immediately eliminated the Putney Gun Club, which was close by, but it's an indoor range for handguns only. The Chester Rod & Gun Club is the least expensive nearby range, but the range is geared toward skeet shooting. The closest prospect was Sportsmen Inc., about fifteen miles from home, but I'd have to be either a member or a guest of one. Friends had given me names of people they knew would invite me, but it wasn't an ask I wanted to make. Even as a guest, I'd have to become an associate member of the National Rifle Association, and the ten-dollar fee would allow Sportsmen Inc. to share my information with an organization I can't support. While originally established in 1871 to "promote and encourage rifle shooting on a scientific basis," the NRA has morphed into a lobbying organization for gun manufacturers, misrepresenting the Second Amendment and promoting political influence over common sense and human life.

The Deerfield Valley Sportsmen's Club offered the best deal on a family membership for two adults and their children under eighteen for a modest price. This good deal got even better if you paid before April 15. I could be there in half an hour, but with membership running from January to December, it hardly made sense for me to join in November. Instead, I headed up the interstate to Hammond Cove, a state-owned and operated safe, accessible, and environmentally responsible shooting range that I'd already paid for through my tax dollars—and funding from the NRA. There was no escaping the NRA, whose powerful lobbying has influenced government policy and gun ownership, saturating the country with the misguided idea that everyone is not only entitled to own firearms, but should be able to use them without oversight of any kind.

I was delighted to have my friend Hilary's company, and the hour-long drive passed quickly. A year earlier, Hilary had expressed interest in joining me for shooting practice. She grew up hunting in Wisconsin and owned a rifle; what she didn't have was time. In addition to her toddler and preschooler, she worked a couple of jobs, milked two goats, kept chickens, and was married to Drew, an advanced medical practitioner who covered the Grace Cottage Hospital emergency department at night. She wanted to hunt and hoped to take it up, maybe in the next year. I recognized the wistfulness in her voice; among the demands of motherhood is perpetually delayed gratification.

We found the Hammond Cove Range located in a no man's land between the interstate and the Connecticut River. At the wooden gate, I showed the range safety officer my hunting license, which allowed me in with Hilary as my guest. The officer directed us to one of the six rifle benches covered by a shed roof. Our bench looked like a modified picnic table anchored to a cement slab. It faced what appeared to be a football field surrounded by a high, earthen berm to absorb bullets and sound, all topped by a chain link fence to keep the field of fire clear. Instead of yard lines, plywood backstops were staggered across the field at twenty-five, fifty-, seventy-five, and one-hundred yards.

About eight people were already set up when we arrived. The safety officer instructed everyone to leave their unloaded firearms on the bench with the action open before Hilary and I headed downrange to staple targets to the backstops at twenty-five and fifty yards. We both planned to warm up with our .22s. My Harrington & Richardson is comfortable the way my two-and-a-half-pound boy's axe is comfortable: not too heavy and simple to use. The .22 takes a single cartridge and has to be emptied and reloaded each time it's fired, which allowed me time to stay calm.

A few more people arrived, including some who headed over to the far end, where there was a high wooden counter, like a bar, for pistol practice. The range officer checked us for the required ear and eye protection and reviewed the range rules. "When I give the signal to fire, the range is hot and everyone must stay behind the firing line. When I give the signal to cease fire, the range is cold. Only when everyone has put down their weapon with the action open will I give the all-clear to head downrange and retrieve your targets."

I braced myself against the bench, looked down the barrel, and squeezed. Guns blasted on either side of me; I couldn't hear the .22's pop. I was a tunnel of concentration, remembering the sequence of bringing the stock to my shoulder, inhaling to aim, and exhaling on the squeeze. My entire focus was on the six-inch circle around the bull's-eye, and I was hitting it. It took more effort to hit the target at fifty yards. Once I found the sweet spot, I was pleased with my aim, and then I reminded myself: This is only the .22.

The range went cold.

I pulled down the used targets and stapled new ones at fifty and seventy-five yards. Back at the bench, I uncased my deer rifle and stared at it. It was a chilly day, but I was suddenly hot: I couldn't remember how to open the magazine. The range officer saw that something was wrong and came over. He showed me how the latch on the trigger-guard pops the trapdoor of the magazine beneath the action, and he did so kindly, with no judgment. I loaded the magazine with five cartridges and chambered the first round.

When the range went hot again, I aimed my rifle and looked for my target through the scope. The target was black, with white circles and a red bull's-eye on a six-inch square. I could see it at fifty yards, but against weathered plywood, it was nearly invisible at seventy-five. The next time the range went cold, the officer handed me a red-on-white paper target the size of a doormat. "It's easier to see a small area on top of a big one."

He was right.

The contrast of the black target stapled to the white one made all the difference. My shots clustered within a four-inch kill zone; I had my aim back. I also knew that seventy-five yards was the very end of my range. I didn't know if it was realistic to expect to find such a long shot in Vermont's dense forest, but I'd done what I could to prepare.

The temperature and sky both dropped while we were shooting, which changed our plans from finding a picnic spot to eating our lunches in the car. I unwrapped my sandwich. Hilary pulled the top off a plastic container filled with roasted vegetables.

"You vegetarian?" I asked.

"Vegan," she answered.

"I thought you kept chickens."

"The kids are omnivores."

"So you feed them meat?"

"When I can find local, organic, ethically raised. That's why I want to hunt."

We ate in silence before Hilary said, "I think I'm going to go raw."

"Raw food diet?" I couldn't think of anything less appealing, except maybe a diet of all processed food.

I'd become a vegetarian in 1975, when a lousy college housing lottery number landed me in Harkness, the natural foods coop on campus. In 1975, natural foods were hippy, not hip. At the beginning of the fall term, we decided we'd eat meat if we could procure a local, grass-fed steer. A carnivore wannabe scoured the countryside for such an animal—and found one. At a post prandial meeting, the researcher explained the situation: The young steer had been raised on pasture all summer, but with winter approaching, the farmer was willing to slaughter, butcher, and sell the meat to us. Otherwise, the farmer would bring the steer into the barn, where it would fatten on grain. We had to vote to kill the animal.

The vote failed.

The animal was still doomed to be slaughtered and eaten, just not by us. I was disappointed—not just for myself, but also for the steer.

That spring, Ralph Nader came to Oberlin to recruit students to help start an Ohio Public Interest Research Group. I don't remember how he segued from Ohio PIRG to food, but he was the first person I ever heard talk about the distance food travels: from field to factory to warehouse to distribution center to grocery store to home—typically 1,500 miles or more. He also noted how fresh produce and unprocessed food was shrinking to the perimeter of the traditional grocery store.

I never forgot Nader's talking points or the food we ate at Harkness, where baking our daily bread began with milling wheat berries into flour, and where we made our weekly tofu, because it wasn't commercially available in northeast Ohio at that time, making it all the more virtuous.

For a while, I was a convert—and tiresomely self-righteous, I'm sure.

So when Hilary said, "I feel so good eating vegan. I might feel even better eating raw," I tried to sound supportive.

"At least you wouldn't have to cook," I said. This, I imagined, was how my friends who bought all their food in a supermarket felt when I told them I'd taken up hunting wild meat. I chewed on that during the drive home.

SEVEN

MY SECOND HUNT

The sixteen-day season started on a fourteen-degree day with the wind chill near zero. I didn't sleep well, so it was a relief to dress and drive to Hilary's. Earlier in the week, she had shown me her land, where she said she saw deer every morning. Another friend who hunted in Wisconsin told me, "Out there you just sit by the river, and when the deer come down to drink, you shoot." Not knowing any better, that's what I expected to happen.

Not in Vermont. When I started reading hunting magazines, I began to understand how hunting in Vermont is different from hunting in the agricultural heartland, in the wide-open Western states, and on private hunting reserves in Texas. In the Midwest, the deer are easily visible when they feed on cropland and feedlots—plots planted specifically to attract deer. Many places out West offer long, clear shots to big game far away, requiring high-caliber rifles, high-resolution scopes, and highly accurate, long-distance aim. In Texas, some ranchers have given up raising cattle and earn more by turning their land into wild game reserves. These reserves vary in style, from the ones where you hook up your RV and cook for yourself, to lavish establishments with attentive hosts, gourmet meals, and price tags to match. Some of these ranches specialize in raising trophy-size bucks and provide guidance to where on the property a hunter might find a specific deer. On some ranches, hunters can drive to hunting stands set up near strategically placed feeding stations. Vermont's cramped woods, wild deer, and uneven terrain make for a hunting experience with markedly different challenges.

Hilary and Drew had recently cleared some of the land near the brook, meaning there was fresh browse where the first succession plants of softwood saplings and wild raspberries had started to colonize the clearing. It looked like a slam-dunk: The deer would stroll into sight and pause to feed and drink. There was even a logging lane that would make it easy to find my seat in the dark and drag my buck back to the truck. Besides, I had Hilary's word that she saw deer from her kitchen window every morning. But the day I scouted with Hilary, I was so intent on learning my way in and out of the woods that I overlooked the complete lack of deer sign: No tracks, no piles of poop, no scrapes on the ground, rubs on the trees or indentations in the leaf litter where deer had bedded down. In a stunning example of naïveté, I assumed that if I found a comfortable place to sit and wait, the deer would come to me, even in the cold.

I have no trouble staying warm and focused while engaged in the heat-generating activities of cross-country skiing or snowshoeing in sub-freezing weather, but there's nothing easy about staying warm while sitting still when the wind chill is zero. It's an endurance test. I fished my chemical hand warmers out of my pack. My fingers were so numb that I couldn't keep the wrappers from crinkling. Had there been any deer in the area, they would have heard me and fled.

The sun rose and I moved, mostly to defrost. Skidder ruts and slash crisscrossed the recently logged land, making for hard going. I scrambled until I found another natural blind and hunkered down, but nothing about my situation felt right. I heard traffic and discovered I was within sight of the road. This wasn't the forest experience I was after. I was also adjacent to a hundred or more acres that weren't posted. Legally speaking, I didn't need permission, but I didn't want to risk disturbing another hunter.

Even before I'd read the story of Atalanta drawing first blood in the boar hunt that ends in Meleager's death, I had recurrent fantasies about taking a deer and enraging a man who claimed it was rightfully his and then stealing it from me. Or I'd shoot a buck with a big rack and a herd of hunters descends on me, a single woman who needs to learn her place. Even as an inner voice tells me to say little, say nothing, play dumb, I still try to talk the guys down, which further enrages the men not only for shooting the buck, but also for being articulate and smart.

These imagined encounters never end well. I recognized them as manifestations of anxiety about trespassing on what I've been acculturated to believe is a man's world: hunting prey. It's a sign of the times. When the hunting season started, high-profile women were speaking out, and powerful men outed for sexual predation were losing their jobs. Part of me was delighted—at last women were holding men accountable and being heard! And part of me was scared. I knew from personal experience that women are one of the species that men prey upon.

When I lived in New York in my twenties, I ran in Riverside Park. In the spring, men would expose themselves, penises emerging with the daffodils. On the sidewalk, guys full of themselves would tell me what they wanted to do with my body as they passed. Worst of all, in the subway, strangers would take advantage of the rush hour crush to press their erections against me. One of the reasons I came to Vermont in 1984 was that I couldn't face another summer of these visual, verbal, and physical insults. Individually, this unwanted attention would possibly have been bearable, but in the aggregate, they amounted to constant assaults. No wonder I questioned the wisdom of being in the woods, potentially putting myself in some man's sights.

On this cold morning, I was feeling momentarily protected from predation, perhaps because I was muffled in long underwear, performance leggings, fleece, and jacket. Despite all my layers, I was still cold, and there were no deer. They're smarter than I was; they were hunkered down. I had yet to learn that conserving energy is the deer's main tactic for winter survival; going indoors is mine. I was home by seven, just as Tim was waking up.

I tried Hilary's land again on Sunday, but it was still too cold. I returned home, where Tim and I worked amicably together, hanging winter curtains, exhuming snow shovels, hauling skis and snowshoes up from the basement. When we stopped for lunch, I confessed that I should have been hunting, and that I really didn't want to go.

"How late can you hunt?" Tim asked.

"Till a half hour past sunset. The sun sets at four-thirty today."

"But it's still light at six."

"I don't write the laws, Tim. I just follow them."

Why was he questioning me?

"But it's still light at six or six-thirty."

Now I was uncertain, so I rechecked the time for that day's sunset. "The sun sets at four-thirty today," I said, an edge in my voice. "Legal hunting ends a half hour after sunset." I'm angered when I have to fight for knowing my stuff. Tim's question triggered all the old feelings of inadequacy that rise when Tim doubts what I know. "Who's the hunter?"

I geared up and walked across our upper field to hunt in the woods on the hill across the road from my house. Both Roger and my neighbor Dean told me that historically there were lots of deer behind the farmhouse that once anchored "the best farm in town," according to the 1874 centennial *History of Newfane.*

My house is at the western end of sixty acres of open land that was once the farm's hayfield, cropland, and pasture. The farmhouse across the road is now a second home to people who live in New York. I'd emailed them. Even though the land wasn't posted, I preferred to have landowners' permission.

Lois replied. She was a financial consultant to high-end international investment banks, so her equivocation came as a surprise when she deferred to her husband. Jim would speak to their caretaker, who also hunted the property.

I live in a town of 1,700 people; I knew their caretaker. Jon was also the fire chief and the man who mowed our lawn. I phoned him, to let him know to expect Jim's call. He said he'd take care of it. He did.

Jim emailed me back, granted me permission to hunt their land, and wished me luck.

That afternoon, I was just glad to be outside. I didn't even care if I saw any deer.

The next day, I didn't hunt. In the morning I wrote; that afternoon, I met with someone at the Department of Corrections about funding for the Brattleboro Community Justice Center; and in the evening I facilitated a discussion about grief with medical professionals, based on their reading of Edward Hirsch's poem "Gabriel."

But in the shower that night, I experienced a pain so sharp that it caught my breath and I nearly fainted. To Tim, I admitted that my breast had hurt the past few days. I'd tried ignoring it, but it wouldn't go away.

His face turned serious as he palpated the area. "When did it start?"

"Ouch!"

"Sorry."

"A couple of days."

"Call Ewa," he said. "You need to be seen."

* * *

It's true that Tim is a family physician; it's also true he's my family and not my physician. I learned this just a few months into our relationship, when I woke with a sore throat. I handed Tim a flashlight and asked him to take a look.

One glance and he said, "You need to see a doctor."

I tilted my head to get a better look at him. "Why?"

"I can't treat family."

He thought of me as family? This was news.

Later that morning, his colleague Bob diagnosed me with quinsy. "It's what George Washington died of," Bob said cheerfully as he shot penicillin into my backside.

I didn't die then, but I might have died a few months later had Tim not been beside me when I woke up and said, "My lips are swelling." I was curious, not worried, but Tim started pulling on his pants.

"Get dressed," he said. "We're going to the hospital."

"What for?"

Angioedema, it turned out. I was having a serious, extravagant, and potentially lethal allergic reaction to the lobster I'd eaten the previous night. Now, when Tim says I need medical care, I follow his advice.

I made an appointment to see Ewa Arnold, my doctor, the following afternoon.

She scolded me for waiting so long. "You should have called! You could have texted me!"

"I'd never do that," I said, trying to smile through my tears. Ewa's both my doctor and a friend.

"You could have emailed me through the portal, then."

I hadn't thought of that.

She examined me, found the spot that took my breath, and went into high gear, blazing past scheduling secretaries until she'd arranged for me to have a diagnostic mammogram and sonogram followed by an appointment with the local breast surgeon the following day.

"We'll get through this," she said. "Let me know how it goes. Message me."

From Ewa's office, I drove ninety miles to the Orwell Free Library, where I gave my transportation and settlement talk to a packed house and spent the night at a friend's, so I wouldn't have to drive the twisty roads home at night.

Thursday, I went straight from Orwell to the hospital in Brattleboro. Ellen, my favorite of all the technicians who've imaged my breasts over the decades, greeted me, putting me at ease. I knew this drill: this wasn't the first time I'd been flagged for diagnostic imaging.

After both a mammogram and a sonogram, I threaded my way through the maze connecting one hospital building to another until

I arrived at the surgeon's office. As arranged, Tim met me there. Even though breast cancer is now treatable with a ninety-five percent survival rate, our personal losses to the disease made lasting impressions: his mother and two of my friends, all when they were younger than me. Statistically and logically, I know I'm more likely to die of cardiac disease than breast cancer, but fear isn't rational, and I'm braver with Tim beside me.

I knew women—friends—this surgeon had treated successfully; I was in good hands. He studied the images on his screen, which showed nothing unusual, then gave me the most thorough breast exam of my life. He found the spot.

"*Ow*," I gasped.

"Is it possible that you've bruised yourself recently?"

Duh! I'd been tucking my rifle tight under my arm while traipsing through the woods; the edge of the scope had bruised my ribs.

I remained calm, and explained that I'm a hunter; it was my rifle.

The surgeon railed against guns. He told me about his residency in Philadelphia, where he treated gunshot wounds every night. I couldn't get a word in edgewise, so I stopped trying. Just as I'm irrationally more frightened of breast cancer than cardiac disease, this surgeon's early exposure to fixing gunshot wounds had shaped his attitude toward all firearms. I understood.

Tim and I celebrated my good health by buying him a new chainsaw for his birthday. As we checked out, I reminded myself that operating a chainsaw has less potential for bodily harm than traveling by car.

We drove home.

* * *

The next day I rose early, enjoyed what was becoming the ritual robing for the hunt, and slipped out the back door. There was no moon, but it wasn't dark. Stars lit my way across our upper field, reminding me of a lesson I learned on the Long Trail: the less light there is, the less light I need.

Just as I acknowledged how stunning the world was by starlight, my neighbor's motion-detection lights blinded me. When sight returned, I crossed the road and entered the woods, where dense pine blocked the stars. The woods *were* dark. I paused for my eyes to adjust, then made my way to an old maple at the edge of a field.

At first, I liked watching the world come into focus as if the sun were on a rheostat and the world's a stage. The problem with this metaphor was that the world is large, and this relatively small patch of ground before me just a proscenium on which I could see only the drama directly before me. The lights were up, but the action hadn't started. Was I waiting for Godot?

As good as I thought this spot would be, I was overcome by uncertainty.

Should I try moving quietly to the place I'd noticed along the stone wall? Or should I climb higher?

I stayed put.

On my way out of the woods a couple of hours later, I flushed two does in a clearing. This was promising: where there are does there will be bucks. I had writing deadlines and a class to teach, but I was encouraged to see deer.

I crossed the road again the following morning, but again, I wasn't sure where to go, and I felt unsettled wherever I sat. By focusing only on the deer, I was losing sight of learning how to read the landscape. I walked out of the woods in time to attend nine o'clock yoga class, then take Dad to the opera.

When I was twelve, Dad took me to see my first-ever live opera. It was a performance of *Carmen* at what was then the new Metropolitan Opera House at Lincoln Center, with chandeliers that rose to the ceiling before the curtain went up. These days, I take Dad to the *Met Live in HD* simulcasts at the Latchis Theatre, in Brattleboro. Dad really only wanted to see his old favorites by Mozart, Puccini, and Verdi. I was glad to see John Adams's *Nixon in China*, and based on the reviews, I had high hopes for this afternoon's production of *The Exterminating Angel*, a new opera by Thomas Adés based on Luis Buñuel's 1962 surrealistic film of the same name. But I never cottoned to this opera's story of high society at a dinner party that turns into a nightmare they can't escape. Nor did I find anything pleasing about the soprano hitting the highest notes in the human range. It was music, but not melodic. Dad dozed through the production. Lucky him. I wished I were hunting.

* * *

As much as I wished I were hunting, it was now the week of Thanksgiving, so I was driving to the airport, shopping, cooking, and generally preparing for a houseful of guests. But guests sleep late, so I slipped outside and crossed the road before anyone was up. I saw from the hoof prints in the frosted grass that deer had been reveling there overnight, which helped me remain patient and optimistic. The morning before Thanksgiving, when I was returning to the house for breakfast, Tim had a phone to his ear and was waving frantically. "She's right here. I'll tell her." He held the handset away from his face and said, "Ed has an eight-pointer in his field. Right now!"

I dropped my pack and ran next door with my rifle. My neighbor was standing on his front porch wearing a fleece pullover and a towel wrapped around his waist. He stepped barefoot on the stone walk and stage-whispered, "It's in back, by the pond! I'd just got out of the shower and saw him standing there."

We snuck around the barn and I saw the heart-shaped rack crowning the buck's head; the rest of him was below the hillside. Even if more of him had been exposed, he was out of my range.

I tried to intercept him across the road, but I didn't see him again. Knowing he was out there gave me new purpose. I went out again that afternoon. Now I was seeing deer sign all over: a scrape, scat, hoofprints, and two does that slipped into the forest and disappeared.

Thanksgiving morning, I hid in a break of trees facing where I saw the buck the day before. I heard gunfire up the hill, where I'd been sitting every morning until today. I returned home and started cooking.

All week, I hunted early and entertained guests late. From Sunday to Sunday, we hosted twenty-five different visitors, put up twelve different overnight guests; changed linens on seven different beds; served fifty-eight dinners; lost count of breakfasts served, lunches eaten, and towels laundered. We ran the dishwasher three times a day, and cut, split, and stacked five cord of firewood. It was great fun.

I was exhausted.

I loved hosting the Destination Thanksgiving, but I was learning that it's not compatible with hunting. I didn't yet know what I could do about that. The last visitors departed by noon on Sunday, which was also the last day of rifle season. I returned to the land across the road and staked out the place where I'd seen another scrape, the sure sign of a buck cruising for a mate. I was still hoping he'd step into my sight and stand still. That this hadn't happened in the previous two weeks didn't deter me from hoping, which is how I discovered that hunters, like writers, are optimists, possibly delusional. How is waiting for a buck to materialize any different from waiting to hear back from an editor considering my work?

Back in the Postal Era, I received plenty of standard rejections from editors, usually a slip of paper preprinted with apologies and regrets. I also received a fair number of personalized letters turning my work down, letters I failed to recognize as encouragement despite their praise of my prose. For a while I had an agent to take the strokes of praise followed by the gut-punch of yet another pass, and I no longer minded the silence between responses so much.

The woods weren't silent. During my second season just ending, I'd heard a tree crash, an owl hoot, a ruffed grouse thrum through the air. Geese honked, chickadees buzzed, and the crows made authoritative announcements. I heard the ragged beech leaves rattle and the brittle oak rustle, and I heard a buck cough, but didn't see him. I also heard gunfire. During the last hour of the season, the woods sounded like a war zone. I thought each shot was my buck going down, until I figured out it was hunters emptying their firearms before heading home.

I stood where I was. The eight-pointer I'd seen four days before might still be alive. That could have been his scrape I saw, where he pawed through the turf and peed. I stood by the patch I'd staked out from every angle on any number of days. I stood downwind and downhill, still expecting, still hoping the deer would move toward the river. I stood like a tree. I stood as dusk fell. I stood until a half hour past sunset before I walked out of the woods and hunting ended for another year.

* * *

I visited Roger when the season was over. He'd shot a 164-pound, six-point buck at Dennis's.

"There's lots of deer up there," he said, referring to the 2,000 acres adjacent to Dennis's camp. "I built a blind with branches to hide my silhouette, so the deer can't see me."

"You built a blind in the dark?" I imagined him cutting brush at four a.m.

"No. The weekend before the season opened, I took a lightweight saw." He made a sawing motion with the side of his palm. "First, I cleared the dead leaves from around the tree so I wouldn't make no noise. Then I piled the branches about this high." He held his hand, palm down, to the middle of his chest. "That's from when I'm sitting," he added. "I always sit with my back against a tree."

Whether I learned this from Roger or discovered the relative comfort of a sylvan backrest on my own, I don't know, but I also liked a seat with a sturdy trunk to lean against.

"I was just sitting there, reading Louis L'Amour." Roger opened his hands like a book and pantomimed reading. "And something told me to look up." He looked up and stroked his beard. "I don't know what it is, but I can be reading and just know when a deer walks up. I looked up and there he was: a six-pointer, looking the other way. I slowly raised my rifle to my chest." He pulled his forearms in close against his body, keeping his eyes on the memory of the deer. "The deer looked my way, but I held still." Roger planted himself. "I didn't move until the buck looked away again. As soon as he did, I raised my rifle and shot." Roger dropped his hands, almost shrugging, *And that was that.*

Would I have the presence of mind to move slowly? I sighed. "At least I saw a buck this year." I conjured the beauty of that buck's face crowned by antlers and blushed to remember that I only saw him because Ed called Tim who told me it was there.

You can't get a deer if you're not in the woods.

I frowned. I should have gone out in the rain. I should have been out every day. "I was only out nine times."

Roger heard the discouragement in my voice.

"I've seen you shoot, Deb. There's no question, you can hit a deer. A deer is a bigger target than a bull's-eye." He looked at me. "But you have to have confidence."

On my drive home, I enumerated what had gone right this season. Except for the bitter cold on opening day, the weather was lovely, from the mid-twenties to forties, and sunny. Granted, I didn't hunt on days it rained, but I was grateful for how the rain silenced the leaves underfoot after it stopped. Soggy leaves don't crackle and snap like dry ones. I saw two scrapes, several does, and one buck. I ventured farther into the woods than ever before and I recognized particular trees. I flushed a ruffed grouse, and I witnessed sunrise and nightfall. I enjoyed how hunting drew me outdoors for hours. Whenever I was hoping and waiting for deer to appear, I experienced boredom; whenever I forgot about the deer, I listened to the woods, observed the life of the forest and the turn of the Earth. That's when I felt a sense of calm and connectedness that I carried with me in my non-hunting life.

But while I was hunting, I lacked confidence. Every time I settled into what looked like a good spot—a place where I could sit against a tree, brace my elbows against my knees and have a clear view and open shooting lanes—the voice of self-doubt questioned my every move.

You're sure this is the best seat? Shouldn't you move farther uphill? Behind that blowdown? Or that one, over there?

Then I'd hear a gunshot: without a doubt, it was some man who'd been hunting his whole life and knew where the deer were and how to stalk them.

What made you think you could learn to hunt? You don't belong in the woods.

* * *

The constant second-guessing was wearing. I should know better than to listen to my inner naysayer. But I had a long history of believing I didn't belong, starting as the only girl in my immediate family.

My parents said they treated us all equally, but Mom also said that if she ever owned a boat she'd name it after her four kids: *Three Hits and a Miss*. My brothers, at least, were consistent: they excluded me for being unlike them, a girl, the oddball. One memorable summer at my Uncle Sam's lake house, my brothers took an unusual interest in setting the table for the kids' lunch, where they doled out paper Dixie cups in red, yellow, green, and blue. Every noon they dealt the same color cup to everyone but me. "Oddball!" they laughed. I held back my tears until one lunch when everyone's cup was red, including mine. When I lifted the cup, lemonade dripped from the fork holes in the bottom.

Michael and David are older, and I'm sure that what I perceived as unfairness was partly the jealousy typical of a younger sibling impatient to grow up. Nevertheless, I wanted the same privileges, like equal pay for equal work. Michael and David were paid handsomely to mow the lawn with the gas mower, a machine I wasn't expected to learn how to use. In contrast, I earned a quarter of what they did for trimming by hand what the mower missed around the trees and gardens on our two acres. My task was Sisyphean; it took longer than mowing. In fact, I rarely finished before it was time to start again, so I didn't even have the satisfaction of momentarily seeing the job done. Who knows? Maybe my folks thought I should learn early on not to expect my work to receive the same recognition or recompense as men's, or that women's work is never done.

Instead of privileges, I had responsibilities, like making dinner when my parents went out. I was also supposed to "make sure the boys clean up the kitchen." The boys didn't clean up, and they didn't listen to me when I told them Mom said they had to. Angry and powerless, I went to my room to read about similarly oppressed girls: Jane Eyre, Mary Lennox, Heidi, and Jo March, all fictional characters who experience existential loneliness. And since my parents told me I was equal to the boys, I also read *David Copperfield* as if I, too, could be the hero of my own life.

When I petitioned my parents to allow me to quit attending Sunday School, they agreed. Unaware of the pervasive sexism in which I was raised, I didn't realize until years later that my parents hadn't expected me to become a bat mitzvah, even though my two older brothers were celebrated for reading their Torah portions when they turned thirteen. All three of my brothers also worked for my father's manufacturing business during the summers, earning workingman's wages. When I asked Dad for a summer job, he said "it was too rough" and there was no "ladies' room" off the manufacturing floor.

"What about the front office?" I asked.

There were no jobs for me there. "The girls don't need any help."

"The girls" were all middle-aged women.

Ironically, my folks had no qualms about sending me off to Minnesota on a twenty-eight-day Outward Bound course when I was sixteen. I was one of eight girls picked up at the airport and plunked in a canoe. We had to paddle our way from the put-in to a campsite on an island we could more easily see than reach. Our two instructors deliberately left us to figure out how to navigate the short stretch of water, pitch tents, cook dinner, and get along. Of all these tasks, it was the last that proved most difficult.

I was a strong member of the group, a capable paddler able to carry the eighteen-foot aluminum canoe on my shoulders over the portages, then double back to help carry the 100-pound packs with our canned food and cast-iron cooking pans. By the end of the second day, I was one of the self-proclaimed elite girls, embedded as one of four in the cool girls' tent.

Five of us were competent, two were eager, and one was timid. Within a few days, the others avoided the timid girl, so I offered to paddle with her in the two-person canoe. That evening, while I was on cooking duty, my tentmates placed my sleeping bag outside the tent, making it clear that I was no longer welcome. I moved into the tent with the less popular girls, becoming an Untouchable for my kindness.

While Outward Bound is known as a wilderness school, and while we did acquire important survival skills, the real curriculum centers on social cohesion, tolerance, and cooperation. Between survival tasks that required cooperation and group meetings, we did become stronger together. But what I remember was the swift establishment of a pecking order, and how, by disrupting it, I became an outlier.

My Outward Bound experience landed me a job as a counselor at a Jewish sleepaway camp in Canada after my sophomore year of college. I'd never been to sleepaway camp. One appealing aspect of this camp was the canoe trip at the start of the summer, where each cabin group spent four days paddling, camping, and bonding. Our first day out was glorious, but on the second day, a cold rain fell. While the girls shivered in the tent, I sawed down a dead tree. The girls were horrified I would do something so unladylike as use a saw and build a fire, even as it warmed them.

Back at camp, they didn't want to ride horseback unless they could shower afterwards; they didn't want to swim unless they could blow-dry their hair. My job was to keep them busy and active, but the girls in my cabin hated me for it. They would have been happy spending the day in their bunks, trading stationery and sharing contraband candy. But my worst offense was being a vegetarian who didn't shave her legs. They didn't believe that someone like me could be Jewish; I appeared too unlike them to belong to their tribe.

By the time I started to hunt, I was used to living a solitary life, even when surrounded by family. By then, the feeling of not belonging was ingrained, and I believed my personal narrative of exclusion. But I always felt that I belonged in Vermont.

I'm not a "native" Vermonter, as those whose families have been in the state for generations often claim to be. I'm a Vermonter-by-Choice who's had to overcome obstacles to make the move from New York to live here: I had to buy a car, and I had to endure my family's disbelief that I could live without home delivery of *The New York Times*. I confess: I miss the newsprint when I light the wood stove. But many people choose to live in Vermont, and no matter how many generations a family of European origin has been working the land, none are "natives." Even Ethan Allen—that Green Mountain Boy—was from away. Only the Abenaki are native to Vermont.

Shortly after my second season of hunting, I stopped listening to self-doubt and started telling myself a story of belonging, a story that predates the European settlement, a story that goes back at least twenty thousand years, when people painted the stories of hunts on cave walls. These paintings affirm that people have been hunting for a long time, and that it's important enough to memorialize. Perhaps the inexplicable force calling me to hunt is hardwired into my limbic brain. Perhaps, despite my membership in the so-called developed world, I'm really answering the primordial call to hunt wild animals. Perhaps I hunt because I'm human.

EIGHT

MY THIRD SEASON

The static of a busy life in civilization dulled my attention to the wild, with one significant exception: a long-anticipated trip to Southeast Alaska. At the end of our Long Trail hike, I promised Jan that Tim and I would visit her. We bought our tickets in January, and planned our trip for the summer solstice.

Meanwhile, after a truly heroic reinvention of himself as a widower and making a new life for himself in Vermont, Dad was becoming too lonely to live. On his ninety-second birthday he told me, "This is the last one."

"Dad, you don't know that! Don't you want to see Jonathan get married?"

He nodded, "June ninth."

"That's right."

The previous fall, Dad caught a cold, took to his bed, and stopped eating. He tried not to eat even after he felt better, but within a week he was up and back on full rations. Nevertheless, he lost all interest in going out and holed up in his room, creating a photo album for each of his five granddaughters, sorting his papers, and giving away his worldly goods.

He offered his belongings to his children, their children, and any other relative who visited. Never known for his patience, he wanted us to cart off the books and take the framed art off the walls right then, and he wasn't easily put off.

"Who's going to take my desk?" he asked me.

"What do you mean?"

"When I'm gone!"

"Not your problem," I reminded him.

His shoulders relaxed, and he turned to me with a sly smile.

Giving away his money was another matter. For years, he'd been saying that he wanted to give it all away before he died, but he was petrified that he might outlive his funds.

I enlisted Tim to help me put Dad at ease.

"Bernie," Tim boomed so Dad could hear. "You have enough money to live for another thirty years."

Dad's eyes widened. "I don't want to live another thirty years!"

"So spend your money!"

One day, I received a call from the manager at the local bank. "Your dad came in and wanted to take all his money out. I told him he needed to consult you."

I had power of attorney and had been paying Dad's bills, but he had access to his account. I don't think the manager had a legal leg to stand on; nevertheless, I was grateful that he knew Dad and alerted me.

Dad said he was going to move his money to a bank down the street. "Who's my power of attorney?" he asked.

"I am. And Michael."

"Do you have a copy of my will?"

I did, but I said, "Michael has it," which was also true. I finally knew better than to walk into this trap.

Even when my father had hearing, he didn't listen to me; when his hearing became impaired, he couldn't. But he always seemed to listen to my brothers and Tim. Back when Tim was in private practice, Dad would ask him about the financial fragility of the medical practice, which I managed. Steam would come out of my ears. The same refrain of *Hell's bells, Nisi,* with which he belittled Mom's navigational skills, rang through the house when he discovered that she'd transposed numbers in the check register, thwarting his effort to balance the bank statement. When Dad asked Tim about our tenuous profitability, the subtext I heard was: *What could she know about finance? She's a girl.*

Tim, bless him, said, "Talk to Deborah. She runs the joint. I just see patients."

I didn't want to experience Dad's ingrained distrust of my financial competence anymore, so I asked Michael to review Dad's will with him. In addition to being male and first-born, Michael is also a lawyer, the executor of Dad's estate, and someone Dad listened to—although Michael might not agree.

Michael drove up on a weekday and went over the papers.

Dad was reassured.

I was more than pleased. I was relieved and delighted that Michael came through when I needed him. I'd always been awed by Michael, my remarkable oldest brother, the one who played first horn in All-State Orchestra, who turned down Yale for Harvard, and who commuted to Midtown in a well-cut suit. For what seemed like the first time in forever, we were in this together, equals: both children of this man who's been a good though sometimes frustrating parent, now sliding into senility.

* * *

In June, friends and relatives gathered in our backyard to witness my brother Jonathan marry Leslie, his wonderful partner of nine years. It was a perfect afternoon. At brunch the next day, Dad said, "I saw everyone I know." In hindsight, these words seem prophetic.

A week later, Tim and I prepared to leave for Alaska, but the night before takeoff, Dad had a stroke.

I called Michael.

"Do me a favor," he said when I explained that Tim and I were supposed to embark on our first two-week vacation in sixteen years. "See if you can delay your trip by a day."

I could, but I wondered if we should even go.

When Mom was dying, my cousin Elaine said, "Go! You still have to live, even when people around you are dying." She should know: She's buried her mother, father, stepmother, both sisters, and countless friends. This is the ache of survival.

Michael was in Vermont by noon the next day. We headed to the hospital, where we found Dad strapped to a chair with a personal minder because he'd shoved the physical therapist who came to evaluate him.

While Dad's words could cause pain, I'd never known him to be physically violent. In fact, at his senior residence he was known for politeness, especially toward women. He routinely helped his tablemates into their dining chairs and then fetched their walkers when the meal ended. But the stroke garbled his speech. Shoving the physical therapist was Dad saying he didn't want rehab; we should let him be.

After our conference with the attending physician, Michael told us, "Go to Alaska. I'll stay and arrange Dad's care."

We left home before seven in the morning and arrived in Juneau at ten o'clock that night. It was the solstice and full daylight when we deplaned.

To see Jan in her natural habitat, meet her old friends and new partner, confirmed that she was thriving. We traveled by ferry, we fished, we feasted, we walked, and we talked. After a few days of visiting, Tim and I left to hike the Chilkoot Trail, the route an estimated seventy thousand prospectors traveled during the great Klondike Gold Rush between 1896 and 1899. It's a thirty-three-mile hike of which thirty-two and three-quarter miles are easy; the quarter-mile Golden Stairs, not so much. Prospectors during the gold rush days crossed the pass in winter, climbing 1,500 stairs chiseled into ice. When we climbed, there was no ice to glue the rocks together. I made slow progress, testing each hand- and foot-hold before making a move while trying to keep three points of contact with the Earth at all times. Tim, of course, scrambled up effortlessly, sending loose rocks plummeting toward me until I shouted, "Don't kill me!"

He didn't.

As soon as I reached the top of the pass I experienced something like post-childbirth amnesia, thinking that climbing the Golden Stairs wasn't so bad. Together, we crossed the international border. It was the end of June, and the Canadian side was a treeless subarctic wilderness of snow, a landscape as brilliant and empty as the bright side of the moon.

After the hike, we returned briefly to Juneau before embarking on the Alaskan Marine Highway to visit Jan's older daughter and her husband. Margaret and Dustin lived outside a remote village on Chichagof Island. There are no cars. We walked most of an hour to reach their home, where they were living without electricity, fridge, internet, or indoor plumbing. The activities of daily living took them outdoors to fetch water, visit the outhouse, tend the garden, hunt in the forest, forage from the sea, gather wood for heat, and walk to visit their homesteading neighbors.

Dustin is an Alaskan hunting guide and Margaret a writer and novice hunter who had recently taken her first deer. The deer are abundant, and the hunting season is months long. The couple rent a freezer in the village that they fill with their venison and salmon. The majority of their diet comes from the landscape around their home. It's delicious.

While in Alaska I checked in with Michael whenever I had cell service. Dad's condition continued to deteriorate. He was no longer eating or responding; he was shutting down, and his advance directive was clear.

"It sounds like it's time for hospice," I said across the continent.

Michael agreed and arranged for Dad to be transferred to Grace Cottage Hospital, where the hospice suite includes a family room connected to the patient's. It's a place where the dying are kept comfortable and the grieving are comforted. It's clear that Dad was dying; this was where I wanted him to be cared for till the end.

As we traveled around Southeast Alaska, I watched whales from the ferry, saw eagles fly, contemplated the vast forest, lifted my eyes to the jagged, snowcapped mountains, and I thought of my father teaching us to sail, taking us skiing, cranking the pasta machine the last time he came to dinner at my house. Between calls, I wondered if he was still alive. I knew that if ever I returned to Alaska, I'd always think, *This is where I was while Dad was dying.* I never imagined that I'd be returning to Juneau nine months later, to deliver a eulogy for Jan.

* * *

Hoping Dad was still alive made the trip home drag. Our flights were on time, but the car battery was dead; we were delayed in long-term parking until two in the morning. Years of night-call have trained Tim to work through hideous fatigue; he drove us home, where we fell into bed at four. I was at Dad's bedside by nine.

I sat with Dad for the next eleven days. I hesitate to say he wasn't conscious, because I can't know for sure. It looked as if he was concentrating on dying, as if dying required everything he had left. I held his hand and played the soundtrack of my childhood, music he introduced to us on vinyl: *The Magic Flute*, Herb Alpert and the Tijuana Brass, the Coldstream Guards, *The Mikado*.

While he slept, sometimes snoring, I reread *War Story*, the collection of the letters he wrote to my mother during The War. It helped me understand why he kept breathing: He was a survivor. I think surviving The War made him genuinely surprised to wake up every morning. I was sure that he wasn't scared of death but frightened of a compromised life.

Dad kept breathing. I sat at his bedside, sometimes numb, sometimes bored, but loath to leave him. The nurses cared for him; the hospital kitchen cared for me, bringing me fruit, cookies, and iced tea. One day, the social worker asked me about Dad's "afterlife."

"What do you mean?" I asked. Did she want to know about Dad's beliefs?

"Do you have a funeral home you want to use?"

Oh! She was talking about his remains! That was easy. "He wants cremation."

Then she asked, "Would you like Hallowell to come?"

"You can arrange that?" I started to cry. "I'd like that very much."

Hallowell is a hospice chorus that practices the therapeutic art of singing for the dying. I love their music, own their CDs, and have heard their *a cappella* singing in concert. They operate as part of the Brattleboro Area Hospice, a volunteer organization that provides non-medical help to the dying, comfort to the grieving, and opportunities to reflect on being mortal, such as the literature-based discussions around end-of-life-care that I've facilitated for healthcare workers, and an obituary-writing workshop for the general public.

Kathy Leo, Hallowell's founder, called to ask what songs Dad might like. I told her how, when we were little, he sang to us at bedtime from the *Fireside Book of Folk Songs*: "Red River Valley," "Camptown Races," "Molly Malone," and "The Riddle Song."

"'The Riddle Song'?"

I sang it to her.

The singers arrived in the afternoon on the ninth day of my vigil. Their voices transformed the smooth surfaces of the hospital room into a space of velvet sound. The music attracted nurses, other patients, and visitors to the door of Dad's room. I sat at his bedside, holding his hand in my right and Tim's in my left. Overnight, the singers learned "The Riddle Song," but instead of just the three verses Dad used to sing, their version had a fourth, about how love is a story that has no end. I wept. When the five singers departed, a sacred silence filled the room.

By now, Dad hadn't eaten in so long that the belly he often struggled to lose had vanished. He was again the broad-shouldered, slim-hipped father of my youth. A voice in my head kept repeating, *Dying is hard*.

His ninety-third birthday was now just a week away. I leaned over and whispered, "If you really don't want another birthday, Dad, you better hurry this up."

The next day, his breathing changed, and his hands were cool. I stayed with him into the night. Near midnight, I tried to sleep in the family room. I looked in on him at three. He was still breathing. I sat with him a few minutes, stroked his forehead and held his hand. I started back to my bed, but stopped and returned to his bedside. He took a breath. Then another. Then none.

I sat with him in stillness.

My Dad.

Eventually, I called the nurse. She felt for a pulse, listened to the silence in his chest, and nodded to me. I phoned each of my brothers. Then I called Tim.

"Are you coming home, then?"

All this time at Dad's deathbed, and I hadn't thought about what would come next. "I can come home?"

"Yes. Come home."

I crawled into bed and wrapped my arms around Tim. "It's our anniversary," I said.

"I know," he mumbled.

Entwined, we slept.

* * *

Previously, when I'd experienced the death of elderly friends, neighbors, and relatives after a long decline, death came as a relief. Dad's was like that, but with more finality. He was the last of his generation in his family, and the last of our parents. Immediately following his passing, we convened at Michael and Judy's to sit *shiva*, the Jewish custom of mourning the deceased. Now, without living parents, I felt enormous gratitude for my brothers, our spouses, and our kids. I am not alone.

A few weeks later, Tim and I hiked Mount Flume in the White Mountains, giving us the first view from a summit since returning from Alaska. It was a good place to acknowledge that I'd moved up in the world, closer to the sky, where heaven is supposed to be. The next day I resumed the activities that support a full life. Yet even as my life returned to normal, Dad showed up in my brothers' assertive voices and in my own syntax and hyperbole, proving he lived on.

* * *

That September, Christine Blasey Ford testified before the Senate Judiciary Committee, accusing Supreme Court nominee Brett Kavanaugh of sexual assault when they were teens. I was listening to the news in the car when I heard a male skeptic say he didn't understand why Ford waited thirty-six years to speak up. I didn't hear any more, because I did understand how that could happen. I'd been silent for fifty.

I wrote a radio commentary not about how I was abused, but about the safety of silence. I knew how hard it was to speak up about sexual abuse, especially for ordinary women, women without celebrity, women who regularly suffer abuse at work, in school, and at home. Women who do speak up are routinely shamed even when their stories are believed. To speak up is to guarantee that one's motives, character, and personal history will be questioned. In my commentary for Vermont Public Radio about how hard it is for women to speak up about past sexual abuse, I wasn't allowed to say that my abuser was my grandfather.

My grandfather was not rich or famous, had never lived in Vermont, and had been dead for forty-five years. Nevertheless, the station wanted to know if anyone who'd known him might be listening. My producer demanded either that I provide proof that this happened or say "a beloved male relative" instead of "grandfather." "Grandfather," she said, "was too particular." But I wasn't willing to tarnish the reputations of all my male relatives to protect the one—and the only one—who abused me.

That I spent ten days negotiating with the station proved the very point of my commentary: To speak up is to risk being victimized all over again. I withdrew the piece and left the station, but I didn't go silently. I narrated what happened, detailing how Vermont Public Radio chose to defend a dead man they didn't know rather than believe a woman whose opinions and work they solicited and broadcast for years. But blaming women for what men do to them has been going on for millennia.

Almost all the translations of the story about Artemis turning Actaeon into a stag after he comes upon her bathing in the forest—stories dating from the Greek poet Callimachus in the third century BCE to the first English translation by William Caxton in 1480 to now—excuse Actaeon's behavior and blame Artemis for hers. They say that Actaeon has simply made a mistake; it was an act of Fate; he's a victim of destiny, not guilt; it's no crime to become lost in the woods. Artemis overreacted; she was excessively cruel; she exhibits remorseless anger. Few versions translate Artemis's actions as justified.

The subtext is that a mortal man's bad behavior is excusable—the result of bad luck, not self-determination—and not even a goddess is entitled to anger or self-defense. Artemis is naked and defenseless while bathing. When she turns Actaeon into a stag, he learns what it's like to live imperiled and voiceless. It kills him. Women live imperiled and voiceless all the time. Mostly, we survive, but it takes a toll.

Readers of the piece published in the local independent weekly responded with an outpouring of confessions from women and men who'd been sexually abused and assaulted by close relatives, partners, and family friends. I received widespread support from readers for speaking out and expressions of dismay and disgust for the radio station.

I had been a regular VPR commentator from November of 2006 until October of 2018, often broadcasting more than twenty commentaries a year. I loved telling stories to create change, and I wasn't willing to be silenced for calling out the silence that perpetuates sexual predation. I'd often accepted the producer's advice about softening my rhetoric, but I wasn't willing to sanitize it. There was no way to sanitize a grandfather cornering his nine-year-old granddaughter and fondling her.

What does my father's death and my leaving VPR have to do with deer hunting? I learned that my father and brothers did listen to me; I learned that in the face of my father's death, my brothers and I are equal; I learned that it was time to tell myself a new story. Leaving VPR, the station that had broadcast my voice for a dozen years, was an act of courage that ironically gave me my voice. I now had the clarity and courage to write this book.

* * *

I initially turned to deer hunting to educate myself in the way of the woods, but this year, just days before opening day, I came down with buck fever: All I wanted to do was shoot a deer. I hardly recognized myself. It's as if the call to hunt that started me on this journey was no longer coming to me from the universe, but from inside my body. At night, I practiced stillness to put myself to sleep, but my cells thrummed as if the particles in my blood were colliding in some approximation of Brownian Motion beneath my skin. The deeper and slower I breathed, the wilder my heart beat, as if I were running through the forest in my dreams. I'd wake before dawn and rise, ready to head out, except that the season hadn't yet started. I daydreamed about seeing a buck and shooting it. I was obsessed. Or maybe I just wanted to get this business of shooting a deer over with, so I could get on with my life. Did I want to give up?

I returned to Roger's for target practice. After hitting my mark with the .22, I loaded my deer rifle. I was working my way farther and farther away from the target, always finding a tree to steady myself, when Roger stopped to watch.

"My aim's off."

He nodded.

I fired.

"Don't lean against the tree."

I glanced a question.

"You want to put the stock against the tree, not your body or the barrel."

It worked.

As always, we talked more than I fired my rifle. This year, Roger showed me how to silence the safety, so I wouldn't scare a buck in my sight with the click.

Hoping this was my year, I asked, "Any tricks to dragging a deer out?" Recovering my quarry was a persistent concern.

"You have to streamline it."

"What's that?"

"You got to make sure its forelegs are tucked in close to its body and its hind legs stretched out straight behind to make it easier to pull the carcass through the woods. That way its legs won't get hung up in trees."

I nodded.

"You got to do it before it stiffens up."

"Okay."

* * *

I woke at three forty-five in the morning on Opening Day. My plan was to hunt from behind the round hay bales stockpiled at the edge of our lower field. I'd seen evidence of deer dancing there; I wanted to catch them at it.

In prehistoric times, this field was at the bottom of a lake. The stony terrace between the lower and upper fields had been the lake's shoreline. From the house on the upper field, the hayfield appears flat, what a Belgian friend once called *la prairie*. But at ground level it's anything but. Undulations in the ground blocked my view, and the space between the hay bales narrowed my field of vision. I tried staking out a place from the upper field, but felt too exposed, so I decamped across the road. Immediately, I saw the white tails of two deer fleeing into the woods.

I had a good time climbing the forested hillside, and a big pile of fresh sign was all the encouragement I needed. Hoof prints dented the soggy earth. I allowed myself to be curious and followed a logging road out to a stream, where the woods were open and bright. After a couple of hours exploring the terrain instead of looking for deer, I decided next time I'd enter from the east, with the wind at my face, downwind from where I'd seen deer. I was thinking like a hunter.

Later that day, I parked at a thirty-seven-acre parcel about a mile from home that belonged to Doug, an out-of-state landowner. He'd placed an ad in the local online newsletter seeking a hunter to help mitigate deer damage to his woods, and I'd answered it. When we spoke by phone, Doug asked why I hunt.

I told him I'm motivated by the ethics of eating local, organic, and foraged food; land conservation, management of the deer herd and the hardwood forest; and by a nagging desire to learn to read the landscape I call home.

He also asked me for references: people who could vouch for my character and my hunting ethics. He phoned both Roger and my friend Dan. A week later, Doug emailed me a map of his land and written permission to hunt on it.

This was my first time there, so my plan was to walk the perimeter. As I opened the passenger door of the pickup, my rifle fell out, landing muzzle-down in sand. As if that weren't bad enough, when I picked the gun up, sand slid down the barrel into the breech. I then tried loading the rifle, only to find I could neither fully chamber the cartridge nor could I remove it. Now I was in trouble.

I left the bolt open and the safety on as I drove home, determined to take care of this problem myself. I was kicking myself for missing a windless afternoon on what looked like good hunting grounds.

In the basement, I spread an old towel on top of the chest freezer with a sandbag to make an improvised gun-cleaning bench. I couldn't get the round out of the chamber, and I didn't want to damage the action. Most of all, I didn't want to become that headline: "Woman Hunter Maimed while Cleaning Rifle."

Since the advent of mandatory gun safety and hunter education, the rate of shooting incidents stemming from hunting has seen a steady decline. But as I was in danger of affirming, most shooting incidents are self-inflicted—exactly what I was trying to avoid. When a hunter shoots someone else, it's usually a hunting buddy. But the majority of hunting incidents are not related to firearms. Currently the biggest cause of hunting injuries of hunters my age is falling out of a tree stand.

I had no interest in hunting from a tree stand.

I worked gingerly to dislodge the round stuck in the chamber. It wouldn't budge. I needed help and called Roger, but he was out hunting. I abandoned the rifle and took refuge in the word shop to write about my gun snafu. I was pleased to find the page where I acknowledged that I'd had a good morning in the field, that I'd been writing well all fall, and that this was a momentary setback.

The physical act of moving my pen across the page diverted me from being sucked into a familiar riptide of self-loathing for letting my rifle fall out of the truck and for ruining my afternoon of hunting, and worst of all, for possibly ruining my rifle. Instead, I reassured myself: I'd figure out how to get my rifle functioning again. I cut myself slack for trying to learn everything about firearms, deer, the woods, and field craft, all in such a short time. It's a lot to learn, but I wasn't giving up. I remembered the stillness of the woods before dawn, and how I witnessed the day's lights come on when the sun came up. My brain lit up. Call Gunther.

I hadn't seen Gunther since we shot his historic rifles in Lester's backyard. He picked up on the first ring, listened to my tale, and said, "Bring the rifle over. Come in through the barn."

I followed Gunther into his wood shop, where he builds furniture. It's a light and spacious space, with all his tools at hand.

I handed him my rifle. He inspected it. "Hmm. Jammed."

"Hmm." I agreed. "Jammed."

He braced the stock between his knees, placed the flat end of a ten-penny nail against the rim of the cartridge and tapped it out with a hammer. The cartridge fell to the floor. "Voilà!"

There was no misfire, no explosion, no one maimed. I was beyond relieved.

Gunther disassembled the action and removed the bolt to make sure it wasn't damaged. He showed me how the spring-loaded pin pops out when the trigger is pulled, just like the spring action of a pen with a retractable point, a tool with which I'm thoroughly familiar.

"Looks good," Gunther said, squinting down the barrel before handing me the rifle. "Nothing a good cleaning won't fix." He told me again how he thinks rifles give hunters an unfair advantage. "To be fair to the deer, you should hunt with a knife."

"Don't worry," I said. "My understanding is that you have to see a deer before you can shoot it."

He chuckled.

"But it's nice to be out in the woods."

"Yeah, that's what my old man used to say. He'd sit on a stump in the sun with his rifle across his lap and take a nap."

"Whatever it takes to sit still."

Sitting still, observing, being present—these are skills I was learning in my yoga practice and applying to hunting. It turns out that these three skills were helping me navigate more calmly and more deliberately through the civilized world as well. They helped me remain calm through this rifle mishap, making it a kerfuffle instead of a fiasco. I had even asked for help without feeling diminished or helpless.

* * *

I returned to Doug's the next day to follow the property line around his land, which was posted according to Vermont's statutes. The signs met the minimum size of 8.5 by 11 inches; the black lettering contrasted with the yellow background; the landowner's name and contact information were legible and dated with the current year. I'd been to the Town Lister's Office for a copy of the tax map so I'd know who Doug's abutters were, and I checked with the Town Clerk, who confirmed that Doug had paid his five dollar annual fee to register that his land was posted, which I appreciated. Knowing I'd find signs at the requisite minimal interval of every 400 feet gave me confidence to set out on my circumambulation, certain that following the signs would be like hiking a blazed trail—except there wasn't a trail.

I was up to my ankles in swampy scrub and engrossed in discovering this parcel from a deer's point of view, looking for places where deer were likely to congregate, feed, and bed down. I started strategizing how I'd find my way here before dawn when I saw not only the next yellow sign marking the property line, but also a swing set in the backyard of a white house.

I didn't want to be near a family home with a rifle, so I cut a corner. The signs petered out. I was bushwhacking through pucker brush when I came upon a homemade deer blind and wondered if I was still on Doug's land. I backtracked until I knew where I was and made my way out.

This was another good learning experience, not a failure. Now I knew that I wanted to hunt on land that isn't hemmed in by civilization. I also had new sympathy for the deer upon whose habitat humans have encroached. It seemed only fair to hunt deer on their turf, where it's wild.

Hunting fragmented parcels of land was like writing only short prose, and I didn't just want to write long, I was ready to. I posted "Goodbye and Farewell" for my readers at *Live to Write, Write to Live*, the blog of the New Hampshire Writers Network, where I'd been writing about the craft and business of writing twice a month for seven years; I cut back on my blog, *Living in Place*. I still had teaching and speaking gigs lined up, but I started accepting fewer. Reducing the many short pieces I wrote would allow me to concentrate on the manuscript I was calling *Learning to Hunt*—and this required me to keep learning to hunt.

Rather than hunt for deer during the week, I hunted for words at my desk. I was working on an essay about how the silence that shrouds sexual abuse protects abusers, allowing the abuse to flourish. Could the hostile questioning of Christine Blasey Ford's integrity and the dismissal of her testimony of abuse at the hands of a Supreme Court nominee have any outcome other than to discourage ordinary women from telling their stories? I argued that the mainstream media works to protect men, even men who aren't powerful, rich, or even alive, like my grandfather.

A colleague who writes edgy feminist essays encouraged me to send the piece to national publications and gave me her list of editors, whose prompt and personal responses were gratifying. After a few passes, however, I realized I'd rather hunt deer than publication.

It was a relief to get back out in the field and only think about one thing: hunting.

* * *

Wet snow had fallen overnight, bleaching the landscape. I crossed the road. A white tail flashed before vanishing into the woods. I followed the tracks. I climbed. I was overdressed. Hot. I turned east and kept climbing, making my way to the ridge, past the trees where I'd sat the previous weekend. I pushed myself to keep climbing until I reached a stone outcrop that gave me a wide view of the spare woods below. Fresh tracks of a large, solitary deer led me to an abandoned hunting camp.

I knew this place. Tim and I had approached it from the other direction on one of our snowshoe rambles. I was in the triangle of woods between my road, the hill road, and a housing development. A dog barked nearby.

A shard of annoyance tore the skin of my thoughts: I'd forgotten to remind Tim to leave me the truck.

I was so hot that I didn't want to gut and haul a deer by myself.

A few friends had offered to come and help if I called them, but how would they find me?

This was no longer fun. I was tired of being alone in the woods. I was tired of trudging through the snow with my rifle. I was tired.

I thought about hiring a guide or signing up for Murphy Robinson's Way of the Huntress, a yearlong program for women learning to hunt. But Murphy's class culminates with a hunt in Northern Virginia. I didn't want to hunt in Northern Virginia. I didn't want to hunt anywhere but here. And I knew there were deer in these woods. I'd seen them.

I gave up and started making my way home.

Tim could see I was discouraged and folded me into a hug. He praised me for my courage and determination. "It's a big undertaking, Deb."

I leaned into him, cheek against his chest, nose near his armpit, inhaling the aroma of my favorite mammal. I relaxed. "I went out early. I found tracks. I found my way. I came home." I wasn't sure if I was talking to him or myself. "I did all those things."

"Umm-hmm."

His hum vibrated against my cheek. I looked up. "But I didn't see the beauty of the woods this morning. I started worrying about how I'd get a buck out. When I do that, I stop being present. Hunting is all about being in the here and now."

He pressed me back into his chest, stroked my hair, and hummed.

* * *

What I needed was hunting ground that wasn't fragmented by houses or close to people or posted against hunting. But I also needed a break, which arrived the weekend between the first and second weeks of rifle season, when Jan and her partner were due for a fleeting visit on their long drive around the lower forty-eight. When the car with the Alaska plates pulled into the driveway, my brain hurt to think how far they'd driven, and my heart sang that they were here.

I gave Jan and Rick a tour of my town and its villages, each with its church dating back to European settlement in the mid- to late-eighteenth century, which seemed ancient to these contemporary Alaskans. My experience of Alaska was the converse: the Tlingit people and their culture is ancient and still very present, whereas Vermont's Abenaki culture is only recently being acknowledged after a long period of disregard by Vermonters of European descent.

I turned in early so I could I slip out before dawn. I knew Jan would sleep until the sun came up. When we hiked the Long Trail, I was always out of my sleeping bag before Jan was awake, and I had the coffee ready by the time she opened her eyes. We switched roles at the end of the day. I'd be snugged into my bag while Jan burned the midnight batteries.

More snow fell overnight. I tried to intercept the deer on their way either to or from the lower field, but there was no cover. Night dissolved into dawn. I was too late. Hoof prints told me the deer had already moved through. I was convinced deer knew how to tell time.

After breakfast, Jan and I took a walk.

"All the times I've been here," she said, "and I've never seen Vermont in the snow. It really is picture-book pretty." She told me a bit about the challenges of traveling with Rick, who wasn't a planner. Jan was. Planning was how she fit seventy-five minutes into every hour.

Jan was an assistant attorney general for the State of Alaska, specializing in family law. Like most lawyers I know, Jan kept a suit and dress shoes in her office to wear to court. But Jan also kept gear for skiing, kayaking, and running. She worked and played hard and was known to change her clothes in the elevator on her way to the courtroom. Famously, she once showed up in court suited but still in her ski boots.

We turned back after four miles and took a turn around the lower field. It was just enough walking to catch up since our visit in Alaska, but not the ongoing conversation of a twenty-five-day hike. "I'm glad we had this time for just the two of us," she said.

"Me, too."

And then it was farewell, which turned out to be goodbye.

* * *

Snow turned to rain, adding to how discouraged I felt. I called Roger.

"You have to have confidence," he said again.

He told me about his thirteen-year-old nephew who tracked and shot a monster buck behind the flood-control dam on the West River. "He'd been tracking that deer all fall, so when they closed school for the snow, he had his dad drop him off up there. He found it, shot it, field dressed it, and covered it with a tarp, covered the tarp with dead leaves, then he went to get help."

Every time Roger tells me a story, I learn something new. This time, it's covering the carcass and going for help. But I wasn't sure I'd ever have a chance to use all this knowledge, nor did I think I'd ever be able to make Roger understand how different it is for a thirteen-year-old who has been learning to hunt since he could walk, and who's probably been around firearms at least as long. I was now sixty-two-years-old; I was a woman new to handling a firearm but with a lifetime of experience being frightened of guns. Did Roger understand how hard this was for me? Did he have any idea how I first needed to overcome feeling that I didn't even have a right to be in the woods, or to carry a rifle, or to hunt a deer? This entire enterprise was so completely foreign to all the expectations with which I'd been raised—foreign to my family of origin, their cultural norms, and their expectations of me based on my gender. Even my friends, husband, and children, who are supportive, wondered what this was all about. On days like today, I wondered, too. Learning to hunt felt just like writing a book: a lonely and difficult enterprise that requires focus, stamina, and persistence. But self-pity is a character flaw, so the next day, I returned to the field.

Over six inches of snow had fallen overnight. The sun was out, but it was fifteen degrees and windy enough for a wind-chill advisory, meaning that the air temperature felt like it was between minus fifteen to minus twenty-four. Nevertheless, that afternoon I drove past Doug's land to my friend Linda's, a mile further up the hill. Linda's family had purchased a defunct farm in the early 1960s, and they spent winter ski vacations and horseback riding summers there. Linda now owns the property, where she built a new house with a magnificent view and lives year-round. She granted me permission to hunt on her hundred acres with one caveat, "You can only hunt on my land as long as you shoot a deer!" Linda is tired of deer ravaging her garden.

I pulled into her long drive and parked on a hill between two open fields. The wind jerked the truck door out of my hand, snaked under my collar, and deafened my ears. I tugged my neck gaiter over my hat, loaded my rifle in the shelter of the cab, and headed into the woods. As if I'd stepped into a sealed room and shut the door, the wind stopped. The trees stood majestic and still, but the snow had altered the landscape beyond recognition.

I'd walked the land with Linda at the end of October, only a few weeks earlier, in a different season. Linda's houseguests from New York and Boston accompanied us as we hiked the trails she'd marked through the forest. The urbanites were curious about why I wanted to hunt. I was more attentive to our conversation than to the land. Besides, with marked trails, I didn't think I could get lost. But when I looked up, I saw we were no longer following the trail with dark green surveyor's tape tied to the trees.

"Are we on a new trail?" I asked. "The color just changed."

"Oh," Linda said. "That's because I ran out of the dark green and just used what I had."

What she had was pale blue.

Because I talked so much, I'd only noted the stream running down the middle of this hundred-acre wood, but gained no clear sense of the boundaries. According to Vermont law, any land that's not posted can be hunted, and more than eighty percent of Vermont's 6.159 million acres are privately held. Since the Vermont constitution guarantees the right to hunt, the onus is on landowners to post their land.

I regrouped as I stood at the edge of the snow-bleached woods and followed Linda's snowshoe tracks until a gust of wind whipped up the snow like a hard-shaken snow-globe. Blinded, I stood still in the whiteout and waited. When I could see again, I strapped on my snowshoes to break trail. I thought I was walking parallel to the stream until I confronted a stone wall, the physical boundary between Linda's land and her neighbor's. Linda and Annie share a common boundary but hold opposing ideas about land use. Linda dislikes deer, and Annie dislikes hunters; neither posts their land. I'm irritated that Annie broadcasts her abhorrence of hunting without posting her land, and I have no intention of hunting on it. On the brighter side, if the land were posted, I'd have to ask Annie's permission to retrieve any deer that died on her property. Since the land isn't posted, I won't have to. But first, I'd have to shoot a deer.

I retraced my steps until I picked up one of Linda's trails, which led me to the stream. I crossed and climbed the opposite side, where I had a good view of the brook sheltered by hemlock, out of the wind. If I were a deer, that's where I'd be. I dug a seat in the snow at the foot of a birch and kept watch.

The wind had died down and the sun was out. I sat in a wonderland, soaking in the splendor. After a while, I consulted my topographical map and tried to figure out where I was. I felt around in my backpack for my compass but came up empty-handed, so I tried using the sun, which should have been in the west this late in the day. The sun was in the wrong place!

I'd recently read about expectation bias and reminded myself the sun doesn't lie. As wrong as it felt, I needed to walk away from the sun to return to the truck. I was irritated that my compass wasn't in my pack. I hate misplacing things. I can't do anything about the location of the sun, but I ought to be able to keep track of my own belongings.

At the start of our hike on the Long Trail, Jan and I were taking too much time breaking camp in the morning. "What we need," I said on our third day, "is a checklist." I gave her the gist of Atul Gawande's *New Yorker* article about how checklists have made anesthesia and surgery safer. That evening, we developed a checklist for getting on the trail each day. Using it, we cut our time by more than half. Since then, I've been more systematic about where I put my keys, wallet, and cell phone when I walk in the door at home, so I can find them again on my way out. The phone is the worst, and there are times when I long for the telephone of my childhood, firmly attached to the wall.

Clearly, I needed a checklist for the daypack I carried when hunting, so I always had my compass with me. But right now, in the woods, I told myself, I can follow my tracks back to the truck. Stay calm and push on.

I resumed following the snowshoe path until I saw big, fresh hoof prints crossing it. I abandoned the packed trail and followed the tracks into the soft snow under the hardwoods. Dainty hoof prints joined the giant heart-shaped ones. Urine punctuated these snowy valentines. I followed this romance, paying no attention to where I was going until a looming fortress of hemlock blocking the sunlight stopped me. I checked over my shoulder. The open hardwoods were still lit, but the sun was grazing the treetops, and I hadn't a clue where I was.

I paused.

I didn't want to backtrack; I wanted to find my way out.

Reason and the sun told me that the road was to the east. I still didn't believe that was the way I'd come.

I consulted the map once more. I was confused but determined not to panic, even though I was feeling unnerved. I didn't have a lot a daylight left; I wasn't prepared to spend the night; and I didn't want to phone home to be rescued.

I checked my pack once more and latched onto my compass. It was there all the time, meaning that I was letting my anxiety cloud my judgment, making things worse.

I walked east, away from the sun. When I came across the snowshoe tracks again, I followed them. They led me to a clearing where daylight lingered and the wind tugged. Exertion and anxiety must have been keeping me warm, because once I paused, I could sense the temperature dropping. I reentered the woods and followed a trail, where I saw one of Annie's red horse-back riding signs. I was on her land, carrying my rifle.

Shit.

This was not where I wanted to be.

But where *was* that?

I wasn't sure. I kept plowing through the snow. Everything looked familiar, but also a bit off. I thought Linda's house would be on my left—until I saw it up the hill to my right. At least I'd found my way back.

Linda was walking down her driveway as I was unloading my rifle. "See anything?" she asked.

"Signs of serious courtship."

"I don't want any deer babies!"

"Well, there's not much chance I can stop that. There's a Lothario out there, already at work."

"Come back and shoot it!"

"I'll try."

But I didn't go back. Deer can disregard the fragmentation caused by property lines. They cross lawns, raid vegetable gardens, and nibble shrubbery without concern about who owns the land they're on. In ways I can't even imagine, they know how to navigate through the landscape to find food, water, shelter, and the society of other deer. I can't forget about land ownership, and I'd just found my way out of the woods by dumb luck.

It was now dusk on Thanksgiving Eve. I expected the first wave of guests to arrive within the hour. In addition to forest fragmentation, I was keenly aware of my fragmented mind. I had to get home.

It's hardly more than a five-minute drive from Linda's house to mine. En route, I was reviewing the order of operations: Stow my hunting gear; change into mufti. Bring the soup up from the downstairs fridge; start it reheating. Braid the challah dough as soon as the bread machine beeps. Prep crudités to go with the hummus and drinks. I reminded myself that ten of the guests were adults; I could delegate. When I turned into my drive, it was full dark, but there was a parked car with Massachusetts plates: my cousins had arrived. I exhaled. Let the party begin.

* * *

I didn't hunt on Thanksgiving Day, and not just because I was overseeing the preparation of a multi-course meal for many, but also because it was simply too cold: The deer would be yarded up, trying to conserve energy in a hemlock grove. The temperature dipped below zero overnight and hadn't yet made it back to fifteen. It felt even colder on account of steady wind punctuated by punishing gusts. It was unlikely that the deer would be out on a day with this much cold wind.

I spent most of the day in the warmth of the kitchen, though I did bundle up and venture out to inspect the footbridge Tim was building across a gully down to the neighbors' swimming hole. He designed and prefabricated sections prior to the four-day weekend during which he was determined to complete it, and he isn't one to let a little wind chill stop him from working outside for hours. Several of the visiting young men joined him. The cold, however, forced the crew indoors to recharge their cordless drills and drivers. Like deer, batteries slow down in the cold; men, not so much. They had the bridge built and decked by the time we pushed the furniture aside, extended the table, and sat down to feast.

Despite the mental fragmentation involved in planning Thanksgiving, I do love the predictability of great food and the small changes in who and how many join us in an orgiastic celebration of gratitude. What was different this year was that there were no elders present. This was my first Thanksgiving without Dad. I was momentarily enveloped in a mourning fog as slick as spilled gravy. When my octogenarian aunt and uncle canceled at the last minute, I unexpectedly found myself among the elders.

With Dad, Aunt Joan, and Uncle Dave in attendance the previous year, our age at the table had averaged seventy-three. This year, it plummeted to twenty-nine. For the first time, I represented the grandparent generation—even though I didn't yet have grandchildren. Fortunately, we were blessed with two two-year-old guests who both contributed mightily to the fun and the din. My cousin's son, Nash, arrived with a mouthful of words like *washing machine, toaster, light,* and *furnace* for the wood stove. When he spied the ceiling fan, we turned it on for a spin.

Dakota, a few months older, is a favorite neighbor whose mother was heavily pregnant with her second child. Jane was in no condition to prepare a Thanksgiving dinner. I invited her to join ours.

"Can my father come, too?"

"Of course!"

"You're sure?"

"Absolutely."

In the hubbub of arriving guests, introductions, and pouring drinks, I pulled Papa Bob aside. "Do you mind telling me how old you are?"

"Seventy-four. Why?"

"I just want to know who's the oldest at the table. I'm pretty sure you're it."

What could he do but take another swig of his Scotch?

Tim and I shared the piano bench at the head of the table. Next to us were the two toddlers in their high chairs; their four parents; and Bob, our sole grandparent. Beyond them sat my brother-in-law, two teens, and five twenty-something adults, one of whom was my middle daughter, Naomi. She was at the foot of the table, where she lit a candle in remembrance of my father. As I watched, I had two thoughts: first, I was looking at a rising generation of smart, passionate people engaged in work to improve the human condition in myriad ways, and second, if I'm lucky, one day when my sun dips below the horizon, these same people will light a candle for me.

* * *

After a morning of farewells and laundry the following day, I drove to the three-hundred-acre parcel where I had permission to hunt but had only scouted briefly the previous year. I'd visited Marie and Ned at their old farmhouse, where they showed me a large map spread across their dining room table and gave me an arm-waving lay of the land, which they clearly knew well. Marie and Ned owned about sixty acres; Alan, a mutual friend, owned the contiguous three hundred acres that had been part of original farm; Steve Franklin, whom I didn't know, owned the land between their properties and the river. All this land was posted "Hunting by Permission Only" and surrounded by more land that wasn't posted at all. Marie said it was great deer habitat, and she and Ned, Alan, and Steve were all interested in having ethical hunters harvest deer for the sake of the trees.

Ned handed me the signed permission form, I said I'd contact Alan and Steve, and I thanked them. I was zipping my jacket to leave when Marie said, "Just please call to let us know when you'll be hunting."

"Sure thing. But it may be before five in the morning. Wouldn't email be better?"

She agreed.

I was nearly out the door when she asked, "Do you know Kelly Price?"

"The game warden?"

"Yes. He hunts here, too. You should call him, and let him know where you'll be."

This felt like micromanagement and part of me wanted to protest, but I wanted to use the fading daylight to look around, so I agreed.

Ned told me he often sees deer at dusk in the northeast corner of the field, where it backs up to the woods. I didn't see any deer sign there, so I continued onto the clearing for one of the two power lines that cross Alan's land. Hoof prints had pounded a game trail under the wires. I made a mental note of four different places with good sight lines.

That evening, I called Kelly Price, explaining that Marie wanted to make sure we stayed out of each other's way.

"A woman hunter!" he crowed. He told me about taking his young daughter out at four-thirty in the morning. "I have a little heater for her."

"Lucky girl," I said. Not on account of the heater, but for having a dad to take her out. "Where will you be hunting?"

He described the location of his blind and said, "I'll be hunting when I'm not working. It's a busy time right now."

"I bet." We told each other where we park our rigs, which is how we'd know if the other was there.

I also emailed Alan and Steve, the other two landowners. Both gladly granted me permission to hunt. Alan with one caveat: no predators. I replied in all honesty that I hoped I wouldn't even see a bear.

Now I had a new worry: What if I do?

* * *

It hadn't been the possibility of confronting a bear that kept me away the previous year; it was my fear of getting lost. This year, I didn't care. Now I wanted to hunt where I wouldn't run into unfriendly boundaries. And after the Thanksgiving hullabaloo, I just wanted to get outside. I didn't even care if I saw any deer.

The windless twenty-degree sunshine seemed balmy after the previous days of biting cold, and I was overdressed. I headed to the northeast corner of the large field, the place Ned said deer congregate at dusk, which was still a couple of hours off. Just inside the woods, I saw a pile of brush that was either slash left by a woodcutter or another hunter's rough blind. In either case, it suited my purposes, giving me both cover and a good view of where I expected the deer to appear.

Almost as soon as I settled in, I heard a truck pull up, doors slam, and male voices heading my way.

Two men. No rifles. Not hunters.

I stood and walked into the field so they could see me in my garish orange.

"Hi," I said. The older man might actually be elderly, the younger one, handsome.

Before I could introduce myself, the younger man said, "I'm sorry. We're probably scaring all the deer away."

"Haven't seen any," I said. "I'm Deborah Luskin," I added.

"Steve Franklin," the handsome one said. "It's a pleasure to meet you!"

"You're the landowner! Thank you for granting permission."

He shook his head. "My land's over there," he waved toward the river. "This is my father," he gestured toward the older man, "Luther."

"Hello."

"Hi," Luther said. "I'm afraid we're ruining your hunting."

"I suppose we should really be wearing something orange," Steve said.

"I would," I said.

"We're hunting for red pine," Luther piped up.

"Dad thinks there's a stand of it here, planted after the 1938 hurricane." Steve's referring to the famous and ferocious hurricane that blew down thirty-five percent of New England's forests.

"I know there's a plantation of it," Luther said. "The question is, can we find it?"

"Would you mind if I joined you?" I asked. "It's a beautiful afternoon, and I'd rather walk with you than wait for the deer."

"By all means," Steve said, and I fell in behind Luther.

We crossed a power-line clearing into a hardwood forest and traversed the south-facing hillside. The snow was ankle deep and sun-softened; there was just enough to hide rocks and deadfalls, making footing tricky. By habit, I became the self-assigned sweep, keeping behind Luther, who wobbled.

"Here it is," he called out.

The afternoon sunshine illuminated the red bark of the red pines. They rose seventy, eighty limbless feet before their topknots of needle-covered branches emerged like bottlebrushes. It was clear by their even spacing and uniform size that the trees had been planted, and that only a couple dozen survived. In 2011, Tropical Storm Irene caused huge damage from flooding but was mild compared to the devastation of the '38 hurricane, which, in addition to heavy rain, blew in with high—and highly damaging—wind.

We climbed over a stone wall before descending a steep bank to a stream. I asked Luther if he'd like me to find him a walking stick when what I really wanted to do was lend him an arm so he wouldn't topple over. It reminded me of encouraging Dad to use a cane, which he resisted, frustrating me.

"Deborah's offering you a walking stick, Dad," Steve repeated, louder. "Wouldn't you like that?"

"No, I'm all right."

Steve looked at me and shrugged. It's a familiar adult-child-of-an-aging-parent gesture. I nodded.

We crossed the power lines again and stopped at the edge of the forest.

"What did you say your name is?" Luther asked.

I gave him my full handle.

"Why's that familiar?" Luther asked, rubbing his gray beard.

"You've heard her on the radio," Steve said.

Luther looked at him. "The radio?"

"Vermont Public Radio," Steve said. "And she writes for the newspaper," he added.

Luther looked at me. "But you *look* familiar."

I knew what was coming.

"Why do you look so familiar?" He jutted his face toward me. "Where do you live?"

I told him.

"You're married to someone famous," he said.

"Dad." Steve nearly drew the word out to two syllables. "*She's* famous."

I looked at Steve and shook my head.

"Who's your husband?" Luther asked.

I told him.

"He's my doctor!" Luther said. He raised his index finger to a scab on his forehead. "He just took a growth off. Here!"

I nodded. I knew this drill.

"He's wonderful."

I agreed.

Steve rolled his eyes.

I smiled at Luther's guileless admiration and delight.

The sun slipped behind the trees, leaving us in shade. "I need to keep moving to stay warm," I said.

We descended through the hardwoods, saying goodbye when it was time to part ways.

I returned to the blind until I heard father and son slam their truck doors and drive away. Shortly after, I followed. I'd had a lovely afternoon, the light was fading, and I was expecting a dozen for dinner.

* * *

Saturday morning, we said goodbye to the last of the guests, and I returned to Dummerston, where I sat from ten to four. I spent the entire day on either side of the power company's cleared easement, where there's good browse, essential now that snow covered the ground. My first seat was one I'd scoped the previous day, at the foot of a huge hemlock standing beside the remains of two stone walls where they cornered at ninety degrees. Like much of Vermont's forests, this land was once cleared for agriculture. The earliest white settlers were subsistence farmers, focused on survival. But that changed in the nineteenth century, when seventy percent of the forests were cleared, first for the Merino sheep craze that lasted from 1810 to 1850, followed by other industries that either required or resulted in cleared land: quarrying slate, marble, granite, and talc; mining copper, which used trees to smelt ore, producing a gas that poisoned forests; and logging, at one time the biggest industry in the state. It's been a long time since this land was either farmed or had its timber harvested. It's now covered in old forest, the kind that can support a moderate number of deer. A middle-aged forest can support very few deer; young forest supports the most.

Even though none of the current landowners hunt, they recognize that hunting is good for the forest. I was trying to do my part: I was well hidden, and I had a good view of the shrub-scrub habitat that deer love, thanks to the cleared land under the power lines. The scrub provides prime habitat for deer, birds, small rodents, rabbits, hawks, bobcats, coyotes, and bears in a cycle of predation and survival.

But I was sitting in shade and started to shiver. A fallen log in the sun on the other side of the power lines beckoned, so I emptied my bladder and crossed the clearing. Just moving warmed me, but it was the sun on my face that made the big difference, and not just physiologically. My spirits lifted in the sunshine, even though I didn't see any deer. I also didn't move from my seat. I was pretty sure it was unrealistic to expect a buck to come to me, but that's what I was hoping. Rather than explore deeper into the woods, I was plotting the best route to drag a buck back to the truck, parked strategically downhill. It didn't look easy.

At four o'clock, I walked out with another forty-five minutes of hunting remaining. It wasn't only that I didn't want to track or field dress a deer in the dark; it was also a matter of my non-hunting life: My brother Jonathan was due to arrive on the five o'clock train.

On Sunday morning, I was out the door at five-thirty and in place a half hour before sunrise on the last day of rifle season. The freezing rain that had iced the landscape overnight was now dripping from the trees. Even the air was soggy, and daylight just a paler shade of gray. But I didn't mind. If I hadn't taken up hunting, I wouldn't have been outside so early or in such weather, and it was beautiful. I was calm. I could see past the gray slush, the gray trees, the gray sky. I saw bronze leaves, pale lichen, dark evergreen, and water-blackened branches. I meditated on the subtlety of color, how it doesn't have to be vivid to breathe life.

Hoofbeats approached from behind, ending my meditation.

I lifted my rifle.

Does.

I watched them run through the woods, cross under the power lines and disappear.

I waited for a buck in pursuit.

None followed.

I traced the does' tracks uphill to thick hemlock shading a stream at the bottom of a ravine. This, I decided, was the place to start next year, and I walked out of the woods for the season.

NINE

ANOTHER DEATH

In February, Tim and I returned from a week of family visits in sunny California to rain sullying fresh snow, sealing us indoors. Our glum endurance of dull weather broke when a bald eagle flew over the sodden snow and landed in a pine at the far end of the hayfield bordering the river. Her head and tail appeared like patches of snow caught on branches drenched silvery with rain. After a while, the eagle flapped to the top of the tallest pine, her head and tail disappearing into the milky sky; only her silhouette was visible: dark, immovable.

She stayed there for hours.

Tim said, "There must be a dead deer in the field."

We pulled on boots and rain gear to go look.

Sure enough, a young doe lay with her body pecked open, her life gone, and a calamity of animal prints in the pink snow.

Later, the eagle perched in a white oak close to the house. I went out to click a photo. She turned her head to face me, and blinked.

Sometime later, the eagle left.

Bald eagles are making a comeback in Vermont, but it's still rare to see one along our small river, especially in February. The previous summer we'd seen innumerable eagles in Juneau, where they appear as common as sparrows do here. In Juneau, eagles perch on the lights that arch over the highway into town, lurk by the salmon hatchery, and—famously—wheel above the city dump.

Since our visit to Juneau, I couldn't see an eagle without thinking of Jan. But that Sunday, I didn't know what that eagle augured. It wasn't just that I didn't have the spiritual literacy to read the flight patterns of birds; I also didn't have any reason to imagine my vibrant friend suddenly lifeless. Gone.

I didn't learn that Jan died until the day after the eagle's visit. When I received the news, I remembered the eagle: how it hung around all day in the rain; how it drew our attention every time it flew past the living-room windows; how it came closer and closer, until it was staring us in the face.

I'm not usually one to interpret birds as messengers from the spirit world. And maybe I'm telling myself this story to feel better. But it's hard to feel better about a loss like this even when I scratch for reasons: Jan died too swiftly to suffer; while alive, Jan vibrated with life and adventure. But the doe lay lifeless, broken open, and I knew: Jan sent the eagle to tell me farewell.

I made the sad and necessary journey to attend Jan's memorial in early April. I traveled alone, stopping in Seattle to visit a college friend whose teenage children I'd never met in a place I'd never been. In Discovery Park, we hiked to Puget Sound through the woods of the Pacific Northwest: bigleaf maple, Douglas fir, western redcedar, and western hemlock. Walking and talking allowed us to close the gap of fifteen years; being outdoors soothed my grief.

The next day I continued to Juneau, where I joined acquaintances I'd met the previous summer; friends and relatives I hadn't seen in almost forty years; and people I knew only from Jan's stories. As often as necessary, I escaped outside to walk in Jan's landscape with people she loved: the coast of Douglas Island with Mary and Nate; the Sheep Creek Trail out from Thane with Michaela; up the Auk Nu Trail to the John Muir Cabin with Jan's hiking club buddies; and to the Mendenhall Glacier with her nieces and a friend from law school.

Over two hundred people came to Jan's memorial. Among the speakers were a Supreme Court Justice who spoke about Jan's thirty-year legal career, which began as a public defender and ended as an assistant attorney general, always advocating for Alaska's most vulnerable citizens; the woman who'd cared for Jan's daughters sang us the song they'd made up while waiting for Jan to fetch them—always arriving at the last possible moment with files akimbo; a colleague from the Hastings Law Review told the story of the officer who stopped Jan for speeding on the night of a big deadline and asked, "Have you been drinking?"

"No!" she answered, offended. "I've been typing!"

He let her off.

I spoke of our long friendship and how, when we came to the end of our long hike, Jan said she felt as if she were starting a new chapter in her life.

* * *

Jan's spirit visited me again in May, when Tim and I signed on with an outfitter for a seven-day hike from the North Rim of the Grand Canyon down to the Colorado River and back. All we had to do was show up in Flagstaff, carry thirty-five pounds in our packs, and hike nine miles a day over uneven ground in potentially hot weather while getting along amicably with others. I was confident in my strong back, optimistic I could get along with others, and outright anxious about the heat.

We left Flagstaff at four a.m. and arrived at the Sowats Point trailhead by noon. While it was only three-and-a-half miles to our first camp, we descended 2,200 feet, most of it within the first mile. From the edge of the canyon, it didn't look possible.

I knew from rock climbing in the U.K., Alpine skiing out West, and hiking in Alaska, that seemingly impossible routes up sheer rock faces, down precipitous slopes, and up vertiginous mountains open up to possibility with the first step. In the Grand Canyon, I had the help of the high-end hiking poles Jan sent as a gift to replace the ones I wore out on our Long Trail hike.

Just a few months after that Long Trail adventure, Jan rafted through the canyon. Now, I channeled courage traversing the same landscape she'd paddled past. As I threaded through slot canyons, stood amazed at thousand-foot waterfalls, withstood hail, and scrambled to safety during a flash flood, I remained slack-jawed with awe and utterly relaxed, even as I climbed out of the canyon in stinging snow. The whole time I was in the Canyon, I felt Jan's joyous energy through the cork handles of those poles. I wasn't yet brave enough to *just say yes*, as she did, but my knee-jerk reaction to challenges, be they on a hike or on the page, was no longer to *just say no*. After Jan's death, I better understood how much I needed to be out of doors, and how finding my way along an apparently unmarked path was no different from writing a book.

Jan often visits me at my desk to remind me: I can do this.

* * *

In June, I had a chance to articulate my recent understanding of death when I introduced Cheryl Strayed, author of *Wild*, at the fortieth anniversary celebration of the Brattleboro Area Hospice. I told the 750 people packing the Latchis Theater in Brattleboro that it's a truth generally avoided we're all going to die because we're afraid of what we don't know. Fear makes us timid. Fear encourages us to seek comfort. Fear can stick us in front of the TV with the doors locked. It can turn life into an endurance test. Yet in the end, we're still going to die. We can't change that, but we can change how we live with fear. "Fear," Strayed writes in *Wild*, "is born of a story we tell ourselves, and so I chose to tell myself a different story." Her mantra while hiking the Pacific Crest Trail is: *I am not afraid*. I told the audience my friend Jan's philosophy in life to *just say yes* allowed her to live without fear. She said yes to entering a 5K snowshoe race on a sparkling February day. A handsome stranger was waiting at the finish.

"Come with me," he said.

Of course, Jan said, "Yes."

The stranger was Death.

She collapsed and died instantly.

* * *

A week after introducing Cheryl Strayed, I was roped into a climbing harness and walking backwards off a granite cliff. Since Jan's death, I had no fear. I changed my story: *I can do this.*

Rock climbing was the activity on the second day of a six-day experiential learning course for educators taught by Misha Golfman, founding partner and executive director of Kroka Expeditions, a New Hampshire-based wilderness school—and so much more. There were nine of us enrolled in the course; we ranged in age from early twenties to mid-sixties. Most had never worn a climbing harness before.

I had, but it had been a while. I first climbed on cliffs above Lake Superior during my Outward Bound course when I was sixteen. I resumed climbing during my junior year abroad, scaling cliffs in Cornwall, Devonshire, Derbyshire, and Wales in my early twenties. I hadn't climbed again until I was in my forties and the mother of three. My daughter Naomi and I spent a Mother's Day weekend with Kroka, climbing local cliffs. As Francis Bacon famously observes, children make us hostages to fate, and I'd become more fearful, more cautious, more susceptible to imaginary worst-case scenarios with the birth of each child. My children tease me about the snow snakes I conjure from anxiety—fantastical serpentine creatures that lurk in my imagination and contaminate my perception of reality.

After changing my story, the snow snakes didn't bother me when I was rappelling off the rock outcrop, but they appeared again when the group embarked on a three-day canoe expedition down the Connecticut River. I love moving by muscle and living outdoors, and I enjoy flat-water paddling, but I dreaded running Sumner Falls in a canoe. My canoeing skills were rusty, and my fear of whitewater robust.

I developed this particular fear when Tim took up whitewater kayaking. Navigating the hazards of a wild river satisfied his need to escape the workaday pressures of saving other people's lives. I was always sure to kiss him as he left—in case he didn't come back—and I spent the hours he was gone planning my widowhood with three young children to raise on my own. He always came back, his skin polished by the river and his smile restored. I couldn't deny him a thrill that washed his spirit, but I declined invitations to join him. Instead, I took up rowing, my shell and sculls turning me into a water strider like those insects whose legs barely dimple the surface as they glide—a flat-water sport.

My task on this canoe expedition was to "sweep," making sure nothing and nobody was left behind when we moved camp. I'd always brought up the rear when we hiked with the kids; being last allowed me both to woolgather and worry. On this trip, I worried. Our group included a few members who'd never before been in a canoe, and one who didn't know how to swim.

We launched. Misha taught us how to read the river and how to use the edge between the current and the calm to navigate. He demonstrated the bracing strokes we'd need to stay upright in whitewater. We practiced how to stay safe if we capsized. It was so hot that capsizing felt good. Nevertheless, I dragged my paddle as we approached the rapids. At the portage, we emptied our gear so we wouldn't lose it if we tipped over. I thought we should just carry the canoes around the rapids despite the abundant poison ivy growing along the path. An itchy rash was more appealing than drowning, and I briefly considered copping out. But when we inspected the rapids from the shore, they didn't look that scary. I zipped up my life vest, buckled my helmet, and acknowledged that I wasn't scared, I was *excited*. This wasn't the first time I'd been taught how to run rapids, but it was the first time that I didn't look only at the swift water. This time, I sought out the edge where the fast water met the calm, and I used it to steer.

I think in metaphors, and seeing how I could use this edge to my advantage was profound. I saw how I'd been allowing fear to be a dam that impeded the course of my life with excess worry. I worried about Tim on his eight-mile commute, I worried about the well running dry, trees crashing onto the house. I worried about things I could do nothing about—except worry. At Sumner Falls, I recognized worry as something that made me feel connected. As we launched, I embraced excitement and crossed the edge where change happens.

The snow snakes melted in the hot sun as I piloted the canoe downstream. In what felt like slow motion, we crossed the fast current, turned downstream in the slower water, glided over a drop, bounced over chop, and pulled into a calm eddy of accomplishment.

I locked in my new knowledge: Fear thrives at the gap between not knowing and learning. It's in this margin between ignorance and experience that I take risks, and by taking risks, learn skills that enable transformation. And not just me: Everyone in the group navigated the rapids successfully. Throughout the rest of our journey, we paddled, watched eagles, and sang.

After learning how to read the river and use the place where fast water collides with slow, I started to see similar margins—not just where the hemlock and oak provide cover and forage for deer, but in the border between exertion and rest, the fertile time between departing and arriving, and the gap between experience and memory—the spaces between.

Despite our partiality for justified margins in print and clear margins in cancer surgery, margins are liminal places, where disparate qualities meet: the river and the riverbank, the ocean and the shore. Margins teem with life and ambiguity: is it a pollywog or a frog? They create the verge between pastures, along fence lines, and beside roads. It's along the margin of memory when I saw one thing and remembered another.

* * *

A few months after the canoe trip, I was driving home on the Dover Road. As always happens as I descend this hill past a particular stone embankment, I remembered the first time I traveled this way. The memory of driving in my grandfather's car and noticing how the slanted evening light tinged the stones a golden orange replays every time I pass this particular stretch of road, but this is the first time I remembered the details.

It was in the mid-1960s, on a summer vacation to visit my aunt and uncle in Vermont. My parents, brothers, and I stayed in a rented house about sixteen miles west of Aunt Joan and Uncle Dave's. Following an afternoon at a lake, my parents, brothers and I returned to our rented house to clean up before heading to Joan and Dave's for dinner. My grandfather met us at the rental. Only now, in recalling these events for the first time in more than fifty years, do I wonder how he came to be there at that moment. Perhaps it was arranged to give me a break from my brothers' relentless teasing that summer, teasing that sometimes caused objects to fly out of my hands: when setting the table, dishes slipped past the counter and cracked; when taking my place at the table, water glasses tipped over; when clearing the table, cutlery clattered to the floor. My brothers called me "Butterfingers." Perhaps my mother asked her father to pick me up to enjoy a moment's peace apart from my brothers.

Grandpa invited me to drive over the hill in his car.

Yes! A chance to sit in the front seat! To have a window! *Relief.*

The road up the hill from the west is neither as steep nor as twisty as the hill down the other side. It was on the descent that Grandpa said, "You're so far away. Come, sit next to me."

We were in his navy-blue Chevy Nova, with a bench seat before seat belts. Ever the obedient child, I slid over.

Grandpa put his arm across my shoulders and pulled me closer. The elbow of his other arm rested on the open window, his hand on the wheel.

"You can be my girlfriend." His hand cupped my new breast.

"It's too hot." I tried wiggling away.

He pulled tighter.

I ducked under his arm and slid back to my side of the bench. I saw the golden glow of evening sun on the rocks piled up the embankment.

For more than fifty years, I remembered that golden light every time I drove past those rocks. I remembered riding in Grandpa's blue Nova. But it wasn't until I'd broken all those years of silence about my grandfather stalking me, cornering me, crossing my boundaries, that I remembered this particular instance of Grandpa feeling me up.

This time, I saw the rocks on the left side of the road, and looked to the right, over the guardrail, across the brook, into the sort of hemlock habitat that deer frequent. I saw the rise and fall of the hills; I saw contours; I recognized the land's orientation to the sun.

TEN

ANOTHER SEASON

By the time my fourth hunting season approached, I'd figured out that preparing to hunt is much the same as preparing to write: clearing the calendar, collecting my tools, doing the research, and sitting alone day after day for hours at a time. To make that possible, I canceled the Thanksgiving lollapalooza and gave myself over entirely to hunting. That Tim was on-call for the holiday made cancelling easier—as if it was on account of his work and not mine that I made the call. Nevertheless, crossing Thanksgiving off the calendar felt radical, and as necessary as protecting my mornings to write.

As in previous years, I headed over to Roger's to reacquaint myself with my rifle. Initially, I handled it with greater confidence but less accuracy. I persisted and found the sweet spot. I showed Roger the target. "The last two are okay," I said, pointing to the bull's-eyes. The other three were just outside center.

"Any one of those shots will kill a deer, Deb."

"Really?"

"They're none of them more than two inches apart."

I looked at him.

He covered the five bullet holes with his hand. "They're all within the kill zone."

I must have frowned, doubting him and myself.

"Killing a deer is easier than hitting a target."

He'd told me this before.

I still didn't believe him.

He wished me luck.

Next, I returned to scout the land across the river where I'd hunted the last three days of the previous season. Alan was selling his 300 acres to the Green Mountain Conservancy (GMC), a local non-profit. In the nineteenth century and into the twentieth, the federal government purchased and protected millions of acres, establishing national forests and parks for the public good. Nowadays, the government leaves conservation to private citizens who are often rank amateurs, like those of us who made up the GMC Board of Directors: Marie, her husband Ned, Steve Franklin, neighbors Mick and Amy—and me. My experience in purchasing property was limited to buying two houses and a commercial building. I had neither knowledge nor experience in land conservation, but I knew that conserving land was important.

Alan's land would become the cornerstone of Deer Run Nature Preserve. In a stroke of remarkable luck, the owner of a contiguous parcel of more than 600 acres offered to sell his land to the GMC at a rock-bottom price. This land was too steep to develop and had no road access, so it wasn't habitable by humans, but it was important habitat for wildlife. Conserving it would protect a critical wildlife corridor between the Connecticut River and the Green Mountain National Forest. The parcel also drains into the West River along almost three miles of shoreline. Conserving this forested land would protect water quality and ameliorate storm damage from more frequent and increasingly violent storms.

But conserving land isn't only good for wildlife, forests, water quality, and climate protection. Land conservation is also essential for humans, because humans also need nature. Studies demonstrate that not only is nature good for humans, but also that lack of it is deleterious. Research into the Japanese practice of *shinrin-yoku* has confirmed the healing properties of *forest bathing*, a bio- and psychodynamic practice developed as an antidote to high-tech life. *Shinrin-yoku* is a form of sensory meditation where a person mindfully immerses herself in the healing atmosphere of the forest to lessen and even prevent the chronic stress responsible for so many of the ailments of modern life, including but not limited to anxiety, depression, distraction, and insomnia. In Japan, doctors prescribe forest bathing for improved health, and people get better.

An unexpected consequence and equally important benefit of *shinrin-yoku* has been a greater appreciation for forests. As people find health among the trees, they've become more aware of the need to protect individual trees from felling and entire forests from development. Forest bathing may prove as important in protecting the natural environment as the natural environment is critical to supporting human well-being.

In the year since I'd last hunted this land, volunteers had built a trail to the top of the ridge, making the trek an easy two-mile hike. The trail deliberately meanders, never exceeding an eight percent grade, so even not-so-hardy hikers can attain long-distance views with modest effort. I envisioned this trail as the landed equivalent of the dotted line on the wide-ruled paper I used in first grade to learn to print. Just as that dotted line helped me space my letters on the page, the trail made it easier for me to know where I was in relation to all that space: The land descends southward from the ridge toward the West River. The sun is the compass needle arcing across the dial of the sky. When clouds block the sun, the rills, brooks, and streams run to the river, pointing my way out. I could imagine finding my way in before daylight and dragging a buck out before dark.

I left the trail to revisit the ravine I had found on the last day of hunting the previous year, a place where I imagined deer picking their way along the streambed, protected between steep banks. I chose the base of a large hemlock with a good view of the gully for my seat and set about dragging fallen branches to create a primitive blind to hide me from the deer. My plan was to sit with my back to the east, so I'd be backlit by the rising sun, which would illuminate the deer on the western slope. I spied an old woods road on the far side of the stream and followed it out. I couldn't ask for an easier dragging route for hauling my deer.

Two days before the season opened, the temperature dropped into the low teens. I remembered how cold I was two years earlier, when the high-tech hunting pants I bought at Dick's didn't keep me warm. I again scouted for trousers sufficiently insulated for sitting on the cold ground. First, I checked the local thrift store, where I found a woolen pair from a men's Brooks Brothers suit, roomy enough to fit over multiple layers of silk, wool, and fleece. They'd do if I couldn't find something better, and they only cost four dollars.

Since lots of Vermont men wear woolen trousers, I tried the men's department at Sam's, where I found two pair that fit: voluminous green ones so stiff and hard to unbutton I'd pee my pants before I'd ever pulled them down, and a pair in gray plaid, slightly softer fabric, with buttons easier to work. They were the smallest in stock, yet big enough to fit over my thickest, warmest insulated leggings. I frowned at myself in the mirror and paid a hundred bucks for warmth, not fashion. Nevertheless, I was pleased with my success and hoped I'd be as lucky finding better glittens. Of all the well-constructed men's handwear Sam's carries—all constructed with technical fabrics that insulate, and shed water—none fit. In the ladies' department, everything was decorative, not functional. Again, I wondered when manufacturers of high-quality gear will realize that the growing number of women hunters is also a growing market for clothes and equipment as well made as what's available for men.

This started me thinking about how many different ways women suffer in a world designed for men, like airbags that injure female drivers because the safety equipment is sized to an average-sized man. This is a dangerous mental groove; it leads me to think about how medication for erectile dysfunction is easy and inexpensive for men to procure, and how contraception for women is expensive and sometimes difficult to obtain. Thoughts like this raise my blood pressure—not good for my health. The best cure for my outrage-induced hypertension is to get outside and walk, so I whistled up the dog and headed to the town forest, a half mile from where I live.

My town didn't set out to create a town forest, but when the highway department needed a new garage, the best location was on ten acres that were part of a 180-acre parcel the seller wouldn't divide. Voters authorized the purchase, and several citizens stepped forward to serve on a conservation commission, created to oversee this public resource. We take for granted that professional, governmental agencies use tax dollars to build and maintain our roads, so it's ironic that our town forest is the result of the new town garage. We have a professional road crew who maintain our bridges and roads, and dedicated volunteers who built and maintain the three hiking trails in the town forest. The trails see heavy use and are my default place to walk in the woods when I don't have time or ambition to wander off-trail. On this overcast, below-freezing day, I calmed myself in these familiar woods as the dog marked what he thought was his territory. Conserved land belongs to everyone.

The day before rifle season started, I slept poorly and woke with a headache. I wrote in the morning and taught in the afternoon. One of the things I wrote was a brief speech to deliver that evening at the forty-fifth annual meeting of the Brattleboro Food Co-op, where I've been a member since 1985. The meeting lasted longer than anticipated, so it was late Friday night when I finally packed for the hunt. This was my fourth season, so by now, I had a system.

At the bottom of my knapsack, I placed the items I'd need to field dress a deer, including nitrile gloves, rags, rope, plastic bags, and my knife, which I'd yet to use. Even though I'd owned it for three years, I hadn't realized that the factory edge it came with had never been sharpened. My brother-in-law showed me how to use a stone to give the blade a razor edge. I hate to imagine the mess and frustration I would have encountered trying to gut a deer with a dull knife. *Yeesh.*

Next, I packed extra socks, gloves, neck gaiter, and fleece hat. On top of that, I crammed my new wool trousers and a heavy fleece jacket, both of which I'd pull on over my base layer after the hot work of climbing uphill to my blind. In the front compartment, I placed my headlamp, compass, map, chemical hand- and foot-warmers, and extra batteries. I set my gear in the front hall, next to the laundry basket containing the clothes I was going to wear out the door. I filled the basket in the reverse order in which I would dress.

* * *

For the fourth year in a row, I went to bed but didn't sleep. My alarm was set for four-thirty, but I gave up at four. I brewed coffee, packed my food and water, and dressed: underwear, silk long johns, sock liners, wool socks, poly-pro quarter zip, fleece-lined leggings, fleece vest, and jacket. My jacket's outermost layer had pockets. I zipped my phone, driver and hunting licenses in one, a bandana in another, and a pee rag in a third.

At the bottom of the basket were my lightweight buff—a versatile cloth tube that can be worn to keep my neck, ears, and head warm; my blaze-orange knit cap; and lightweight gloves. I took my rifle out of its case and slid it into a gun sock, then pocketed five cartridges in my safety vest. I became quieter, calmer, and clearer as I stepped into each layer. I mentally reviewed what I'd packed as I laced my boots.

I was ready.

Even at this hour, there was traffic on the state highway, all pickup trucks. I imagined they were all hunters, like me. I crossed the covered bridge over the West River and turned north. No traffic on this dirt road. The houses were dark, the stars bright.

It was twelve degrees and crystal clear. The moon was four days past full, and the trees cast shadows. I loaded my rifle by the truck's dome light. Roger's tradition is to kiss the last cartridge in, for good luck. Not mine.

I walked along a wooded path beside an open field and stopped when I came to the power line clearings. I paused there, and said my prayer for the hunt.

I'm not usually big on prayer, but Murphy Robinson, with whom I'd stayed in touch since taking the Huntress Intensive, recently emailed a videoed recitation of their Huntress Prayer. While my skills for finding, shooting, and field dressing a deer were still untested, I had growing confidence in my ability to learn them. I was less sure about my readiness to take a deer's life with dignity. I felt the responsibility acutely. It's a subject that Murphy deals with as no other hunter I know. At the Huntress Intensive, we discussed ways to honor the deer's sacrifice, and ways to prepare our own souls to be in right relationship with the hunt.

I now had three seasons of experience in the field and clarity about my motives: to learn from Vermont deer how to read the landscape and then to eat the landscape by eating the deer. What I wasn't sure about was whether I was spiritually prepared to take and honor a deer's life.

I was standing at the edge of the power lines with a full view of the starred universe.

I was humbled by the night sky and took a deep breath.

I exhaled long and slow.

I'm just a small link in the great chain of being, a part of nature, doing my best.

Another deep inhale and long exhale.

I'm going into the woods to hunt deer.

I inhaled again and exhaled a prayer:

May the buck that steps in front of my bullet die swiftly.

May I be nourished by his sacrifice.

May I honor him by telling his story.

Selah.

I crossed under the wires, stepped into the dark woods, and crashed into branches, announcing myself to woodland creatures near and far.

This wasn't going to work.

I backtracked to the clearing under the power lines and followed a game trail by moonlight. The hike warmed me, but as soon as I stopped moving, I was cold. When I reached the height of land, I sat on one of the giant trees the power company had felled and unlaced my boots, slipped one off, stuck my leg into my woolen trousers, returned that foot to my boot. I did the same on the other side. I shrugged off my jacket; pulled on my fleece, and zipped up my layers. I retied my boots and crossed into the hemlock. Their needles muffled my footsteps, and enough moonlight shone through the branches for me to find my way to my primitive blind. It was five-thirty. Legal hunting starts a half hour before official sunrise, which would occur at six thirty-seven. I had time to fade into the landscape.

The moon slipped below the hill I was facing. I watched the sunrise indirectly as daylight hit the western slope and night's shadow receded, turning the hillside golden. I hadn't anticipated this beauty or that my seat would be in the shade. Even swaddled in layers, I was cold. Nevertheless, I sat and waited for the deer, which did not appear.

At nine o'clock, I moved into the sunlight and took a seat on a stone near where the two power lines cross. These power lines were built in the 1960s and expanded in this century. Like most power lines, these are now an accepted feature of the viewscape. I suspect future generations will become similarly used to wind turbines and solar arrays.

One of the unintended consequences of these power lines is how they now provide the shrub-scrub habitat once common near crop fields, in orchards, and beside pastures, when there were more farms. It's habitat essential to Vermont wildlife, especially birds. As part of the application for the conservation easement, the Green Mountain Conservancy hired a pair of ornithologists to conduct a bird survey. They counted over seventy species of birds feeding and breeding in these power corridors, including several species now rare in Vermont.

Not only did these wide clearings provide important habitat for wildlife, they'd become the x- and y-axes that helped me navigate this land. The double high-tension lines ran north-south; the single high-tension line, east and west. They crossed at a skewed angle, so they divided these three hundred acres into unequal quadrants. Once I thawed out, I followed a faint path uphill in the northeast quarter. Where the path faded, I bushwhacked. I was pretty sure I'd intersect the blazed trail higher up.

I did.

I stepped out of the hardwood onto the trail, which threads through hemlock, bringing relief from the noisy crackle of dry leaves I'd been tromping through. These woods were dark, cool, and quiet, but devoid of deer sign: not a rub, not a scrape, not even a pile of pellets. I saw light ahead and left the trail to enter a beautiful clearing—the sort of place deer like to browse. I scanned for cover and saw what looked like a car battery tucked into the base of a large, lone oak. It was a stone so precisely rectangular I couldn't tell if it was deliberately chiseled or a random act of nature. It was a perfect, south-facing seat. I took it.

I sat in the sunshine, quieted myself, and waited.

Nothing.

The next morning was even colder, so I didn't head out until after sunrise. Instead of following the trail, I climbed straight up the eastern property line, so steep in places I had to kick the toes of my boots into the earth to gain purchase on the slippery leaves. When I reached a plateau, I cut west.

I still saw no sign of deer, possibly because I made so much noise walking through dried leaves. But I wasn't even seeing hoof prints or deer poop—reliable signs of deer passing through. I noted places I could perch, but instead of looking for deer, I pulled out my compass and bushwhacked due west. My hunch paid off: I found the oak with the stone seat, this time approaching it from the opposite direction. I sat on the stone and basked in my orienteering success. I named this tree "The Stone Oak."

The one-degree morning warmed to the mid-thirties by midday. Balmy. I didn't move. I heard woodpeckers, turkeys, crows, wind, water, a single gunshot. I sat for ten minutes—or maybe it was sixty; doped by the sun and the aroma of rotting leaves, I'd stopped telling time. Eventually, I moved on, continuing west until I intersected the trail and started following it down. Willow, Steve Franklin's dog, came running up, followed by a young girl.

"You must be Ginny," I said, introducing myself. "I work with your dad." Steve is vice-president of the GMC board.

"He's coming behind me, with my grandparents," Ginny said. "They're slow."

"Good to know," I said. "Have a good hike."

I continued a long way before running into the rest of the family. Luther, Steve's father, recognized me. "How's the hunting?"

"I'm having a great time exploring the woods." I grinned at him.

Luther grinned back.

We continued in opposite directions.

At the power lines, I climbed onto logs felled ten years earlier, when the transmission wires were doubled. From where I was sitting, I could see a game trail, but my eye was drawn to the sky, where a hawk rode a thermal. I watched it bank, catching the light as it made wide, lazy loops before fading into the sky.

By late afternoon, clouds descended, and a line of people in orange vests paraded toward the beaver pond. Too many people around to shoot at anything—as if there were any deer to shoot at, which there were not. I joined Marie, who lives nearby. Her daughter and a daughter-in-law with young kids had already fed apples to the beavers. The children were now exploring an alder swamp. The little girls were accompanied by their aunt, a naturalist. These children were being nurtured in nature. I was stabbed with envy, wishing the adults in my childhood had encouraged curiosity instead of warning me about the perils of sunburn, riptides, poison ivy, and ticks. For the first time, I realized I'd been taught to be fearful of the natural world. I was unlearning that fear now.

I visited long enough to catch sight of the beavers. As I said goodbye, the naturalist asked, "Did you see the scrape by the gate?"

"I came from the other direction, but I'll check it on my way out. Thanks."

If she hadn't alerted me, I probably wouldn't have seen where a buck had swiped right—scraping the ground and filling it with his scent—letting the does in the area know that he was interested in hooking up. I headed back to the truck in the gloaming of dusk. In my diary, I noted: *No deer. Changing weather. A good day in the woods.*

On another day, I gave myself permission to explore without the expectation of shooting a deer—an activity I'd heard other hunters refer to as "taking your rifle for a walk." I passed by the scrape I'd seen before, but didn't see any other sign. I wondered what else I wasn't seeing.

I circumambulated the southwest quadrant, where I hadn't yet explored. It was rough going down steep terrain through a tangle of pucker-brush before entering a grove of old-growth hemlock that blocked the sun. Moss thrived in the deep shade like green velvet, carpeting the ground and upholstering the scattered boulders and fallen trees. I stepped into the sunshine at a high plateau, what I'd heard called a savannah at a GMC board meeting: a mostly flat area with stately oak trees, tall and well-spaced, so that light penetrated the canopy, allowing tall grass to flourish. I sat with my back against one of the great trees, and watched for deer. I saw none. I continued following the boundary, which passed a giant erratic—a boulder the size of a garden shed—carried and abandoned by the last glacier. I was now on the backside of the beaver pond and sat for a spell.

And so it went all afternoon: I walked, I sat, I took note. I found places to watch for deer, and when I became cold or bored, I walked to warm up and inspect stone walls, communities of trees, and the contours of the land. In one area, I saw flags a state biologist had placed to mark two different endangered plant species whose presence would add muscle to our application for a state conservation grant. But I saw no sign of deer in these woods, and at some point, I stopped thinking about them. It was dusk before I called it a day.

* * *

I've rarely welcomed the sound of rain pounding the roof as I did the next morning. By thirteen minutes into legal hunting, I was in the middle of yoga practice, stretching my aching body and quieting my noisy mind. As much as I enjoyed developing my routine of dressing, packing, arriving at my hunting grounds, loading my rifle, and heading into the woods, I was ready for a reprieve from traipsing through the woods looking for non-existent deer.

The rain turned to snow, dropping a couple of wet inches. When the snow stopped that afternoon, I suited up to hunt across the road. The rain had silenced the leaf litter. Where the snow stuck, I saw deer tracks and pellets. My buck lust spiked and my insecurity bloomed. No matter where I chose to sit, I saw another place that looked better and moved there. A dog barked. I hoped the sound would move the deer my way.

After a few restless hours, the overcast sky dimmed. I made a last stand beside a young pine at the edge of a meadow where I'd often seen deer sign and fleeing deer. The field glowed as the day faded. I was waiting for a deer—any deer—to walk into the clearing just to reassure me these animals exist.

I heard them and froze.
They stopped just behind me.
I couldn't see, but I knew they were there.
Close.
I stood absolutely still.
One huffed; its breath warmed my ear.
I shifted.
Hoofbeats faded into the woods.
I was suffused with delight as I floated home in the dark.

I was back across the road before six the next morning, walking into the mist hanging in the trees. I waited by an apple tree at the edge of the field and witnessed daybreak. I was too late; the deer had already moved up the hill, so I followed their tracks along a stream and then a stone wall until I nearly tripped over a newly split log. I looked up: A house. A woman and her dog, both wearing orange vests. Neither saw me. I ducked behind a tree until they went inside, then climbed to the ledge outcrop near the abandoned hunting camp where I'd been before. I saw fresh deer sign, but this time I suspected the dogs were barking at me, meaning I was close to the backyards of a nearby development, a kind of rural suburbia. Houses now hemmed in what had been historically good hunting ground. The line between wilderness and development is porous; wildlife adapts, and so did I. I didn't feel safe hunting in this margin between wild and civilized, so even though it was only ten in the morning, I headed in.

 I returned to Deer Run the next afternoon, where I was less likely to see people. I followed the eastern property line beside a stream until I came to an unusually well-built stone wall at ninety-degrees to a stream. My map confirmed that the wall marked the corner not just between two different landowners, but also the boundary between two towns.

 I'd begun to consider the hubris of private land ownership, particularly of wild land. But this wall indicated a political boundary, one of particular interest to me, as the 600-acre parcel GMC was negotiating to purchase and conserve spanned this boundary. In the past two weeks, I'd made evening presentations about the proposed purchase at four meetings, introducing the project to each town's conservation commission and select board—all served by volunteers.

 In one town, a member of the conservation commission wanted to know who would pay the taxes on the land.

 We would. The Green Mountain Conservancy was creating an endowment to do so.

 In the other town, a select board member asked for clarification. "You call yourselves the Green Mountain Conservancy, but you're establishing Deer Run Nature *Preserve*. Conservation and preservation are not the same. Which are you doing here?"

Deer Run Nature Preserve is a conservation project whose name was chosen for the way it sounds. The well-intentioned amateurs behind its creation must not have been thinking about the differences between conservation and preservation when they named this project, but the differences are significant, as I learned in hunter education. *Conservation* is the wise use of natural resources, while *preservation* protects natural resources from being used at all. I also had to learn some of the finer points of conservation as it relates to wildlife.

Conservation of natural resources is now a field of scientific research, but the concept of regulating the human use of nature is documented in the Bible and has doubtless been around even longer. Preservation is a newer concept that protects nature by attempting to eliminate all human impact, as if nature can be put up in jars or exhibited in a museum. Once we assured the select board that our intent was to conserve the land rather than preserve it, they were happy to support the project.

I found a place along the wall with the wind in my face and a clear view of where deer might move down the mountain toward the river—if there were any deer. After a while, I pulled out my phone and played an online word game against the computer. Tempting as it was to check email, I kept the phone in airplane mode. I'd hate to scare a deer with a ringtone.

Near sunset, I packed up and hiked down, crossed under the power lines and stopped. This was the gloaming hour, and deer are crepuscular animals that move at twilight. I hunkered behind a blowdown as the world faded with the light. Inexplicably, it gave me a certain satisfaction to witness the day end.

* * *

Since the deer weren't in the woods, neither was I. Over the weekend, Tim helped me put up strawberry-rhubarb jam with homegrown fruit from the freezer. Holiday gifts. I baked a cheesecake for the Green Mountain Conservancy's upcoming annual meeting, which would start with a potluck supper.

Monday morning, I advanced some of the legal paperwork of revising our wills, a task we started in January and aimed to finish before the year ended. I'd already completed and registered my advance healthcare directive for my end-of-life care should I be unable to advocate for myself. I remembered my father, who was a generous man, especially when it came to educating his children, nieces, nephews, and granddaughters. But his best and last gift was the clarity of his living will.

I rewarded myself with an afternoon at Deer Run. The morning clouds gave way to sun. I'd planned to hike to the ridge, but I stopped in the sunshine overlooking the ravine I'd staked out on Opening Day. It was pleasant, and I was content sitting on a comfortable boulder, immersed in the sensations of being in the forest—my own version of *shinrin-yoku*.

I heard them before I saw them: two does traversing the ravine opposite me. They were heading toward the power lines. Even at this distance, they looked big, healthy. I peered through the woods in the direction they'd come. Were there more? Was there a buck? The two does moved without urgency; friends out for a walk. And so, the tenth day of the sixteen-day season came to an end. But I felt alert now that I'd seen deer—as if I'd woken up from a hundred year sleep.

* * *

On Day Eleven, icy fog obscured the morning light, but the forecast was for sun. I arrived on the land at eight and walked through frozen mist that turned golden as it thawed. Even the fallen leaves shimmered in a kaleidoscope of topaz hues. My plan was to hunt the ridge, but I was stunned by the morning's beauty and sat on the boulder above the ravine where I'd seen the two deer the previous day.

The cathedral light invited me to wander. I followed a trickle of a stream, crossed it, and climbed a rock outcrop. The mist shimmered and glowed until I stepped into the hemlock, where I saw the pink tape flagging the trail ahead. I knew exactly where I was. To my right: the clearing with the stone oak.

Two whitetails vanished into the hemlock, probably does.

I looked around. In the soft loam at my feet was an unmistakable, brand-new scrape. I was alert as never before. I wasn't anywhere near the buzzing power lines, but I was humming with the hunt.

I left the trail and walked until I came to another hardwood clearing surrounded by hemlock and sat on a log that had fallen beside a stump tall enough to hide my silhouette. I stilled myself in the pale sun; even motionless, I was warm. I kept my eyes trained on the landscape in front of me when hoofbeats approached from behind. Four does arrived, saw me, and screeched to a halt, like in a *Road Runner* cartoon. The lead deer, larger than the others, advanced and stamped her forefoot. The three others did the same. I didn't crack a smile, but I wanted to grin.

The big girl stomped again. So did the other three, like the kangaroos in *Horton Hears a Who*, when one after another echoes, "Me too!"

I still didn't move.

The lead doe snorted. So did the others.

It took effort not to laugh.

The face-off continued: the dominant doe stamped and huffed just three or four feet from me. The others lost interest and pawed the nearby leaf litter for acorns. The doe snorted once more and ran back up the hill with her followers close behind.

I was elated by this face-to-face encounter with charismatic megafauna in the wild. As far as I was concerned, I was done for the day. I felt the way I feel when I finish reading a really good novel: a bit stunned as I leave the imagined world created with words and step back into the ordinary world I live in. Dishes. Laundry. But I promised myself I'd hike to the top of the ridge, so I shouldered my daypack and rifle.

The higher I climbed, the snowier the woods, the brighter the sun, the bluer the sky, the lighter my heart. Heart-shaped hoof prints pocked the snow. Being so close to those deer and winning the game of chicken with the lead doe was all so magical that I no longer cared if I saw a buck. But I didn't want to leave the woods. Sunlight gleamed on the oak leaves where snow had melted. I was so charmed by those girls and the beauty of the day that I climbed the meandering trail still grinning. Near the top, I glimpsed the ski slopes at Stratton, some twenty miles away. The view was high-definition. Stunning.

A stone monument whose origin is lost to time marks the end of the trail. I leaned my rifle against it and set my daypack down. "I'm here," I announced to the white pine, then sat on the dry needles, pleased with myself for persevering.

I snapped a photo of the view, of my rifle and pack leaning against the stones, and then took a selfie, which I examined to see if I'd been visibly changed by my encounter with the four deer.

I didn't look different. I was smiling. Happy.

Trucks rumbling on the state highway below interrupted my thoughts. The GMC's annual meeting was that evening, to be followed by finalizing the plans for a public hearing scheduled for a few days after hunting ended. I'd already done the publicity for the event, writing press releases and mailing invitations. Tonight's meeting would be my chance to nail down the details for the event itself.

I sighed, packed up, and started down.

The landscape shimmered in sunlight. Deer tracks perforated the snow every which way. It was just past noon, and even though I was heading downhill, I was hot and thirsty and ready to head home. But two stone outcrops separated by a river of leaves invited me up to a shaded plateau. It was cooler there. I sat on a log lodged into a three-trunked tree, slipped off my pack and unscrewed my water bottle. As I brought the bottle to my lips, I moved my head to the left. Through the woods, I saw the profile of a deer.

I replaced the cap on my flask and put it on the ground, keeping my eyes on the doe. Another nose followed.

Does it have antlers?

Oh fuck.

It does.

I lifted my rifle and put my eye to the sight, but saw nothing.

Not again!

I removed the lens cap from the scope. The doe was heading away at a diagonal.

I shifted the gun to the other side of the tree.

She sensed the movement. Curious, she approached me, then veered to my right.

The buck gave chase, taking the shortcut across my line of fire.

Am I going to shoot him?

That's what I'm here for.

He's running.

I've never shot at a moving target.

I trained my muzzle on the kill zone and pulled the trigger.

He leapt, landed, and leapt again.

How could I miss?

Before I finished asking the question, he flopped on his side. Bounced. Stilled.

I didn't miss.

Before I was thirsty; now I was parched. I drained my water bottle.

My thirst persisted.

At the Huntress Intensive, Murphy taught us to wait a half hour to give the buck time to die, and just a few weeks earlier, my brother Jonathan sent me an article about a hunter in the Ozarks who assumed the buck he shot was dead and immediately went to check on it. The buck wasn't dead, and it gored the hunter, who now was.

I texted Ian, my future son-in-law. He and Ruth had said they'd help drag a deer out of the woods.

My text didn't go through.

Shit. No reception. Now what?

I checked again.

This time, I turned airplane mode off and texted Ruth: *Can you and Ian help drag a deer out of the woods?*

She called.

I had enough presence of mind to say, "If you and Ian don't have any safety orange, stop at Sam's and buy some. A hat, a vest—something—and a tarp to drag it out."

"It will take us a while."

"That's okay. I have to field dress the deer."

I must have babbled, because Ruth said, "Hey Mom, it sounds like you need to spend some time with your deer. Calm down."

"Yeah."

I gave her directions to where I was, not far off the blazed trail.

The buck fell not even twenty feet from where I sat.

I approached him from behind, amazed that I remembered this safety precaution. A plume of bright blood bloomed from his nose.

His chest was still and his eyes open. I touched one eye with a stick. When he didn't blink, I knelt by his head and placed my hand on his head as in benediction, but I touched a tick and pulled back. *Eww.*

Okay, this wasn't the spiritual moment I'd hoped for, but My Buck was beautiful, even in repose. I counted six points: three long tines on one side, and three broken stubs on the other. A fighter. And he had died swiftly, for which I was grateful. I snapped a photo of him stretched out on a carpet of leaves, as if he's relaxed, asleep.

I put my phone away. My work began.

First, I tied my tag with my name and license number to his antler. I filled in the date and time of day, twelve-thirty p.m. I pulled the buck's hind legs downhill, as I remembered from the field dressing video. Next, I gathered my kit from my knapsack beside the log where I'd leaned my rifle. Seeing the gun triggered a memory of the hunter's ed film about a hunter who's just shot her first deer. She's so excited that she's waving her rifle in her partner's face. The rifle's still loaded, and she hasn't clicked the safety back on. I didn't want to be that hunter, so I checked my safety. It was on, but the rifle was still loaded and I was done for the day. I emptied the magazine, dropping the four live cartridges in one pocket, and the empty casing in another. A souvenir.

I knelt next to the buck and pulled on nitrile gloves. I felt for his breastbone and started peeling off his skin with my razor-sharp knife. I was making good progress, but something wasn't right.

I paused.

How am I supposed to do this?

I retrieved my phone and turned it on. I was high up on the ridge where no one lives, but I had five bars of reception and downloaded the Vermont Fish and Wildlife field dressing video I'd watched before. I watched it again. Rodney Emmett, the conservation officer who does the demo, has a calm and reassuring voice. I returned to My Buck and punctured the skin, then unzipped his belly without nicking his innards. There was almost no blood.

I checked the video once more, stopping it after the next step: gently nudging the guts partway out of the cavity. I knew what came next, but I watched more of the video just to be sure. Cutting away the diaphragm from the ribs has to be done by feel. I rolled up my sleeves and, keeping the back of my hand and the flat of my blade against the buck's ribs, sliced through the muscle. It was wet and warm inside the buck, and when I finished separating the diaphragm from the ribs, all the blood flooded out.

I mistook blood clots for the liver and tried to collect them in a plastic bag before I realized my mistake. My hands were too bloody to work the phone, so I removed my gloves to watch the next step: reaching as far up the throat as I could to cut the windpipe. I pulled on new gloves. The windpipe felt like plastic; the heart like a ball. The liver was unmistakable—and huge. I carried these organs over to some snow and wiped them off, bagged them, and dug them into the snow to cool off.

A bleat.

The doe was back.

She bleated again, looking for her buck.

My heart cracked. I felt for her. I know what it's like to have a man disappear at an intimate moment. All those years when Tim took night call, he'd answer the phone and leave our bed for the hospital, no matter what. But he always came back.

She bleated again.

When I told her, "I'm sure you'll find another buck," it sounded as feeble as telling a broken-hearted friend, "You'll find someone else, someone better."

The doe turned and ran off.

I watched the end of the video. My Buck's bladder was empty, but his rectum was full. I squeezed the pellets away from his anus and cut through the rectum. Now all the innards were severed, forward and aft. I slid them out of the deer and down the slope, out of the way.

I collected my bloody gloves and rags, rubbed snow on my hands to clean them as best I could, wished I had some water, I sat down to wait.

Ruth and Ian arrived a few minutes later.

"Wow."

"Well done."

I hardly registered their reactions because Ian handed me a liter of water and I drank it all.

Ruth asked, "Do you want a picture with the deer?"

"I don't think so."

"You sure? Don't you want one kneeling beside it?"

I knew the shot she was suggesting. It's a classic, with the hunter showing off the deer's head and antlers. I looked around at the peaceful afternoon and shook my head. "It feels like an invasion of privacy. I don't want to gloat."

Ian asked, "How do we get him out?"

"I don't know. I've never done this before."

We rolled the buck onto the tarp. I thought we could just drag him straight down the hill, but when we tried bushwhacking, we got hung up on the blowdowns. I suggested we follow the hiking trail to the power lines.

Ruth and Ian started dragging. I tried to help, but they had this. I saw how they worked together, communicating wordlessly, each knowing how the other thinks—a sign of how their relationship had developed over eight years of adventures, from working together overseas to through-hiking the Appalachian Trail. I felt privileged to have them on my side.

Even dragging the buck down the power line trail was hard. The tarp shredded. It took hours to drag the deer out. We loaded him into the truck and drove directly to the reporting station at the local general store.

ELEVEN

TELLING THE STORY

There were three generations of women behind the counter at the store; the youngest a six-year-old girl. The girl's mother did the computer work to report my deer; her mother phoned her husband to come weigh My Buck.

"Earl will be here in a minute," she said.

The storekeepers were very kind, and I wished I knew the women's names. One family had run the store for almost fifty years. Since they sold it, it has changed hands more times than I can remember and I'd lost my connection to the place. I rarely shopped there anymore.

Earl arrived and congratulated me. "A scrub buck," he said, pointing at the broken points on the left antler.

"Does he still count as a six-pointer, even though they're damaged?"

"Seven," he said.

"Seven points?"

He showed me a nub of a new point emerging on the damaged side.

"Does that count?" It wasn't protruding a full inch, and I didn't think I could hang my wedding ring on it, which Helen once told me is how you test for a legal point.

"We'll give it to you."

I doubted this was fair. "Six is enough."

I backed the truck to the scale. Earl showed me how to cut a slit between the tendon and the knee of the hind legs so we could hang the buck from the gambrel attached to the hoist.

"Any guesses?" he asked.

Ruth, Ian, and I all estimated the buck's weight. I was right on the money: one-forty.

Men I didn't know crowded around the scale and congratulated me. The storekeeper came out with a camera and snapped a photo of me holding the buck's head while the buck hung from the scale. It joined the photos of all the other hunters who had reported their kills at this station this season. At first glance, every photo looked pretty much the same: a bearded man in camo standing next to a buck or a bear. But on closer inspection, I saw a few boys, some teens, and a handful of women. There must have been close to a hundred all together. Mine was tacked up at the end of a row about waist-high. I was inordinately proud to join these hunters on "The Wall of Game."

Ruth and Ian bought beer, and I was tempted to crack one open when we returned home, but I was still hoping to make the GMC board's annual meeting, scheduled to start within the hour. Before I could go, I somehow had to get the buck out of the truck and hang it to cool.

I had an idea about how to go about this: install heavy-duty hooks in the ceiling of the garage. I even found two such hooks in the basement workshop, but as usual, I couldn't find the bits and chocks and batteries for any of the drills, which my husband and his brother use all the time. By default, I've spent my lifetime depending on the men in my life to hang things for me, things like pictures, shelves, hooks, and now, a deer. I must have thought it was gender-specific, because I expected Ian to know how to hang a deer, so I deferred to him. Meanwhile, I was keeping an eye on the clock.

Ian didn't like my hook idea and scrounged around for something else that might work. I called Roger. I was ready for his outgoing voice-mail message, which has been the same since answering machines used cassette tapes: *You know what this is and you know what to do.*

"Hi Roger. It's Deb. I know how to shoot a deer, and I figured out how to field dress it, but I haven't a clue how to hang a 140-pound six-pointer."

I hadn't eaten since breakfast; it was now after six pm. I was still thirsty. My mind skipped like a scratched vinyl LP. Water. Meeting. I shot a buck. Water. Meeting. I shot a buck.

Ian told me I had to decide if I was going to go to the meeting or take care of my deer. My brain skipped some more. I have to go to this meeting. I'm responsible for the public meeting next week.

I told Ruth and Ian that if we couldn't hang the deer, we could lay him out on a table in the garage, where it was about thirty degrees. There was a homemade plywood table with folding legs in the basement. It weighed a ton, but Ruth and Ian easily carried it upstairs.

Meanwhile, I called Clark—carpenter, neighbor, and friend—who arrived with his van full of tools. He had My Buck strung up by its hind legs in no time. I promised him a venison dinner.

Roger called back. I told him we'd got the deer hanging. He said to make sure I removed the entire windpipe or it would taint the meat. He wanted to come over, but I told him I was about to leave for a meeting. Before I left, I yanked on the few inches of windpipe still inside the deer and cut it off.

Ruth, Ian, and I were a dirty, hungry, thirsty mess. Ruth showered upstairs. Ian ate peanut butter on crackers.

"You're really going to this meeting?" Ian asked through a mouthful of crumbs. I looked at the peanut butter jar on the kitchen counter. I should have been hungry, but I wasn't.

"I have to." That was my brain stuck in another groove, a groove about being responsible to others before myself, a hard habit to break.

Ruth and Ian traded places. I showered downstairs. Five minutes later, I was out the door with the cheesecake and showed up just as the others were finishing dinner. I answered questions about my hunt while our host asked, "What can I get you to drink?"

"Water."

He filled a tall glass from a dispenser on the fridge door. I don't usually like cold water, but I drank this and refilled the glass five more times during the evening. I was barely able to pay attention to the annual reports. After the annual meeting, we held our regular monthly meeting. As usual, we meandered off the agenda. At last, we arrived at the item I was there for. I went down my list of tasks and recruited volunteers to set up chairs, bring printed handouts, a clipboard and pen; bake cookies; buy paper cups and sweet cider; bring the projector and screen; and decide the order of speakers. That done, we adjourned.

I could have stayed home with My Buck.

* * *

Back home, Tim and I admired My Buck hanging in the garage. I told him the story, from having given up hunting for the day, hiking up to the monument, following an instinct to the plateau, sitting on a log behind a multi-trunked tree, reaching for my water bottle, seeing the doe's head, then the buck's; lowering the water bottle and raising my rifle; shifting to the other side of the trunk; asking myself if I was going to shoot; taking aim; pulling the trigger; wondering why the buck didn't drop; watching it fall over and bounce; texting Ian with my phone in airplane mode; turning the phone on; walking over to the buck; seeing the plume of bright blood.

"A lung shot," Tim said.

I told him about watching the video and gutting the deer; Ruth and Ian's heroic drag; taking it to the big-game reporting station; and Clark coming over to help hang it up. It's a story I would tell again and again, each time engraving the event in my memory, where it will live with other life-and-death moments: surviving a spectacular fall down an icy ski slope without injury; nearly drowning in a riptide off the Mediterranean coast; seeing the stain of a miscarriage, giving birth to each of my children, sitting with Dad while he was dying; and now, shooting my first buck.

"When I saw that photo," Tim said about the snapshot I texted, "I knew you'd done it. It was so peaceful. Well done."

I was no longer thirsty, but Tim poured me a drink. "Here, bourbon to calm you."

It didn't.

I didn't sleep.

In the morning, I went out to look at My Buck.

I'd never seen a wild animal so close up; he was more beautiful than I could have imagined. He hung by his hind legs from a beam nine feet from the ground with his nose nearly touching the cement floor, his body stretched out as if to flee. Each hollow hair on the thick fur was tan and gray with black flecks at the tip except for his belly and the underside of his tail, which were pure white. Antlers crowned his head, appearing regal even in death.

I went to my word shop and sat at my desk, but I couldn't concentrate.

I texted Dennis, who helped me the first year I hunted.

He replied immediately. *Patience, persistence, and you will persevere. You finally got your ten-second window and made it happen.*

He asked for more pictures. I'd only taken the one of the buck lying as he'd fallen. I didn't want to take photos while My Buck's spirit was still hanging about the woods. But now that the buck was hanging in the garage, I shot photos of his head and antlers, a close-up of the entrance and exit wounds, his handsome face, so noble and still. I sent this *memento mori* to Dennis, along with a brief version of the hunt. I asked, "How long should the deer hang?"

Dennis texted back. "A week if the weather's below forty and the garage isn't heated."

It wasn't.

"The fur keeps it cold."

I returned to my desk in the studio.

Now I can write the book.

But I kept going back to the garage to visit the deer.

I called Mike Fontaine, who processes wild game as his father did before him. I asked if he could butcher it for me.

"Sure," he said. "Do you want me to take off the hide?"

"No. My daughter and I will skin it." As much as I wanted the pelt, I promised it to Ruth, as reward for dragging the deer's dead weight for most of two miles.

Mike told me to bring it over any afternoon the following week.

I was in love with My Buck and could think of nothing else except Thanksgiving. Now that I'd shot the deer, I wanted all the people I love to show up and party. But it was too late; everyone had made other plans. And as much as I wanted to feast with our friends, I was also tired and glad the holiday would be a quiet one.

Mark and Kathy, our friends from Maine, arrived Friday. If there was turkey at that fabled but apocryphal Puritan Thanksgiving, there was probably also venison, but I wasn't ready to eat My Buck yet, and not just because Dennis recommended the meat hang and cure for a few days. I bought a turkey, made cranberry sauce, roasted Brussels sprouts, and baked a pumpkin pie not because I thought it had anything to do with the Puritans, but because it's how my family has been celebrating since arriving in America. We ate our fill and played Scrabble. Everyone admired the buck. My Buck.

* * *

It snowed overnight. I was out shoveling the path to the studio when my neighbor Dean pulled in to plow. He leaned out the open window. "I hear you got a deer!"

"How do you know?" It's spooky how word spread.

"I heard at Thanksgiving."

It took me a moment to make the connection. "Oh, right. Mike is your brother-in-law." Mike, the guy who's going to butcher the buck.

I nodded toward the open garage door. "He's hanging right there."

Dean peered in. "You haven't skinned him yet?"

"No, I'm letting him hang."

"You're going to have a hell of a time getting that hide off once it's cold."

"Oh." My heart sank. Dennis said to leave the fur on. "I'll figure it out."

"Well, good luck." Dean backed up and started pushing the snow off the drive.

I had thought that different hunters giving me authoritative but differing advice would end once I shot a buck, but no such luck. Maybe a hunter who grew up in a family where hunting is handed down just does what his father did without thinking about it. I didn't have that tradition. Despite all the unsolicited advice, I had to figure out what to do for myself.

Same with the testicles. When Roger shoots a buck, he hangs its balls in a tree. This was too primitive for me. I preferred the method from the Fish and Wildlife field-dressing video and left the buck's courting tackle intact until I could watch the next video, where Rodney Elmer—the same, calm, matter-of-fact conservation officer—demonstrates how to remove the deer's parts along with the hide.

I asked Tim to hold the carcass still while I climbed a step stool and started to operate. Tim has never performed an orchiectomy, but he'd dissected corpses in med school, performed surgery in residency, done vasectomies in his practice, and is male, so he knows his way around the anatomy. He talked me through the procedure. I removed the penis, testicles, bladder, anus, and all the tubing in one piece. The surgery was a success. It helped that the patient was already deceased.

* * *

Eight days after I'd shot the deer, Ruth and I skinned it. On account of what my neighbor Dean had said about it being harder when the deer is cold, I stapled a tent of plastic around the deer and hung a drop light inside overnight, so the cold fat, which acts like glue, would warm up.

I only needed to watch the video about skinning the deer once. I had sewn clothing and undressed babies, skills that translate to skinning a deer. Ruth and I each worked a side, starting at the hindquarters, near the ceiling. We teased the hide away from the flesh, revealing the buck's muscles, each one distinct, working the hide loose to the shoulders, then down the front legs. I made a vertical slit through the skin up the throat, and a horizontal one around the top of the neck, as close to the head as I could. We pulled the hide off. Undressing the deer was intimate work giving us a privileged view: My Buck, naked.

Next, I sank the knife around the base of the skull all the way down to the spine. Ruth steadied the hanging carcass by the front legs while I twisted the head until I hit resistance. "Can you twist in opposition?"

She nodded and walked the body one way, while I twisted the head in the other. I grabbed the base of the antlers for better torque and pulled against the bone till it cracked, then I cut through the connective tissue. Success left me holding the head by the antlers. I placed it on the table. The buck's beautiful dark eyes stared at me. I turned the head to face the wall.

Naked. Headless. My Buck had shape-shifted from the-deer-I-shot into the-venison-I'm-going-to-eat. It was gruesome.

We lined the truck bed with the plastic sheeting that served as the warming tent, lowered the carcass, and wrapped it. It's just a short ride to Mike's place, but everything I'd learned about harvesting wild meat includes keeping it cold, dry, and clean. The temperature was below freezing and not snowing. The plastic would keep it clean.

Deer hides and heads were heaped outside the door of the shed where Mike processes game. I was glad I'd saved My Buck from that indignity. Mike hooked the carcass onto the overhead trolley by its hind legs, and my deer became just another carcass hanging in the cooler. I consoled myself: It's the carcass of an animal that lived in the nearby woods, was never dosed with antibiotics or growth hormones, was never crowded into a feed lot, and died swiftly while in hot pursuit of a doe. He had a good life, and now his flesh will nourish mine.

* * *

I had just enough time to change into clean jeans, gather my wits, and meet my helpers at the hall where we were hosting our public information meeting about adding 626 acres to the newly established Deer Run Nature Preserve. By the time we were ready to start, it was standing room only. Over seventy people came out to learn about this project. In small-town Vermont, that's a big crowd. People from the Land Trust, the Vermont Agency of Natural Resources, and members of the GMC board spoke. I facilitated the Q&A. Afterwards, people drank cider, ate cookies, and chatted.

No one asked me about the land deal. All my neighbors wanted to talk about was my deer.

These were community members: people I greeted at the post office, people who came to town meeting, people who read my columns, heard me on the radio, or knew me because Tim had delivered their babies, sewed up their gashes, set their broken bones, and cared for their parents right up to the end. I was astonished that my hunting success was an important piece of local news.

Matt, a neighbor, congratulated me. We hadn't seen each other since the community cider press in October, when he gave me his phone number if I ever needed help dragging a deer. He wanted to hear the story, right up to delivering the deer to Mike's that afternoon.

"Are you going to mount it?" he asked.

I shook my head. "I just want the antlers and skull. I'm going to bury the head and let the worms clean it for me."

The next day, I buried the buck's head in the vegetable garden. I lined the hole with empty beehive supers, which I covered with hardware cloth, hoping this would keep out the mice. It was a relief to have the deer out of sight. I'd been unable to eat his heart, liver, or flesh while he'd been hanging by his hind legs in the garage, empty of his insides but with his beauty intact.

The head buried, I finally returned to work, reestablishing my routine after what seemed like two weeks of Sundays since shooting the deer. I felt jet lagged without ever having changed time zones. I was at my desk when the phone rang.

"Jon and I were talking, and we don't think you should bury the head." Thanks to caller ID I knew who was on the line.

"Oh, hi Matt." In the nearly thirty years we've been acquainted, we had never before spoken by phone. Jon is the fire chief who also mows our lawn and takes care of the property across the road, where I sometimes hunt; he's also Matt's cousin. I was touched that they were concerned about preserving the buck's head and antlers.

"The mice will eat the antlers. There won't be nothing left."

All my insecurities resurfaced. "What should I do?"

"Boiling it is best."

"I'm not sure I have the stomach for that. Can I hang it in a tree?"

"You can try, but the squirrels might get it."

"Thanks, Matt."

I abandoned my desk and dug up the buck's head. Tim would help me string it up, even though that seemed ghoulish. In the meantime, I placed it on the roof of the woodshed on the north side of my writing studio, where I peeked at it every time I fed the wood stove. My Buck looked as noble and serene as ever. But it snowed overnight, and the next day, he was just a lump.

* * *

Roger greeted me with a bear hug when I showed up to tell him about the hunt. "I knew you could do it! When I saw how you can shoot, I knew you could do it."

"You were right. Shooting a deer is easier than hitting a target, even a deer on the run."

"I was going to drive down to see it, but you had a meeting or something."

"Yeah," I said. "I'm sorry I didn't just blow off the meeting." I was still kicking myself about that.

I showed Roger the photo I took of the deer after he fell and told him the story. By now, I'd told the story so many times that I repeated key phrases. Then I showed Roger the photos of the deer hanging in the garage: the antlers, the face, the small hole where the bullet went in, and the ragged one where it came out.

"You must have been close."

"He ran right in front of me." I was sitting at Roger's dining table and pointed to the staircase on the other side of an easy chair and sofa in the living room. "I don't think he was much farther away than that wall. But he kept going. I thought I'd missed him." I replayed the deer running past me in the video of memory. For the first time, I saw that his forelegs and hind legs came together in pain. He landed, leapt again. The next time, he barely rose off the ground. "But before I could figure out what was happening, he dropped dead." He fell flat on his side with such force that he bounced.

"You must have got him through the heart or lungs. It was a good shot."

I told Roger about how people I didn't know had been congratulating me on shooting the deer and then giving me conflicting instructions about processing the antlers. "I want to preserve the antlers."

"That's easy. I'll show you."

I followed him out to Antler Alley. Roger pulled a pair of six-point antlers off the wall and turned it over.

"You can do this yourself." Roger held the mounted antlers and mimed a sawing motion with the edge of his palm across where the deer's forehead used to be. "First, you got to saw through the skull, and then you have to scrape off all the hair and the flesh. It's a bit of a job."

I wasn't sure I was up for this. Peeling off the skin was one thing, peeling off My Buck's face—quite another. "I was hoping to keep the antlers and skull intact."

"A European mount."

I'd heard this term before, but it didn't mean anything to me. My face must have looked blank.

"Come upstairs, I'll show you."

I followed Roger back into the house, through the living room and up the stairs to the second story he'd added to accommodate his museum. Both he and Janis are collectors, and the walls are covered with 110 original paintings by the Maine wildlife and landscape artist Yodeling Raymond "Slim" Clark. The rest of the space is filled with a miscellany of art and artifacts: a flight of hand-carved shore birds, a crew of fisherman statues, a tribe of carved Indians, antique glassware, tins, and an extensive collection of all things chicken—antique stoneware chicken fountains; scales for grading eggs; hen-, rooster-, and egg-shaped salt and pepper shakers; and a flock of chicken statuary.

I loved looking at all the old-time stuff, but I always returned to where a herd of nine bucks are mounted on the wall. These are big, Canadian whitetails that Roger shot in Alberta, Saskatchewan, or Quebec, except for the ninth, a monster mule deer he shot in Wyoming.

I followed Roger down the narrow aisle to a shelf with six bear skulls in a line. He picked one up and held it out for me to inspect close up. It was right out of Georgia O'Keeffe.

"Yeah, that's what I want."

"This is better than boiling. See here," he tilted the skull. "See them little bones and compartments?"

I did see: a delicate honeycomb of cartilage inside the bear's nose.

"You don't get that if you boil the head, and those little partitions, that's what gives a bear or a deer such a good sense of smell."

"So what's the secret to cleaning a skull like that?" It's just what Roger wanted me to ask.

"It ain't no secret. It's beetles."

"Beetles?"

"Yeah. There's this special kind of flesh-eating beetle that will clean a deer skull down to the bone. You send your deer's head off to this place. They put the head in a box with these beetles. A couple of months later, this is what you got left."

A tag threaded through an eye socket read, "Skulls Unlimited." I looked them up online. They use dermestid beetles for custom skull cleaning. Cleaning a whitetail deer head cost $149, plus the cost of shipping the head FedEx Air.

I didn't really care about all the fine channels of cartilage inside the buck's nose. I just wanted to hang his skull and antlers above my desk in the word shop.

"What about The Rustic Moose?" It's the local taxidermy shop. My kids have been there and reported the place is a marvel. They've come home with bobcat faces for costumes and antler chews for the dog.

"You could use him," Roger said.

I could tell he was unenthusiastic and let the subject drop. Roger was loyal to the taxidermist he's used for years and years and wouldn't trust anyone else with his mounts. But I wasn't interested in stuffed heads. I'm not that kind of hunter, and I don't expect I ever will be.

* * *

I'd driven past The Rustic Moose thousands of times, but this was the first time I'd parked and pushed open one of the windowless doors, entering a room stuffed with mammal heads, pelts, antlers, and a couple of live hunters shooting the breeze. Their conversation stopped when they saw me.

A tall man with wild gray hair flowing into his shaggy beard stepped out from an office farther back.

"Tom?"

"Yeah." He smiled. "Whaddaya got?" He nodded at the grain bag cradled in my arms.

I walked past the two men and felt their eyes on me as I pulled My Buck's head out of the bag.

"I just started a boil, so this will have to wait till next week." He looked at a calendar on the desk and told me when it would be done.

He didn't ask for my name, phone number, or money. "Call first. Make sure I'm here."

"Great. Thanks." I almost turned to go. "Can I look around?"

"Please do."

There was another room in back, bigger than the first, with even more taxidermy on the walls and displayed on tables that divided the room into aisles. I patted skunk skins, raccoons, gray squirrel, and bobcat. Deer, bear, and moose stared me down with their glassy eyes. I inspected lamp bases fashioned from the forelegs of whitetails and other questionable décor. I tried to imagine living in a time when animal skin was the premium fabric against water and cold, the gold standard that wool, down, and polyester fleece have tried to best.

I had to pass by the hunters again on my way out. "You shoot that?" one asked.

"I did. My first."

"Congratulations."

On my way home, I stopped at Mike's to pick up my meat, which filled two large boxes, and a twenty-pound bag of ground venison, half of which we turned into Italian sausage, both hot and sweet. On my brother-in-law Andrew's birthday later that week, we feasted on venison steak. It seemed appropriate to take the first bite during a celebration, a way of honoring My Buck, now on my plate. I closed my eyes and imagined the acorns, blackberry leaves, deer moss, and twigs the deer had eaten. I chewed on the flavors of the landscape I call home and felt blessed.

TWELVE

READING THE LANDSCAPE

Shooting, gutting, dragging, hanging, skinning, and ultimately eating My Buck was like hiking along a high, exposed ridge, complete with a long and sustained view of endless possibility. But just as hikes don't end on mountaintops, hunting didn't end with a single meal of venison.

Deer hunting in November is now an integral part of my rural life. I've gained enough woodland literacy not just to find my way in the woods, but also to find the deer. Instead of only seeing the raised flags of fleeing whitetails, I routinely have close encounters. One morning, I spied a giant buck ambling downhill as I was walking up. The slant of light shone on the bare trees between us. He moved silently, like a shadow, then disappeared. One afternoon, I heard what sounded like a bark and a squeal. I peered through the trees and witnessed a buck dismounting a doe. At dusk, as I walked down a trail on my way out of the woods, a petite doe rushed past within arm's length. I stopped, turned, and came face to face with a young buck. We stared at one another. His nose and eyes—his whole face—was a delicate version of a Jersey calf, crowned by four arching points.

You are too young to be chasing that doe. She's too young!

The buck ran into the woods and stood behind a hemlock, his head and neck visible.

I'm not going to shoot you.

I walked on, and he took off after the doe.

I've now seen a herd of does in a hayfield at daybreak and a sorority of does ambling through the forest in the rain. One afternoon I found a scrape line, where a buck had marked his territory. Before long, I heard a rush of hooves and caught sight of a buck on the fly, running downhill in giant leaps, barely touching the ground. As if charmed, I've now seen more deer in a single season than I saw in my first four.

Maybe I see more deer because I spend more time in the woods, or maybe I walk and sit more quietly, or maybe I now have a better idea of where the deer are. Now I wander through the forest, learning the land in daylight and dark, in fair weather and rain. I no longer worry about getting lost or about finding the best place to stake out. I'm content just to see deer, but deer aren't all I see. I'm starting to recognize fauna other than deer. One of my favorites is the Bruce spanworm, also known as "Hunter's Moth." These tiny white moths fly in clusters, like small patches of fog at ground level. This moth is better known in its larval stage as the tiny green inchworm that appears in the spring. The inchworm feeds on the buds and new leaves of deciduous trees, pupates over the summer, and emerges as a moth after its predators have flown south for the winter. It's a survival tactic that works: Bruce spanworms are found across North America, just like white-tailed deer. I enjoy their company in the otherwise still forest.

* * *

I took up hunting to learn to read the landscape, to harvest local wild meat, and to overcome my fear of getting lost. I accomplished all that—and more. I learned about Artemis, hunter of game. But she was much more than a hunter. The ancient Greek poet Homer called her Mistress of Animals. She protected the forest, trees, and vegetation—wild nature—upon which all life depends. When the king of Calydon makes offerings of thanks to the goddesses and gods for his rich surplus of grain, wine, and olive oil, he neglects to burn incense to Artemis. She sends the boar to Calydon as a reminder and a warning: wild nature is the foundation of agriculture. When a king enjoys a rich harvest but fails to honor the natural world for sustaining life, the forest will be trampled, warriors will die, and mothers will murder their children.

* * *

I spent untold hours sitting in the woods. Occasionally I was bored, especially when I became impatient to shoot a deer. But when I was simply present and observant, I started to see connections I'd never before noticed. One day, sitting on a ledge beside a hemlock rooted just below me, my knee rested against the tree's trunk, and I felt the tree sway, as if it moved to a rhythm I couldn't hear.

The tree creaked, and I heard my own voice rise, filled with gratitude. It's trees that shelter me in my wooden house, trees that make my piano sing, and trees that I burn to keep me warm indoors. Trees contribute their needles and leaves to the forest floor. When trees die, they lie down and enrich the earth; alive, they carry the wind; they sigh and creak. Trees are guardians of the forest, hosts to insects, home to birds and small mammals; they provide shade, store water, and clean the air. It's the color of trees that gives Vermont its Franco-English name—the Green Mountain State.

By learning to hunt I'm becoming observant of the natural world the way that searching for words allows me to consider nuances of meaning. I'm learning to be more attentive, to develop an intimacy with the forest and the weather and with the deer, my allies in education and in concern for the forest—their home, my solace, our planet's lungs.

I have so much more to learn, and the time I have left diminishes daily. Sixteen days of rifle season isn't long enough for full immersion in the forest of home. To extend my hunting season, I've started hunting with a bow. It allows a single shot at close range, requiring both more skill and more patience than I currently have—and I'm willing to learn.

I am still learning to hunt.

Perhaps most significantly, learning to hunt has forced me to change my narrative. While I'm sitting alone in the woods, I don't feel lonely; I feel connected—connected to the many people who helped me learn this ancient skill, to my local community of hunters, and to the long lineage of mythic hunters going back to the start of time, including Artemis, the young hunter and the ancient goddess, protector of wildlife, goddess of childbirth: Death. Nature. Life.

Learning to hunt has also included lessons in humility and wonderment. Learning to hunt has required me to admit my ignorance, to acquire new skills in a foreign language, to face my fears, and to acknowledge mortality—mine, My Buck's, and the natural cycles of birth and death evident throughout the forest, which is a bible of decay, survival, and regeneration.

Everything that lives also dies; everything we eat was once alive—meat, fruit, vegetables, grains. And yet we must eat to stay alive. Hunting for meat has brought me closer not only to the source of my food but also to untamed nature, what we humans so often think we can control. Learning to hunt is an ongoing education in learning how to live in a more balanced relationship with both the nature of the material world and my own human nature.

I have so much to learn from nature, including how to accept death. While I'm alive, I will keep hunting for deer and for words. I will acknowledge that I'm one among many. I will strive to stay curious, remain calm in the face of ignorance, welcome new knowledge, and seek ways to live more lightly on this earth.

Enjoy more about
Reviving Artemis:
The Making of a Huntress

Meet the Author
Check out author appearances
Explore special features

Photo credit: Kelly Fletcher

AUTHOR BIO

DEBORAH LEE LUSKIN moved from New York City to Vermont in 1984 to write, keep bees, and raise daughters. She has been an editorial columnist, radio commentator, pen-for-hire, and blogger. Her first novel, *Into the Wilderness*, won the Independent Publishers Gold Medal for Regional Fiction.

Luskin has also enjoyed a long career as an educator, teaching writing and literature-based humanities classes to gifted elementary writers, college students, new adult readers, life-long learners, healthcare workers, and prison inmates. She holds a PhD in English Literature and expected to become an academic, not a deer hunter. She lives in Vermont with her husband, their dog, usually a cat, and a variable number of chickens.

ACKNOWLEDGMENTS

I may have gone into the woods by myself on Opening Day, but I did not learn to hunt alone. This story is populated with the many people who supported me as I learned to hunt. In addition to my mentors, Roger Brown and Murphy Robinson, I am indebted to everyone mentioned in this book for forcing me to abandon my lifelong belief that I'm a loner, and to acknowledge that I live in a robust community of friends, neighbors, naturalists, conservationists and wildlife professionals, and—now—hunters. Learning to hunt has forced me to change my personal narrative from one of exclusion to one of belonging. The magnitude of this paradigm shift is not to be understated.

The same must be said for writing this book. While I wrote most of this book alone in my writing studio, I wrote in community during the pandemic via Zoom with the playwrights at Z Space in San Francisco; I am sustained by the community of writers who attend the Rosefire Writing Circle every Friday; and I have more friends than can be named here. I thank them all.

I benefitted from comments offered by the following generous readers of different drafts: Tom Bedell, Michelle Dussault, Myra Fassler, Michael Fleming, Castle Freeman, Becky Karush, Leslie Katz, Linda LaKind, Jonathan Luskin, Joyce Marcel, Meg Ostrum, Vincent Panella, Sarah Stern, Walter Slowinski, and Jennifer Weltz. They gave feedback with enough encouragement to rewrite again, again, and again. I have Molly Hill, proprietor of Wild Book Company, to thank for pointing me to Sibylline Press.

Just as I had willing mentors teach me to hunt and talented readers to help me tell this story better than I could have on my own, I have also been the lucky beneficiary of the expertise, wisdom, and embrace of the sisterhood at Sibylline Press, proving yet again the power of mutual support and teamwork.

Finally, I thank Miriam, Naomi, and Ruth for teaching me the new ways of the world, and Timo, for more than I can say.

STUDY GUIDE QUESTIONS

1. Did you have a favorite scene? What did you like about it?

2. What does Luskin mean by "reading the landscape" and "eating the landscape"?

3. Do you see ways in which learning to hunt has liberated Luskin from learned limitations based on gender, social expectation, and/or education?

4. How does Luskin balance owning and hunting with a rifle with her support for limitations on gun ownership?

5. What does Luskin mean by "the ache of survival"?

6. What are some of the contradictions Luskin confronts in her quest to learn to navigate through the forest?

7. Artemis is the goddess of the hunt, the wilderness, wild animals, nature, vegetation, childbirth, care of children and chastity. What did you learn about this goddess from reading *Reviving Artemis*? How do the stories about Artemis inform Luskin's story?

8. Have you ever surprised yourself by pursuing something foreign to your upbringing and well outside your comfort zone?

9. Has reading *Reviving Artemis* led you to question any opinions and/or beliefs about hunting, how you source your food, and/or how you spend time in nature?

10. If you could name only one thing this book is about, what would it be?

Sibylline Press is proud to publish the brilliant work of women authors over 50. We are a woman-owned publishing company and, like our authors, represent women of a certain age.

ALSO AVAILABLE FROM
Sibylline Press

Other People's Kids: A Novel
By Kim Culbertson
FICTION
392 pages, Trade Paper, $22
ISBN: 9781960573438
Also available as an ebook AND AUDIOBOOK

After a violent incident at her prestigious Bay Area school, English teacher Chelsea Garden returns to her rural hometown seeking refuge and a fresh start. There, she reconnects with a burned-out principal and an old flame, both working at the local high school. *Other People's Kids* follows three educators at different stages of their careers as they navigate second chances, personal crossroads, and the risks of starting over.

Collateral Stardust: Chasing Warren Beatty and Other Foolish Things
By Nikki Nash
MEMOIR
280 pages, Trade Paper, $19
ISBN: 9781960573421
Also available as an ebook AND AUDIOBOOK

Raised in a chaotic, bohemian Hollywood household, teenage Nikki Nash becomes fixated on a bold mission: meet and win over Warren Beatty. With determination and a detailed plan, at eighteen, working in a restaurant near the Beverly Wilshire, her long-shot dream collides with reality. While Warren remains ever present in her life, this is really the story of one woman navigating Hollywood as a producer, comedian, and actor in the eccentric fringes of L.A., brushing up against fame, danger, and dysfunction.

Seeds of the Pomegranate: A Novel
By Suzanne Samuels

HISTORICAL FICTION
416 pages, Trade Paper, $22
ISBN: 9781960573445
Also available as an ebook and audiobook

After illness derails her dreams of becoming a painter in Sicily, Mimi Inglese immigrates to New York, only to be dragged into her father's criminal underworld. When he's imprisoned, she turns to counterfeiting to survive, using her artistic gift to forge a path through Gangland chaos. As violence closes in, Mimi must risk everything to escape a life built on desperation and reclaim the future she once imagined.

You Could Be Happy Here: A Novel
By Erin Van Rheenen

FICTION
280 pages, Trade Paper, $19
ISBN: 9781960573476
Also available as an ebook and audiobook

When Lucy loses her mother and discovers her real father may be a man from her childhood summers in Costa Rica, she sets out to find him—and herself. But the village she returns to is no longer the paradise she remembers, and her search raises more questions than answers. *You Could be Happy Here* is a story of identity, belonging, and redefining home in a world that no longer fits the past.

The House of Cavanaugh: A Novel

By Polly Dugan

FICTION
248 pages, Trade Paper, $18
ISBN: 9781960573469
Also available as an ebook and audiobook

In 1964, Joan Cavanaugh has a secret affair that leads to the birth of a daughter whose true paternity she takes to her grave. Fifty years later, when 23andMe unearths the buried truth, the foundations of two tightly connected families are deeply shaken. *The House of Cavanaugh* is a gripping story of hidden pasts, unraveling loyalties, and what it really means to be family.

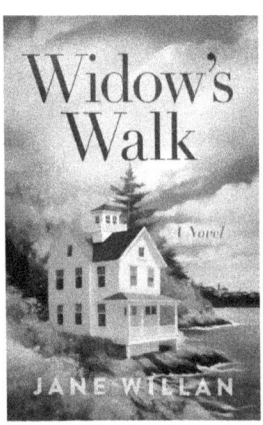

Widow's Walk: A Novel

By Jane Willan

FICTION
336 pages, Trade Paper, $20
ISBN: 9781960573452
Also available as an ebook and audiobook

When new Reverend Miranda McCurdy brings progressive change to a tradition-bound coastal church in Maine, her efforts spark fierce resistance—especially after she challenges the town's beloved Thanksgiving pageant. As the congregation splinters and a woman seeking sanctuary raises the stakes, Miranda must choose between fleeing back to her old life or staying to fight for the community she's slowly come to love. A stray dog and a mysterious stranger may tip the scales in this story of conviction, belonging, and second chances.

 For more books from **Sibylline Press**, please visit our website at sibyllinepress.com

www.ingramcontent.com/pod-product-compliance
Lightning Source LLC
Chambersburg PA
CBHW031314160426
43196CB00007B/534